The Beatitudes in Chinese

Jesus' Sermon on the Mount

Jesus' Sermon on the Mount

Mandating a Better Righteousness

Jack R. Lundbom

Fortress Press
Minneapolis

JESUS' SERMON ON THE MOUNT

Mandating a Better Righteousness

Cover image: Sankt Matthæus Kirke, Copenhagen, Denmark. /Altarpiece – "Sermon on the Mount" – detail By Henrik Olrik

Cover design: Alisha Lofgren

Library of Congress Cataloging-in-Publication Data

Print ISBN: 978-1-4514-9302-3

eBook ISBN: 978-1-4514-9422-8

The paper used in this publication meets the minimum requirements of American National Standard for Information Sciences — Permanence of Paper for Printed Library Materials, ANSI Z329.48-1984.

Manufactured in the U.S.A.

This book was produced using PressBooks.com, and PDF rendering was done by PrinceXML.

To

Elder Lindahl

Contents

Preface

In a day when many in the church are trying to decide how low the bar of Christian living may be set, I find myself moving in the opposite direction. In my view, the bar must be set considerably higher than where most people—in the church and in the larger American society—are setting it. We need more than a minor correction. In both church and society revolutionary change is required so as to set our course on a new path. Our troubled situation, which has been developing over many years, has led me to take a new look at Jesus' Sermon on the Mount, which, more than any other biblical passage is the defining document for the church. If properly interpreted, it can give us the best chance of providing the remedy we need.

Biblical scholars will know much of what is contained in this book, but I hope that students, pastors, and laypeople will profit not only from the exegesis of the Sermon but from the rabbinic literature cited throughout. Much of the latter has long been available in English but is seldom read as background for the Sermon on the Mount. My hope, then, is that people everywhere, believers and nonbelievers, will find the present study informative and useful.

It is many years since I taught a course on Christian Origins at the University of California, Berkeley, where, in the first term given over to a study of the New Testament Gospels, I focused on Matthew and the Sermon on the Mount. In subsequent years I have held teaching positions in Old Testament, and my writing has been mostly—but not exclusively—on Old Testament books and Old Testament subjects. Material in the present book has been presented in lay seminars, adult Sunday School classes, and in sermons. The essays in chapters 1–3, prepared originally for a Lay School of Theology at the Lutheran Theological Seminary at Gettysburg, Pennsylvania, in July of 2006, are included here to put the Sermon on the Mount in a larger perspective. The essay on the *Imitatio Dei* (chapter 4) is presented for the first time. Remaining chapters are a verse-by-verse commentary on the Sermon.

It gives me great pleasure to return in this book to a study of the Sermon on the Mount, which has been a favorite of mine ever since Confirmation days, when I first began to read the Bible on my own. Jesus' words "Do not be anxious about your life . . . " in Matt. 6:25–34 still move me deeply.

Portions of the essays "Rhetoric and Composition in Matthew" (chapter 1) and "New Covenant in Matthew" (chapter 2) were published earlier in my *Biblical Rhetoric and Rhetorical Criticism* (Sheffield: Sheffield Phoenix Press, 2013), 313–22, and *Writing Up Jeremiah* (Eugene, OR: Cascade Books, 2013), 160–71, and the essay "At What Elevation Is Jesus' Sermon on the Mount?" (chapter 3) appeared originally in *Currents in Theology and Mission* 36 (2009): 440–54. All are reprinted with permission.

The Beatitudes in Chinese on the overleaf are provided by my good friend the Rev. Wing Han Jessica Wong, pastor in Hong Kong and a former student of mine at the Lutheran Theological Seminary, Hong Kong.

I am dedicating this book to Dr. Elder Lindahl, for many years Professor of Theology at North Park College in Chicago. I came to know Elder first in a Sunday school class on Christian ethics taught at the North Park Covenant Church, Chicago, and he has been a valued friend ever since. Elder has a mind transparent and radiant as clear Swedish glass, having the uncommon ability to make profound ideas simple and easy to understand. He is also a Christian gentleman and a man of deep faith, which count even more among those who know him than academic excellence.*

Biblical quotations unless noted are from the New Revised Standard Version (NRSV), with the exception of quotations from Hosea in Chapter 1, which are my own translation.

Jack R. Lundbom

*Word came that Dr. Elder Lindahl passed away on November 3, 2014. Peace be to his memory.

Abbreviations

Ancient Sources

Old Testament Apocrypha

Macc.	Maccabees
Sir.	Wisdom of ben Sirach (Ecclesiasticus)
Tob.	Tobit
Wis.	Wisdom of Solomon

Old Testament Pseudepigrapha

As. Mos.	*Assumption of Moses*
Let. Arist.	*Letter of Aristeas*
2 Bar.	*2 (Syriac Apocalypse of) Baruch*
4 Ezra	*4 Ezra (2 Esdras)*
Ps. Sol.	*Psalms of Solomon*
Sib. Or.	*Sibylline Oracles*
Slav. En.	*2 (Slavonic Apocalypse of) Enoch / Book of the Secrets of Enoch*
T. Abr.	*Testament of Abraham*
T. Ash.	*Testament of Asher*
T. Ben.	*Testament of Benjamin*

T. Iss.	*Testament of Issachar*
T. Job	*Testament of Job*
T. Jud.	*Testament of Judah*
T. Levi	*Testament of Levi*
T. Naph.	*Testament of Naphtali*
Vis. Ezra	*Vision of Ezra*

Josephus

Ant.	*Jewish Antiquities*
Apion	*Against Apion*
War	*The Jewish War*

Philo

Agr.	*De Agricultura (On Husbandry)*
Cher.	*De Cherubim (On the Cherubim)*
Decal.	*De Decalogo (The Decalogue)*
Deus.	*Quod Deus Immutabilis Sit (On the Unchangeableness of God)*
Ebr.	*De Ebrietate (On Drunkenness)*
Fug.	*De Fuga et Inventione (On Flight and Finding)*
Her.	*Quis Rerum Divinarum Heres (Who Is the Heir of Divine Things)*
Mig.	*De Migratione Abrahami (On the Migration of Abraham)*
Post.	*De Posteritate Caini (On the Posterity and Exile of Cain)*
Praem.	*De Praemiis et Poenis (On Rewards and Punishments)*
Spec. leg.	*De Specialibus Legibus (On the Special Laws)*
Vit. Mos.	*De Vita Mosis (On the Life of Moses)*

Dead Sea Scrolls

1QH	*Thanksgiving Hymns (Hodayot)*
1QM	*War Scroll*
1QS	*Manual of Discipline/Rule of the Community*
4Q473	*The Two Ways*
CD	*Damascus Document / The Zadokite Document*
MD	Manual of Discipline / Rule of the Community

Rabbinic Works

Ab.	*Abot*
Ab. R. Nat.	*'Avot de Rabbi Nathan*
Ab. Zar.	*'Abodah Zarah*
Apoc. Mos.	*Apocalypse of Moses* (in *The Books of Adam and Eve*)
'Ar.	*'Arakin*
b.	*Babylonian Talmud*
B. Bat.	*Baba Batra*
B. Meẓ.	*Baba Meẓi'a*
B. Qam.	*Baba Qamma*
Ber.	*Berakhot*
Beṣ.	*Beṣah*
Cant. Rab.	*Canticles Rabbah*
Deut. Rab.	*Deuteronomy Rabbah*
Ecc. Rab.	*Ecclesiastes Rabbah*
'Erub.	*'Erubin*
Exod. Rab.	*Exodus Rabbah*
Gen. Rab.	*Genesis Rabbah*
Git.	*Gittin*

Ḥag.	*Ḥagigah*
Ḥul.	*Ḥullin*
j.	*Jerusalem Talmud*
Ket.	*Ketubot*
Lev. Rab.	*Leviticus Rabbah*
m.	*Mishnah*
M. Qat.	*Mo'ed Qatan*
Mak.	*Makkot*
Meg.	*Megillah*
Mekh.	*Mekhilta according to Rabbi Ishmael*
Men.	*Menahot*
Midr.	*Midrash*
Midr. Ps.	*Midrash Psalms*
Ned.	*Nedarim*
Num. Rab.	*Numbers Rabbah*
P. Ab.	*Pirke Abot (= m. Abot)*
Pes.	*Pesahim*
Pes. R.	*Pesiqta Rabbati*
Qid.	*Qiddushin*
Sanh.	*Sanhedrin*
Shab.	*Shabbat*
Sheq.	*Sheqalim*
Shir.	*Shirata*
Sifre Deut.	*Sifre Deuteronomy*
Sot.	*Sota*
Suk.	*Sukkah*
T	*Targum*

T^{Nf}	*Targum Neofiti*
T^{PsJ}	*Targum Pseudo-Jonathan*
Ta'an.	*Ta'anit*
Tanh.	*Tanhuma*
Yeb.	*Yebamot*
Yom.	*Yoma*

Early Christian Literature

Dial. Trypho	Justin Martyr, *Dialogue with Trypho*
Did.	*Didache*
Eus. Hist.	Eusebius, *Ecclesiastical History*
Eus. Prep.	Eusebius, *Evangelical Preparation*
Shep. Herm.	*The Shepherd of Hermas*

Greek Sources

Aristotle

Art Rhet.	*The 'Art' of Rhetoric*
Nic. Eth.	*The Nicomachean Ethics*

Herodotus

Hist.	*The History*

Isocrates

Nic.	*To Nicoles*

Plato

Phae.	*Phaedo*

Roman Sources

Seneca

Benef   *De Beneficiis (On Benefits)*

Pliny

Nat. Hist.   *Natural History (Naturalis Historia)*

Tacitus

An.   *The Annals*

Modern Sources

AB	Anchor Bible
ANET[3]	James B. Pritchard, ed., *Ancient Near Eastern Texts Relating to the Old Testament* (3rd ed. with Supplement; Princeton: Princeton University Press, 1969).
APOT	R. H. Charles, ed., *The Apocrypha and Pseudepigrapha of the Old Testament* (2 vols.; Oxford: Clarendon, 1913).
AramB	Aramaic Bible
AThR	*Anglican Theological Review*
BA	*Biblical Archaeologist*
BASOR Supp	Bulletin of the American Schools of Oriental Research, Supplementary Series
BDB	F. Brown, S. R. Driver, and C. A. Briggs, *A Hebrew and English Lexicon of the Old Testament* (Oxford: Clarendon, 1962).
BWCC	*A Book of Worship for Covenant Churches* (Chicago, 1964).

CBQ	*Catholic Biblical Quarterly*
CovH	*Covenant Hymnal* (Chicago, 1931, 1950, 1996).
Dict Talm	Marcus Jastrow, *A Dictionary of the Targumim, the Talmud Babli and Yerushalmi, and the Midrashic Literature* (2 vols.; London: Luzac, 1903; repr., New York: Pardes, 1950).
DJD	Discoveries in the Judean Desert
EncJud	*Encyclopaedia Judaica* (ed. C. Roth and G. Wigoder; Jerusalem, 1971–73).
ET	*Expository Times*
Gk.	Greek
Heb.	Hebrew
HTR	*Harvard Theological Review*
HUCA	*Hebrew Union College Annual*
IB	George A. Buttrick, ed., *The Interpreter's Bible* (12 vols.; New York: Abingdon-Cokesbury, 1951–57).
IEJ	*Israel Exploration Journal*
Int	*Interpretation*
JB	Jerusalem Bible
JBC	Raymond E. Brown, Joseph A. Fitzmyer, and Roland E. Murphy, eds., *Jerome Biblical Commentary* (Englewood Cliffs, NJ: Prentice Hall, 1968).
JBL	*Journal of Biblical Literature*
JJS	*Journal of Jewish Studies*
JQR	*Jewish Quarterly Review*
JR	*Journal of Religion*
JSOTSup	Journal for the Study of the Old Testament, Supplement Series
JThS	*Journal of Theological Studies*
KJV	The Authorized King James Version (1611)
LCL	Loeb Classical Library
LXX	Septuagint, according to Alfred Rahlfs, ed., *Septuaginta II* (8th edn.; Stuttgart: Württembergische Bibelanstalt, 1965).

MSS	Manuscripts
NEB	New English Bible
NEngH	*New English Hymnal* (Norwich, 1986).
NIB	Leander E. Keck, ed., *The New Interpreter's Bible* (Nashville: Abingdon, 1994–2004).
NRSV	New Revised Standard Version
NTS	*New Testament Studies*
NovT	*Novum Testamentum*
NT	New Testament
OT	Old Testament
OTL	Old Testament Library
OTP	James H. Charlesworth, ed., *The Old Testament Pseudepigrapha* (2 vols.; Garden City, NY: Doubleday, 1983–85).
RSV	Revised Standard Version
SBLDS	Society of Biblical Literature Dissertation Series
SEÅ	*Svensk Exegetisk Årsbok*
TDNT	Gerhard Kittel and Gerhard Friedrich, eds., *Theological Dictionary of the New Testament* (trans. G. W. Bromiley; 10 vols.; Grand Rapids: Eerdmans, 1964–76).
TDOT	J. Botterweck, Helmer Ringgren, and H.-J. Fabry, eds., *Theological Dictionary of the Old Testament* (trans. J. T. Willis, G. W. Bromiley, and D. E. Green; 15 vols.; Grand Rapids: Eerdmans, 1974–).
VT	*Vetus Testamentum*
ZNW	*Zeitschrift für die neutestamentliche Wissenschaft*

The Sermon on the Mount

Matthew 5 [1]When Jesus saw the crowds, he went up the mountain; and after he sat down, his disciples came to him. [2]Then he began to speak, and taught them, saying:

> [3]"Blessed are the poor in spirit,
>> for theirs is the kingdom of heaven.
> [4]"Blessed are those who mourn,
>> for they will be comforted.
> [5]"Blessed are the meek,
>> for they will inherit the earth.
> [6]"Blessed are those who hunger and thirst for righteousness,
>> for they will be filled.
> [7]"Blessed are the merciful,
>> for they will receive mercy.
> [8]"Blessed are the pure in heart,
>> for they will see God.
> [9]"Blessed are the peacemakers,
>> for they will be called children of God.
> [10]"Blessed are those who are persecuted
>> for righteousness' sake,
>> for theirs is the kingdom of heaven.

[11]"Blessed are you when people revile you and persecute you and utter all kinds of evil against you falsely on my account. [12]Rejoice and be glad, for your reward is great in heaven, for in the same way they persecuted the prophets who were before you.

[13]"You are the salt of the earth; but if salt has lost its taste, how can its saltiness be restored? It is no longer good for anything, but is thrown out and trampled under foot. [14]You are the light of the world. A city built on a hill cannot be hid. [15]No one after lighting a lamp puts it under the bushel basket, but on the lampstand, and it gives light to all in the house. [16]In the same way, let your light shine before others, so that they may see your good works and give glory to your Father in heaven.

[17]"Do not think that I have come to abolish the law or the prophets; I have come not to abolish but to fulfill. [18]For truly I tell you, until heaven and earth pass away, not one letter, not one stroke of a letter, will pass from the law until all is accomplished. [19]Therefore, whoever breaks one of the least of these commandments, and teaches others to do the same, will be called least in the kingdom of heaven; but whoever does them and teaches them will be called great in the kingdom of heaven. [20]For I tell you, unless your righteousness exceeds that of the scribes and Pharisees, you will never enter the kingdom of heaven.

[21]"You have heard that it was said to those of ancient times, 'You shall not murder'; and 'whoever murders shall be liable to judgment.' [22]But I say to you that if you are angry with a brother or sister, you will be liable to judgment; and if you insult a brother or sister, you will

be liable to the council; and if you say, 'You fool,' you will be liable to the hell of fire. [23]So when you are offering your gift at the altar, if you remember that your brother or sister has something against you, [24]leave your gift there before the altar and go; first be reconciled to your brother or sister, and then come and offer your gift. [25]Come to terms quickly with your accuser while you are on the way to court with him, or your accuser may hand you over to the judge, and the judge to the guard, and you will be thrown into prison. [26]Truly I tell you, you will never get out until you have paid the last penny.

[27]"You have heard that it was said, 'You shall not commit adultery.' [28]But I say to you that everyone who looks at a woman with lust has already committed adultery with her in his heart. [29]If your right eye causes you to sin, tear it out and throw it away; it is better for you to lose one of your members than for your whole body to be thrown into hell. [30]And if your right hand causes you to sin, cut it off and throw it away; it is better for you to lose one of your members than for your whole body to go into hell.

[31]"It was also said, 'Whoever divorces his wife, let him give her a certificate of divorce.' [32]But I say to you that anyone who divorces his wife, except on the ground of unchastity, causes her to commit adultery; and whoever marries a divorced woman commits adultery.

[33]"Again, you have heard that it was said to those of ancient times, 'You shall not swear falsely, but carry out the vows you have made to the Lord.' [34]But I say to you, Do not swear at all, either by heaven, for it is the throne of God, [35]or by the earth, for it is his footstool, or by Jerusalem, for it is the city of the great King. [36]And do not swear

by your head, for you cannot make one hair white or black. [37]Let your word be 'Yes, Yes' or 'No, No'; anything more than this comes from the evil one.

[38]"You have heard that it was said, 'An eye for an eye and a tooth for a tooth.' [39]But I say to you, Do not resist an evildoer. But if anyone strikes you on the right cheek, turn the other also; [40]and if anyone wants to sue you and take your coat, give your cloak as well; [41]and if anyone forces you to go one mile, go also the second mile. [42]Give to everyone who begs from you, and do not refuse anyone who wants to borrow from you.

[43]"You have heard that it was said, 'You shall love your neighbor and hate your enemy.' [44]But I say to you, Love your enemies and pray for those who persecute you, [45]so that you may be children of your Father in heaven; for he makes his sun rise on the evil and on the good, and sends rain on the righteous and on the unrighteous. [46]For if you love those who love you, what reward do you have? Do not even the tax collectors do the same? [47]And if you greet only your brothers and sisters, what more are you doing than others? Do not even the Gentiles do the same? [48]Be perfect, therefore, as your heavenly Father is perfect.

6 [1]"Beware of practicing your piety before others in order to be seen by them; for then you have no reward from your Father in heaven. [2]So whenever you give alms, do not sound a trumpet before you, as the hypocrites do in the synagogues and in the streets, so that they may be praised by others. Truly I tell you, they have received their reward. [3]But when you give alms, do not let your left hand know

what your right hand is doing, [4]so that your alms may be done in secret; and your Father who sees in secret will reward you.

[5]"And whenever you pray, do not be like the hypocrites; for they love to stand and pray in the synagogues and at the street corners, so that they may be seen by others. Truly I tell you, they have received their reward. [6]But whenever you pray, go into your room and shut the door and pray to your Father who is in secret; and your Father who sees in secret will reward you. [7]When you are praying, do not heap up empty phrases as the Gentiles do; for they think that they will be heard because of their many words. [8]Do not be like them, for your Father knows what you need before you ask him.

[9]"Pray then in this way:
Our Father in heaven,
hallowed be your name.
[10]Your kingdom come,
your will be done, on earth as it is in heaven.
[11]Give us this day our daily bread.
[12]And forgive us our debts,
as we also have forgiven our debtors.
[13]And do not bring us to the time of trial,
but rescue us from the evil one.
(For the kingdom and the power and
the glory are yours forever. Amen.)[1]

[14]For if you forgive others their trespasses, your heavenly Father will also forgive you; [15]but if you do not forgive others, neither will

---

1. NRSV has this in a footnote.

your Father forgive your trespasses. [16]And whenever you fast, do not look dismal, like the hypocrites, for they disfigure their faces so as to show others that they are fasting. Truly I tell you, they have received their reward. [17]But when you fast, put oil on your head and wash your face, [18]so that your fasting may be seen not by others but by your Father who is in secret; and your Father who sees in secret will reward you.

[19]"Do not store up for yourselves treasures on earth, where moth and rust consume and where thieves break in and steal; [20]but store up for yourselves treasures in heaven, where neither moth nor rust consumes and where thieves do not break in and steal. [21]For where your treasure is, there your heart will be also.

[22]"The eye is the lamp of the body. So, if your eye is healthy, your whole body will be full of light; [23]but if your eye is unhealthy, your whole body will be full of darkness. If then the light in you is darkness, how great is the darkness! [24]No one can serve two masters; for a slave will either hate the one and love the other, or be devoted to the one and despise the other. You cannot serve God and wealth.

[25]"Therefore I tell you, do not worry about your life, what you will eat or what you will drink, or about your body, what you will wear. Is not life more than food, and the body more than clothing? [26]Look at the birds of the air; they neither sow nor reap nor gather into barns, and yet your heavenly Father feeds them. Are you not of more value than they? [27]And can any of you by worrying add a single hour to your span of life? [28]And why do you worry about clothing? Consider the lilies of the field, how they grow; they neither

toil nor spin, [29]yet I tell you, even Solomon in all his glory was not clothed like one of these. [30]But if God so clothes the grass of the field, which is alive today and tomorrow is thrown into the oven, will he not much more clothe you—you of little faith? [31]Therefore do not worry, saying, 'What will we eat?' or 'What will we drink?' or 'What will we wear?' [32]For it is the Gentiles who strive for all these things; and indeed your heavenly Father knows that you need all these things. [33]But strive first for the kingdom of God and his righteousness, and all these things will be given to you as well. [34]So do not worry about tomorrow, for tomorrow will bring worries of its own. Today's trouble is enough for today.

7 [1]"Do not judge, so that you may not be judged. [2]For with the judgment you make you will be judged, and the measure you give will be the measure you get. [3]Why do you see the speck in your neighbor's eye, but do not notice the log in your own eye? [4]Or how can you say to your neighbor, 'Let me take the speck out of your eye,' while the log is in your own eye? [5]You hypocrite, first take the log out of your own eye, and then you will see clearly to take the speck out of your neighbor's eye.

[6]"Do not give what is holy to dogs; and do not throw pearls before swine, or they will trample them under foot and turn and maul you.

[7]"Ask, and it will be given you; search, and you will find; knock, and the door will be opened for you. [8]For everyone who asks receives, and everyone who searches finds, and for everyone who knocks, the door will be opened. [9]Is there anyone among you who, if your child asks for bread, will give a stone? [10]Or if the child asks for a fish,

will give a snake? [11]If you then, who are evil, know how to give good gifts to your children, how much more will your Father in heaven give good things to those who ask him! [12]In everything do to others as you would have them do to you; for this is the law and the prophets.

[13]"Enter through the narrow gate; for the gate is wide and the road is easy that leads to destruction, and there are many who take it. [14]For the gate is narrow and the road is hard that leads to life, and there are few who find it.

[15]"Beware of false prophets, who come to you in sheep's clothing but inwardly are ravenous wolves. [16]You will know them by their fruits. Are grapes gathered from thorns, or figs from thistles? [17]In the same way, every good tree bears good fruit, but the bad tree bears bad fruit. [18]A good tree cannot bear bad fruit, nor can a bad tree bear good fruit. [19]Every tree that does not bear good fruit is cut down and thrown into the fire. [20]Thus you will know them by their fruits.

[21]"Not everyone who says to me, 'Lord, Lord,' will enter the kingdom of heaven, but only the one who does the will of my Father in heaven. [22]On that day many will say to me, 'Lord, Lord, did we not prophesy in your name, and cast out demons in your name, and do many deeds of power in your name?' [23]Then I will declare to them, 'I never knew you; go away from me, you evildoers.' [24]Everyone then who hears these words of mine and acts on them will be like a wise man who built his house on rock. [25]The rain fell, the floods came, and the winds blew and beat on that house, but it did not fall, because it had been founded on rock. [26]And everyone

who hears these words of mine and does not act on them will be like a foolish man who build his house on sand. [27]The rain fell, and the floods came, and the winds blew and beat against that house, and it fell—and great was its fall!"

[28]"Now when Jesus had finished saying these things, the crowds were astounded at his teaching, [29]for he taught them as one having authority, and not as their scribes."

Introduction

If the Sermon on the Mount is to be properly understood and is to challenge people to aim for a better righteousness, which is my purpose in writing the present book, it requires clarification and careful attention especially at two points. The lead articles in Part 1 discuss these issues in some detail. First, it must be remembered by people living in a modern culture where most things are read, not heard spoken aloud, that the Sermon on the Mount was created in an oral culture where people would only hear it when it was read aloud in public worship or on some other occasion. Hearing, not seeing, was everything. Chapter 1, "Rhetoric and Composition in Matthew," discusses the oral provenance of the Sermon, giving particular attention to the balancing of "blessings" and "woes" in Matthew's Gospel. This Gospel is a new covenant document, about which the New Testament is otherwise almost completely silent, and Matthew in his composition is seen to have given a new twist to the Old Testament covenant document of Deuteronomy. Chapter 2, "The New Covenant in Matthew," discusses further the new covenant in early Christianity, putting it in the context of other biblical covenants.

Second, modern interpretation of the Sermon largely takes the words of Jesus, as presented by the Gospel writer Matthew, as being completely out of reach, making the Sermon for many a great teaching but one that cannot be taken seriously. But if one cannot live by this Sermon, then why even try? Chapter 3, "At What Elevation Is Jesus' Sermon on the Mount?" and chapter 4, "*Imitatio Dei* in the Sermon on the Mount," seek to correct this misinterpretation. The *Imitatio Dei* concept in Judaism (given that Latin title in Christianity) helps explain Jesus' directive in Matt. 5:48: "You, therefore, must be perfect as your heavenly Father is perfect." It is somewhat of an irony that the Sermon must be brought down from unreachable heights before it can become the teaching it was meant to be, namely, one intended to raise the level of human behavior above the mediocrity attributed here to the Pharisees and the Gentiles.

Part 2, the verse-by-verse commentary on the Sermon, proceeds with these larger points as background and interprets the various teachings of the Sermon in the light of teachings in the Old Testament and in rabbinic Judaism, both of which are often insufficiently known and understood by the majority of people reading Jesus' Sermon on the Mount.

PART I

The Sermon on the Mount and the Gospel of Matthew

Rhetoric and Composition in Matthew

Structure in the New Testament Gospels

Each of the Gospel writers in the New Testament gathered existing traditions about Jesus, which doubtless circulated for a time in oral form, and structured a selected number into a written Gospel. The structures facilitated an oral reading of the Gospels to members of the early church.

Mark, in the first part of his Gospel, after an initial word on the preparatory work of John the Baptist, reports the many healings, exorcisms, and nature miracles performed by Jesus, but the disciples are nevertheless unable to perceive who Jesus is (Mark 1:16—8:26).[1] Those much less acquainted with Jesus respond with far greater insight, for example, the cleansed leper in Galilee, where Jesus' ministry begins (Mark 1:40-45). A turning point in Mark's Gospel comes in the episode at Caesarea Philippi, where Peter confesses Jesus to be the Christ (Mark 8:27-33). Now comes a sudden change in

---

1. Theodore J. Weeden, *Mark—Traditions in Conflict* (Philadelphia: Fortress Press, 1971).

the disciples; they have a greater capacity for discernment—however, Peter's understanding of messiahship is not that of Jesus. For Jesus, it involves suffering and death.

In the second part of Mark's Gospel, this latter teaching is fulfilled. Judas betrays his master, resulting in Jesus' capture, suffering, and death (Mark 14:10—15:47). The Gospel ends with a brief report of Jesus' resurrection on Easter morning, but the women closest to Jesus, who were told to report the good news to the disciples and Peter, are unwilling to tell anyone (Mark 16:1-8). Mark's strange ending has a point to make, however. A contrast is being drawn between the leper whom Jesus healed in Galilee and what happened subsequently (Mark 1:40-45). Jesus told the fellow not to tell anyone but to go show himself to the priest, but instead he went out and told the good news to everyone (v. 45). The contrast makes an *inclusio* for the entire Gospel, which is another device giving structure to the completed work. The verses in Mark 16:9-20 are a later addition.[2]

Luke, more the historian than any of the other Gospel writers, structures his Gospel and a second work on the Acts of the Apostles by giving prominence to geography and the Jerusalem temple in getting the good news out to the world. His Gospel begins and ends in Jerusalem, more specifically in the Jerusalem temple, where another tie-in between beginning and end is discerned.[3] At the beginning, the aged Zechariah receives a divine visitation, and after his tongue is loosed, he prophesies and exclaims, "*Blessed* be the Lord God of Israel" (Luke 1:64-68). Then at the end of the Gospel, Luke has Jesus *blessing* the disciples at Bethany when he leaves them. He says, "Then he led them out as far as Bethany, and lifting up his

---

2. See Jack R. Lundbom, "Closure in Mark's Gospel," *Seminary Ridge Review* 9, no. 1 (2006): 33–41; reprinted in Lundbom, *Biblical Rhetoric and Rhetorical Criticism* (Hebrew Bible Monographs 45; Sheffield: Sheffield Phoenix Press, 2013), 323–31.

3. Lundbom, "Closure in Mark's Gospel," 38 (in *Biblical Rhetoric*, 328–29).

hands he *blessed* them. While he was *blessing* them, he withdrew from them and was carried up into heaven. And they worshiped him, and returned to Jerusalem with great joy, and they were continually in the temple *blessing* God" (Luke 24:50-53).

After Jesus' departure, the disciples must remain in Jerusalem until the Holy Spirit is poured out upon them (Acts 1:4-5). Once this takes place, the good news can go forth from Jerusalem to all Judea, to Samaria, and to the end of the earth (Acts 1:8). This is the controlling structure of Luke's Gospel and Acts.

The Gospel of John is more theological in nature, not history per se, even though it does report the miracles, sufferings, death, and resurrection of Jesus. It contains yet another structure. After introducing Jesus as the incarnate Word of God (John 1:1-14), John the Baptist as forerunner to this Word (John 1:15-34), and Jesus' calling of his disciples (John 1:35-51), John anchors his Gospel in a "Book of Signs" (chapters 2–12), after which he follows with a "Book of the Passion" (chapters 13–20).[4] At the end of the Book of the Passion, Jesus' signs are again given prominence. John says in conclusion:

> Now Jesus did many other signs in the presence of his disciples, which are not written in this book. But these are written so that you may come to believe that Jesus is the Messiah, the Son of God, and that through believing you may have life in his name. (20:30-31)

Chapter 21, reporting a Galilee resurrection appearance of Jesus, is a later addition.

---

4. C. H. Dodd, *The Interpretation of the Fourth Gospel* (Cambridge: Cambridge University Press, 1953), 292, 297, 379.

Structure in the Gospel of Matthew

Matthew structures his Gospel as a "new covenant" document for the nascent church, about which more will be said in the following chapter. In this Gospel, the "church" gets explicit mention. There is another tie-in between beginning and end, although the final verses of this Gospel are taken by many as a later addition (Matt. 28:18-20).[5] For Matthew, Jesus is "Emmanuel," "God with us" (1:23), and at the end of the Gospel the great biblical affirmation, "I will be with you," is brought in to show that God, in Christ and in the Holy Spirit, will continue to dwell with his people to the close of the age (Matt. 28:20).

The structure of Matthew is more developed than is the structure of any other Gospel. Benjamin Bacon of Yale divided this Gospel into five books, which he believed were modeled on the five books of the Torah: Genesis through Deuteronomy.[6] This made Matthew into a "new Torah," or a "new Law." Each little book within the larger book contained a narrative section, a sermonic section, and then a closing formula stating that Jesus had finished his teaching. Bacon's outline is the following:

---

5. J. C. Fenton, "Inclusio and Chiasmus in Matthew," in *Studia evangelica: Papers Presented to the International Congress on "The Four Gospels in 1957" Held at Christ Church, Oxford* (ed. Kurt Aland; Texte und Untersuchungen zur Geschichte der altchristlichen Literatur 73; Berlin: Akademie-Verlag, 1959), 174–79; Fenton, *The Gospel of Saint Matthew* (Pelican New Testament Commentaries; Baltimore: Penguin Books, 1963), 43; Charles H. Lohr, "Oral Techniques in the Gospel of Matthew," *CBQ* 23 (1961): 410; H. B. Green, "The Structure of St. Matthew's Gospel," in *Studia evangelica IV: Papers Presented to the Third International Congress on New Testament Studies*, part 1, *The New Testament Scriptures* (ed. F. L. Cross; Berlin: Akademie-Verlag, 1968), 58; Lundbom, "Closure in Mark's Gospel," 37–38 (in *Biblical Rhetoric,* 327–28).

6. Benjamin W. Bacon, *Studies in Matthew* (New York: Henry Holt, 1930), 80–90.

Book I	3–4	Narrative
	5:1—7:27	Sermon: The Sermon on the Mount
	7:28-29	"And when Jesus finished these sayings . . ."
Book II	8:1—9:35	Narrative
	9:36—10:42	Sermon: The Missionary Discourse
	11:1	"And when Jesus had finished instructing his twelve disciples . . ."
Book III	11:2—12:50	Narrative
	13:1-52	Sermon: Parables on the Kingdom
	13:53	"And when Jesus had finished these parables . . ."
Book IV	13:54—17:21	Narrative
	17:22—18:35	Sermon: Church Administration
	19:1	"Now when Jesus had finished these sayings . . ."
Book V	19:2—22:46	Narrative
	23—25	Sermon: End Times/Farewell Address
	26:1	"When Jesus finished *all* these sayings . . ."

The addition of "all" in the final formula shows that a climax has been reached. Bacon's view was widely accepted, with minor reservations and modifications.[7] But not everyone was convinced that the five books of the Gospel were a conscious attempt on the writer's part to put forward a "new Torah." There are other collections of five books, for example, the Psalms and the Megilloth. But the main problem is that the structure left out material at the beginning and end of the Gospel. According to W. D. Davies, "On Bacon's view of Matthew,

---

7. See, for example, Joachim Jeremias, *The Sermon on the Mount* (trans. Norman Perrin; London: University of London, Athlone Press, 1961), 16–17.

the birth narratives are outside the main scheme of the work and, what is more important, the Passion of Jesus and his Resurrection are reduced to mere addenda."[8]

A better outline for Matthew was proposed by Charles Lohr, who argued that the Gospel was structured into a large chiasmus.[9] Chiasmus is a crosswise rhetorical figure well known from classical literature, found by Nils Lund to exist in large panels of both the Old and New Testament discourse. Lund showed how words and ideas often build up to a center point, which is frequently the climax, and then repeat in reverse order to the end.[10] Lund found this structure in the Gospels, particularly in Matthew.[11] It is an old rhetorical structure, Semitic in origin,[12] with Lund calling it "the gift of the East to the West."[13]

Lohr's structure, like Bacon's, alternates narrative and sermon, as follows:

1–4	a	Narrative: Birth and Beginnings
5–7	b	Sermon: *Blessings*, Entering the Kingdom
8–9	c	Narrative: Authority and Invitation
10	d	Sermon: Mission Discourse
11–12	e	Narrative: Rejection by Present Generation
13	f	Sermon: Parables of the Kingdom

8. W. D. Davies, *Invitation to the New Testament* (Garden City, NY: Doubleday, 1966), 214. This point was also made by H. B. Green, "Structure of St. Matthew's Gospel," 49.

9. Lohr, "Oral Techniques in the Gospel of Matthew," 427. Chiastic structures have also been proposed by Fenton, *Gospel of St. Matthew*, 15–17; H. B. Green, "Structure of St. Matthew's Gospel," 58; M. Eugene Boring, "The Gospel of Matthew," in *NIB* 8: 113; and Tyler J. VanderWeele, "Some Observations Concerning the Chiastic Structure of the Gospel of Matthew," *JThS* 59 (2008): 669–73.

10. Nils W. Lund, *Chiasmus in the New Testament* (Chapel Hill, NC University of North Carolina Press, 1942; repr., Peabody, Mass,: Hendrickson, 1992.

11. Nils W. Lund, "The Influence of Chiasmus upon the Structure of the Gospels," *AThR* 13 (1931): 27–48; Lund, "The Influence of Chiasmus upon the Structure of the Gospel according to Matthew," *AThR* 13 (1931): 405–33.

12. Lund, "Influence of Chiasmus upon the Structure of the Gospels," 28.

13. Nils W. Lund, *Outline Studies in the Book of Revelation* (Chicago: Covenant Book Concern, 1935), 4; Lund, *Chiasmus in the New Testament*, viii.

14–17	e'	Narrative: Acknowledgment by Disciples
18	d'	Sermon: Community Discourse
19–22	c'	Narrative: Authority and Invitation
23–25	b'	Sermon: *Woes*, Coming of the Kingdom
26–28	a'	Narrative: Death and Resurrection

Here all the Gospel material is accounted for, and while some descriptive titles proposed by Lohr may not reproduce exactly what Matthew had in mind, they are convincing in the main. One sees very clearly how the "woes" of chapter 23 intend to balance the "blessings" of chapter 5, where also in chapters 5-7 the emphasis is on entering the kingdom, while in chapters 23-25 it is on the kingdom coming in days ahead. The kingdom of heaven, which is the "rule of God," is both a present and a future reality. The parables of the kingdom in chapter 13 are also seen to be the center and climax of Matthew's Gospel.

Blessings and Woes

Especially noteworthy in this structure is the balancing of "blessings" and "woes."[14] This has to be intentional, and it is what makes Matthew's Gospel into a "new covenant document, about which more will be said in the following chapter.

In Luke's Sermon on the Plain one cannot miss the contrasting of blessings and woes (Luke 6:20-26), but in Matthew they are separated by so much intervening material that the contrast is nearly lost—and for many readers of the Gospel it is lost. Luther, for example, went to

---

14. Lohr, "Oral Techniques in the Gospel of Matthew," 427; see also Isabel Ann Massey, *Interpreting the Sermon on the Mount in the Light of Jewish Tradition as Evidenced in the Palestinian Targums of the Pentateuch: Selected Themes* (Studies in the Bible and Early Christianity 25; Lewiston, NY: Edwin Mellen, 1991), 120.

Luke 6, not to Matthew 23, to cite the woes on those whose behavior was the opposite of what was being taught in the Sermon.[15] This is a good reason, incidentally, for hearing Matthew's entire Gospel read aloud from start to finish. In a single reading one will perceive that the woes on the Pharisees and scribes stand in contrast to the blessings pronounced upon the new people of the kingdom. The woes of chapter 23, as Moshe Weinfeld points out, are firmly rooted in Jewish teaching about hypocrisy.[16] They are the following:

> But woe to you, scribes and Pharisees, hypocrites! *For you lock people out of the kingdom of heaven.* For you do not go in yourselves, and when others are going in, you stop them.
> Woe to you, scribes and Pharisees, hypocrites! For you cross sea and land to make a single convert, and you make the new convert twice as much a child of hell as yourselves.
> Woe to you, blind guides, who say, "Whoever swears by the sanctuary is bound by nothing, but whoever swears by the gold of the sanctuary is bound by the oath." You blind fools! For which is greater, the gold or the sanctuary that has made the gold sacred? . . .
> Woe to you, scribes and Pharisees, hypocrites! For you tithe mint, dill and cummin, and have neglected the weightier matters of the law: justice and mercy and faith. It is these you ought to have practiced without neglecting others. You blind guides! You strain out a gnat but swallow a camel!
> Woe to you, scribes and Pharisees, hypocrites! For you clean the outside of the cup and of the plate, but inside they are full of greed and self-indulgence. You blind Pharisee! First clean the inside of the cup, so that the outside also may become clean.
> Woe to you, scribes and Pharisees, hypocrites! For you are like whitewashed tombs, which on the outside look beautiful, but inside they are full of the bones of the dead and of all kinds of filth. . . .
> Woe to you, scribes and Pharisees, hypocrites! For you build the tombs of the prophets and decorate the graves of the righteous, and you say,

15. *Luther's Works,* vol. 21, *The Sermon on the Mount (Sermons) and The Magnificat* (ed. Jaroslav Pelikan; St. Louis: Concordia, 1956), 11, 44.
16. Moshe Weinfeld, "The Charge of Hypocrisy in Matthew 23 and in Jewish Sources," *Immanuel* 24–25 (1990): 52–58.

"If we had lived in the days of our ancestors, we would not have taken part with them in shedding the blood of the prophets." (Matt 23:13–36)

These are contrasted with the blessings beginning the Sermon on the Mount, commonly called the "Beatitudes." They are the following:

Blessed are the poor in spirit, for theirs is *the kingdom of heaven.*
Blessed are those who mourn, for they will be comforted.
Blessed are the meek, for they will inherit the earth.
Blessed are those who hunger and thirst for righteousness, for they will be filled.
Blessed are the merciful, for they will receive mercy.
Blessed are the pure in heart, for they will see God.
Blessed are the peacemakers, for they will be called children of God.
Blessed are those who are persecuted for righteousness' sake, for theirs is *the kingdom of heaven.*
Blessed are you when people revile you and persecute you and utter all kinds of evil against you falsely on my account. Rejoice and be glad, for your reward is great in heaven, for in the same way they persecuted the prophets who were before you. (Matt 5:3–12)

These woes and blessings contain some striking contrasts:[17]

17. Adapted with minor changes from Fenton, *Gospel of St. Matthew*, 368.

Woes	Blessings
"You lock people out of the *kingdom of heaven*" (23:13)	"poor in spirit/those persecuted . . . theirs is the *kingdom of heaven*" (5:3, 10)
"you make the convert . . . a *child of hell*" (23:15)	"peacemakers . . . will be called *children of God*" (5:9)
"*blind* guides . . . *blind* fools . . . *blind* . . ." (23:16-19)	"the pure in heart . . . will *see* God" (5:8)
"you have neglected . . . *mercy* (23:23)	"the *merciful* . . . will receive *mercy*" (5:7)
"you clean the outside of the *cup* and of the *plate* . . ." (23:25)	"those who *hunger and thirst* after righteousness . . . will be filled" (5:6)
"you are like whitewashed *tombs* . . . full of *the bones of dead men*" (23:27)	"those who *mourn* . . . will be comforted" (5:4)
"you will build the *tombs* . . . and decorate the *graves* . . ." (23:29)	
"that upon you may come all the righteous blood shed on *earth*" (23:35)	"the meek . . . will inherit the *earth*" (5:5)

The Kingdom of Heaven

In Matthew's Gospel the term "kingdom of heaven" appears prominently at the beginning, middle, and end (5:3, 10; 13:1-52; 23:13). The Sermon on the Mount pronounces blessings on those entering the kingdom, while chapters 23–25 state that, when the kingdom comes (in its fullness), the blessed will enter into the joy of their master, while those receiving woes will reap a dreadful reward.

The kingdom is also featured at the center of Matthew's Gospel, where it is portrayed in parables (chapter 13). This becomes a "turning point" of the Gospel.[18] Our concern here is with the six parables at the core of the chapter, which appear to manifest another rhetorical structure.

---

18. Lohr, "Oral Techniques in the Gospel of Matthew," 428; Jack Dean Kingsbury, *The Parables of Jesus in Matthew 13* (Richmond, VA: John Knox Press, 1969), 13.

We are accustomed to hearing that a parable is told to convey a single point, which is true, although parables may contain allegorical traits as Jewish stories often do.[19] But here six parables are grouped in pairs, so that two parables—not one—are intended to convey a single point.[20] We notice in other Gospels, too, that Jesus is said to have told two parables in succession, for example, the parables of the mustard seed and the leaven (Luke 13:18-21); two parables of the feasts (Luke 14:7-14); the parables of building a tower and a king going to war (Luke 14:28-32); the parables of the lost sheep and the lost coin (Luke 15:3-10); and the parables of the unrighteous judge and the Pharisee and the tax collector (Luke 18:1-14). But what makes the present structure different is that one of the pairs is here broken up to frame the whole: The parable of the good and bad seed is placed at the beginning, and the parable of the good and bad fish is placed at the end. The structure, then, is the following:

a   Parable of the Good and Bad Seed (13:24-30)

    b   Parable of the Mustard Seed (13:31-32)

    b'   Parable of the Leaven (13:33)

    c   Parable of the Treasure Hidden in the Field (13:44)

    c'   Parable of the Costly Pearl (13:45-46)

a'   Parable of the Good and Bad Fish (13:47-50)

---

19. Floyd V. Filson, *A Commentary on the Gospel according to St. Matthew* (Harper's New Testament Commentaries; New York: Harper & Brothers, 1960), 158.

20. Filson notes that the parables of the mustard seed and the leaven make one point, viz., that great developments come from small beginnings, and that the parables of the treasure hidden in the field and the costly pearl emphasize a single truth—the supreme worth of the kingdom (*Gospel according to St. Matthew*, 162, 164). Sherman Johnson says, too, that the mustard seed and the leaven are twin parables, so also the hidden treasure and the costly pearl ("Matthew," *IB* 7:414). He speculates, too, that Matthew may have rewritten Mark 4:26-29 into the parable of the good and bad seed in order to provide a twin parable to the good and bad fish (p. 239).

The parables at beginning and end both speak about the final separation of the righteous from the wicked at the end of the age (a and a'); the parables on the mustard seed and the leaven speak about the spectacular growth of the kingdom (b and b'); and the parables on the treasure hidden in the field and the costly pearl speak of the kingdom's infinite worth (c and c').

Matthew is adopting here a rhetorical form in Hebrew poetry used by the Old Testament prophet Hosea. Hosea writes his poetry in ordinary parallelism of bicolons and tricolons, but in some oracles he will break up a bicolon, putting a single colon at the beginning and a single colon at the end.[21] Two of these structures appear in Hosea 4, the first one in vv. 4b-9a:

> [4b]Your *people* are like the contentions of a *priest.*

> [5]You shall stumble by day;
> > and the prophet also will stumble with you by night,
> > > and I will destroy your mother.
> [6]My people are destroyed for lack of knowledge;
> > because you have rejected knowledge,
> > > so I reject you from being priest to me.
> And since you have forgotten the law of your God,
> > I will forget your children—even I.
> [7]The more they increased, the more they sinned against me;

21. See David Noel Freedman, "Prolegomenon" to George Buchanan Gray, *The Forms of Hebrew Poetry: Considered with Special Reference to the Criticism and Interpretation of the Old Testament* (1915; repr., Library of Biblical Studies; New York: Ktav, 1972), xxxvi–xxxvii (reprinted in Freedman, *Pottery, Poetry, and Prophecy: Studies in Early Hebrew Poetry* [Winona Lake, IN: Eisenbrauns, 1980], 46); Jack R. Lundbom, "Contentious Priests and Contentious People in Hosea IV 1-10," *VT* 36 (1986): 52–70 (reprinted in Lundbom, *Biblical Rhetoric*, 216–31); and Lundbom, "Poetic Structure and Prophetic Rhetoric in Hosea," *VT* 29 (1979): 300–308 (reprinted in *Prophecy in the Hebrew Bible: Selected Studies from Vetus Testamentum* [ed. David E. Orton; Brill's Readers in Biblical Studies 5; Leiden: Brill, 2000], 139–47; and in Lundbom, *Biblical Rhetoric*, 232–39).

I will exchange[22] their glory for shame.
⁸They feed on the sin of my people;
they are greedy for their iniquity.

^{9a}Therefore it shall be like *people,* like *priest.* (Hos. 4:4b–9a)

And again in 4:11–14:

¹¹New wine takes away the mind of *my people.*

¹²They inquire of their thing of wood,
and their staff gives them oracles
For a spirit of whoredom has led them away,
and they have gone a–whoring out
from under their God.
¹³On the tops of the mountains they sacrifice,
and on the hills they burn offerings,
Under oak, poplar, and terebinth
because their shade is good!
Therefore your daughters play the whore,
and your sons' brides commit adultery.
¹⁴I will not punish your daughters when they play the whore,
nor your sons' brides when they commit adultery.
For those men over there go aside with whores
and sacrifice with sacred prostitutes.

A people without sense will be thrust down. (Hos. 4:11–14)

---

22. *Tiq soph* [scribal correction]: "They exchanged."

Another broken bicolon structure occurs in Hos. 8:9-13:

> [9]For *behold* they have gone up to *Assyria,*
>
> A wild ass off by himself.
>> Ephraim has hired lovers.
> [10]Even though they hire among the nations,
>> now I will gather them up,
> So that they soon writhe under the burden,
>> king and princes.
> [11]Indeed Ephraim has multiplied altars,
>> altars for sinning they have become to him
>>> altars for sinning.
> [12]Though I write for him multitudes of my laws,
>> they are regarded as something strange.
> [13]Sacrifices they love, so they sacrifice,
>> and flesh they eat.
> Yahweh takes no delight in them.
> Now he will remember their iniquity
>> and punish their sins.
>
> *Behold* they will return to *Egypt.* (Hos. 8:9-13)

Matthew, in similar fashion, breaks up a pair of parables, putting one at the beginning and one at the end. The parable of the sower (Matt. 13:3-9) becomes a cover parable used to introduce six other parables on the kingdom. The chapter as it now stands adds in addition some interpretation: (1) an explanation to the disciples as to why Jesus speaks in parables (13:10-17); (2) an allegorical interpretation of the parable of the sower (13:18-23); (3) another explanation as to why Jesus speaks in parables (13:34-35); (4) an allegorical interpretation of the parable of the good and bad seed (13:36-43); and (5) a concluding word about scribes properly trained for the kingdom of heaven (13:51-52).

Structure in the Sermon on the Mount

The Sermon on the Mount is likewise well structured within Matthew's Gospel, where it is not at all difficult to delimit pericopes. The Sermon consists of the following sections:

1. Introduction. Jesus teaches on the mountain; primary audience is the disciples (5:1-2).
2. Eight Blessings (5:3-12). Blessings 1 and 7 contain Matthew's key term, "kingdom of heaven," which could make an *inclusio* for a core of seven blessings.[23] Blessing 8 shifts to direct address and expands: "Blessed are *you* . . . rejoice and be glad. . . ." In Hebrew poetry, the final line in a series often varies the repetition,[24] is longer than the other lines,[25] and shifts to direct address.[26] The shift to direct address makes a heavier "ballast statement," which is another rhetorical feature in Hebrew poetry bringing discourse to a dramatic conclusion.[27] Matthew Black

23. Hans Dieter Betz, *The Sermon on the Mount: A Commentary on the Sermon on the Mount, Including the Sermon on the Plain (Matthew 5:3—7:27 and Luke 6:20-49)* (Hermeneia; Minneapolis: Fortress Press, 1995), 142, 146.

24. David Noel Freedman, "Deliberate Deviation from an Established Pattern of Repetition in Hebrew Poetry as a Rhetorical Device," in *Proceedings of the Ninth World Congress of Jewish Studies (Jerusalem, August 4-12, 1985). Division A, The Period of the Bible.* (Jerusalem: World Union of Jewish Studies, 1986), 45–52 (reprinted in *Divine Commitment and Human Obligation: Selected Writings of David Noel Freedman* (ed. John R. Huddlestun; 2 vols.; Grand Rapids: Eerdmans, 1997), 2:205–12).

25. David Daube, "Three Questions of Form in Matthew V," *JThS* 45 (1944): 21-23; Daube, *The New Testament and Rabbinic Judaism* (London: University of London and Athlone Press, 1956), 196–201.

26. Jack R. Lundbom, *Jeremiah: A Study in Ancient Hebrew Rhetoric* (SBLDS 18; Missoula, MT: Society of Biblical Literature and Scholars Press, 1975, 77; 2nd ed., Winona Lake, IN: Eisenbrauns, 1997), 103.

believed that the Beatitudes were originally cast in poetic form in Hebrew or Aramaic.[28]

3. Disciples Are to Be Salt and Light in the World (5:13-16). The two segments have parallel beginnings: "You are the salt of the earth"/"You are the light of the world." The section concludes by calling those seeing "your good works" to "give glory to your Father in heaven."

4. Mandating a Better Righteousness (5:17-20). The concluding verse appears to be another ballast statement. Jeremias says that v. 20, "Unless your righteousness exceeds that of the scribes and Pharisees, you will never enter the kingdom of heaven," is the theme of the Sermon on the Mount, which would point to its being a particularly weighty statement.[29] What follows are the antitheses that develop this statement on a "better righteousness."

5. What about Anger? (5:21-26). Here begins the first of five "You have heard that it was said . . . But I say to you" introductions, delimiting the section to vv. 21-26 and making it clear that Jesus has provocative anger in mind. The section concludes with a ballast statement employing the emphatic "truly," which is the Hebrew "'āmēn!"

---

27. Ballast lines were first recognized by George Adam Smith, *The Early Poetry of Israel in Its Physical and Social Origins* (Schweich Lectures, 1910; London: Henry Frowde, Oxford University Press, 1912), 20–21, 77, and were identified elsewhere in Hebrew poetry by James Muilenburg, "Form Criticism and Beyond," *JBL* 88 (1969): 9-12 (reprinted in *Hearing and Speaking the Word: Selections from the Works of James Muilenburg* [ed. Thomas F. Best; Scholars Press Homage Series; Chico, CA: Scholars Press, 1984], 27–44; and in *Beyond Form Criticism: Essays in Old Testament Literary Criticism* [ed. Paul R. House; Sources for Biblical and Theological Study 2; Winona Lake, IN: Eisenbrauns, 1992], 49–69). In one of Smith's ballast lines, Deut. 32:14b, a shift to second person address occurs. For ballast lines in the Song of Moses, see also Jack R. Lundbom, "Structure in the Song of Moses (Deuteronomy 32.1-43)," in Lundbom, *Biblical Rhetoric*, 133–36; and Lundbom, *Deuteronomy: A Commentary* (Grand Rapids: Eerdmans, 2013), 859–62.

28. Matthew Black, "The Beatitudes," *ET* 64 (1952–53): 125–26.

29. Jeremias, *Sermon on the Mount*," 22–24.

6. Beware of Lust (5:27-30). Introduced by "You have heard that it was said . . . But I say to you." The balance in vv. 29-30 aids in delimiting the unit—"right eye"/"right hand," also the repeated conclusion: "it is better for you to lose one of your members than for your whole body to go into hell."

7. What about Divorce? (5:31-32). Introduced by an abbreviated "It was also said . . . But I say to you," with the section also delimited by content to vv. 31-32.

8. Better Not to Use Oaths (5:33-37). Introduced by "You have heard that it was said . . . But I say to you," with the section also delimited by content to vv. 33-37.

9. How to Handle Insult (5:38-42). Introduced by "You have heard that it was said . . . But I say to you," with the section also delimited by content to vv. 38-42.

10. Love Your Enemies (5:43-48). Introduced by "You have heard that it was said . . . But I say to you," with the section also delimited by content to vv. 43-48. The concluding verse, "Be perfect, therefore, as your heavenly Father is perfect," is another ballast statement, this one summing up the entire Sermon on the Mount. See further chapter 4 on the "*Imitatio Dei*."

11. Beware of Public Piety (6:1-18). Here three teachings have parallel introductions: "So when you *give alms*" (v. 2); "And whenever you *pray*" (v. 5); and "And whenever you *fast*" (v. 16). Matthew supplements the central teaching on prayer with his presentation of the Lord's Prayer (vv. 9-13), on either side of which is more expansion (vv. 7-8, 14-15). Ulrich Luz thinks that the Lord's Prayer is the central text of the Sermon on the Mount, which it may be.[30] The section is also structured with an *inclusio*:[31]

---

30. Ulrich Luz, *Matthew 1–7: A Commentary* (trans. James E. Crouch; Hermeneia; Minneapolis: Fortress Press, 2007), 172.

> 6:1   Beware of practicing your piety before others in order to *be seen* by them; for then you will have *no reward* from your Father in heaven.

> 6:18   . . . and your Father who *sees* in secret *will reward you.*

12. Where Your Treasure Is (6:19-21). A teaching on the laying up of treasure, concluding with another ballast statement: "For where your treasure is, there your heart will be also."

13. Single-mindedness to God and to others (6:22-24). Two teachings on single-mindedness, each of which concludes with a ballast statement: "If then the light in you is darkness, how great is the darkness!" (v. 23b), and "You cannot serve God and wealth" (v. 24b).

14. Do not worry about Your Life (6:25-34). The three basic human concerns, "What you will eat," "What you will drink," and "What you will wear" balance the section at beginning and end (vv. 25, 31). Concerns of food and clothing are met with parallel responses: "Look at the birds of the air . . ." (v. 26) and "Consider the lilies of the field . . ." (v. 28). Concluding the section is a ballast statement: "But strive first for the kingdom of God and his righteousness, and all these things will be given to you as well." Verse 34 is a later add-on.

15. Beware of Making Judgments (7:1-5). This section is delimited by content and parallel questions: "Why do you *see the speck* in *your neighbor's eye,* but do not notice the *log in your own eye?*" (v. 3), and "Or how can you say to your *neighbor,* Let me *take the speck* out of *your eye,* while the *log is in your own eye?*" (v. 4). Delimiting the section to 7:1-5 makes it clear that the opening

---

31. Eugene M. Skibbe, "Pentateuchal Themes in the Sermon on the Mount," *Lutheran Quarterly* 20 (1968): 47.

"Do not judge" is not absolute but simply a cautionary word about hypocritical judgments.

16. Give Not Away What Is Holy (7:6). A teaching on the infinite worth of the kingdom: It is not to be given to those who will cheapen or ruin it. The section is a chiasmus: give *dogs*/throw before *swine*/they [*swine*] trample/they [*dogs*] turn to rend.

17. Ask and It Will Be Given You (7:7-12). A teaching stressing the need to search out the kingdom, employing three verbs: ask, search, and knock. It concludes with the Golden Rule, which is another ballast statement in the entire Sermon on the Mount (v. 12). The reference to "the law and the prophets" in v. 12 may also tie in structurally with "the law and the prophets" in 5:17.[32]

18. Enter by the Narrow Gate (7:13-14). A wisdom teaching on the "two ways" and the "two gates": the gate is wide and the way broad (not easy) leading to destruction; the gate is narrow and the way confined (not hard) leading to life.

19. Beware of False Prophets (7:15-20). Another wisdom teaching, this one discriminating false from true prophets. Prophets, like trees, are known by their fruits. The false prophet bears bad fruit, and the true prophet good fruit. The unit concludes with a ballast statement: "Thus you will know them by their fruits" (v 20).

20. Hearing and Doing Is Everything (7:21-27). This concluding teaching develops another wisdom theme, and has two parts: (1) a warning that not everyone speaking the name of the Lord or doing deeds of power/mighty works in his name will enter the kingdom of heaven, only the one who does the will of the Father who is in heaven; and (2) a parable on the two houses: one a house on rock built by the wise man, the other a house on sand

---

32. Luz, *Matthew 1–7*, 173.

built by the foolish man. Jesus expects the assembled to hear and do what he has taught in the Sermon. The parable ends with a ballast statement similar to the one in 6:23: "and great was its fall!" (7:27b).

21. Conclusion. Jesus finishes his teaching on the mountain; the background crowds are astounded because he taught as one with authority (7:28-29). This conclusion balances the introduction in 5:1-2.[33]

Proclaiming Matthew's Gospel in the Early Church

One may well ask why Matthew structured his Gospel and also the Sermon on the Mount in the way that he did. Tradition has it that Matthew was a tax collector, thus a trained scribe (Matt. 9:9), which could account for his attention to balance, order, and good written form. (In the Old Testament, the book of Jeremiah is more ordered than any of the other prophetic books, probably because Baruch the scribe—and also his brother Seraiah—had a hand in the composition [see Jer. 36:4-8, 32; 51:59-64]).[34]

But there may be another reason for Matthew giving structure to his Gospel, which would obtain also for other Gospel writers, and that would be the need for Gospels to be read aloud in their entirety to gathered assemblies—worshipers in the early church primarily, but also others interested in hearing the faith that this new church was proclaiming. Nils Lund maintained that larger chiastic structures served a liturgical function in the Jewish community.[35] For example,

---

33. Luz, *Matthew 1–7*, 173.
34. Jack R. Lundbom, *Jeremiah 1–20: A New Translation with Introduction and Commentary* (AB 21A; New York: Doubleday, 1999; repr., New Haven: Yale University Press, 2009), 85, 92–101; Lundbom, *Jeremiah 21–36: A New Translation with Introduction and Commentary* (AB 21B; New York: Doubleday, 2004; repr., New Haven: Yale University Press, 2007), 581–94; Lundbom, *Writing Up Jeremiah: The Prophet and the Book* (Eugene, OR: Cascade Books, 2013), 46–86.

he argued that the book of Revelation—which he believed was structured into a large chiasmus—was to be read aloud to a gathered congregation on the eve of persecution.[36] Lund also thought that the chiastic structure might serve as a mnemonic device in a culture still largely oral.[37] Lohr, too, argued that, in writing his Gospel, Matthew adapted existing traditions to the traditional style of oral literature.[38]

Reading the inspired Word of God aloud to worshiping congregations had been going on for centuries. The Deuteronomic law, once put into written form, was to be read aloud every seven years at the Feast of Booths. Everyone was to be present—men, women, small children, even sojourners residing in the land (Deut. 31:9-13). When the first Jeremiah scroll was written in 605 B.C.E., it was read aloud to a gathered assembly on a fast day in 604 B.C.E. The one reading it was a prominent Jerusalem scribe, Baruch ben Neriah (Jer 36:1-8). Paul's letters, likewise, were read in their entirety to gathered congregations of Christians. The tradition of reading Scripture aloud in worship has been carried on down through the ages, only now only small portions are read; seldom if ever are entire books read.

In the spring of 2011, when the four hundredth anniversary of the translation of the King James Bible was marked in England, a continuous reading of the entire KJV took place in Great Saint Mary's Church, Cambridge. People from the various Cambridge churches were invited to read portions of the KJV. My church, Saint Mark's, took part. The committee planning the event estimated that the Gospel of Mark would take about ninety minutes to read. Matthew would take a bit longer.

---

35. Lund, "Influence of Chiasmus upon the Structure of the Gospel according to Matthew," 406–7; Lund, *Chiasmus in the New Testament*, 93.

36. Nils W. Lund, *Studies in the Book of Revelation* (Chicago: Covenant Press, 1955).

37. Lund, "Influence of Chiasmus upon the Structure of the Gospels," 48.

38. Lohr, "Oral Techniques in the Gospel of Matthew," 404.

Matthew's Gospel was written so as to be read aloud to a congregation gathered for worship, its structure containing messages that people today will likely miss if they read the Gospel silently or hear only small portions read aloud in public worship.

2

The New Covenant in Matthew

The new covenant promised by Jeremiah (Jer. 31:31-34) is well understood by Matthew and has been incorporated into the writing of his Gospel. Matthew shows how this new covenant has been fulfilled in the ministry of Jesus and the establishment of the nascent church. The new covenant has important precedents in the Old Testament, where a number of covenants define the relationship God has with certain individuals, the nation Israel, and indeed with all of creation.

Covenant in Ancient Israel

The idea of "covenant" is central to the faith of both Jews and Christians. It is said to be the central idea in the Bible, one scholar having designated it the controlling concept for illuminating the entire Old Testament.[1] Christian Scripture became the "New Testament," where Latin *testamentum* translated the Greek διαθήκη,

---

1. Walther Eichrodt, *Theology of the Old Testament* (trans. J. A. Baker; 2 vols.; London: SCM Press, 1961–67).

meaning "covenant." From Paul we get the term "Old Testament"; in 2 Cor. 3:14 he refers to reading the "old covenant" (παλαιᾶς διαθήκης) in the synagogue. Use of the term "old covenant" was then carried on by the Church Fathers, and survives in our own day.

In the Old Testament, God makes not one but a number of covenants: with individuals, with a chosen people, with royal and priestly lines, and with the whole of creation. The covenant made with Abraham, repeated to Isaac and Jacob, was that Abraham's descendants would be in number like the stars of the sky or the sands on the seashore; that Abraham would be a blessing to all people on the earth; and that descendants of him and Sarah would one day return to possess the land in which they were presently sojourning (Genesis 12; 15; 17).

With David, God made a covenant that his royal line would continue in perpetuity. Nathan the prophet delivered this promise to David in 2 Samuel 7, and it is repeated in Psalm 89:

> You said, "I have made a covenant with my chosen one,
>> I have sworn to my servant David:
> 'I will establish your descendants forever,
>> and build your throne for all generations.'" (Ps. 89:3-4)

With the zealous priest Phinehas, who plunged a spear into an Israelite man and a Midianite woman for worshiping Baal of Peor, and thereby stayed a plague that had claimed twenty-four thousand lives, God made a covenant ensuring permanence to the Aaronic line of priests (Num. 25:11-13).

Earlier still, in hoary antiquity, God is said to have made a covenant with Noah after the great Flood, promising that as long as the world endures there will never again be a flood like the one just sent. This covenant was with all humanity, Israelites and non-Israelites. More than that, it was with every living creature that came out of Noah's ark—beasts, birds, and other living creatures. It was a covenant with the entire created order (Gen. 9:8-11).

All these covenants were given unconditionally and in perpetuity, which is to say, they could not be broken and thus would never end. Yes, they were preceded by acts of faith (Noah; Abraham) or devotion (David; Phinehas ["zeal"]), and were confirmed by signs (rainbow; circumcision); still no conditions were set forth. Maintenance of the covenant did not depend on Abraham's obedience or any other act. The same was true with Noah and David, both of whom acted badly after covenants were made with them. Noah got drunk after planting a vineyard and drinking the wine, and David committed adultery with the wife of Uriah the Hittite and then planned Uriah's murder as a cover-up. Phinehas, so far as we know, did not commit any subsequent sin, but his priestly line fell into a sorry state. Read Hosea and Jeremiah to see their assessments of the priesthood (Hos. 4:6; 5:1; 6:9; Jer. 5:31; 6:13; 23:11). This type of covenant, in which a sovereign—here the Lord God—obligates himself but does not set forth statutes that the subordinate must obey, was unique in the ancient world.[2]

The covenant occupying center stage in the Old Testament, however, is the one that God makes with Israel. It was formalized at Mount Sinai, where God gave Israel the Law, the core of which was the Ten Commandments (Exod. 20:1-17; Deut. 5:1-22). Unlike the other covenants just named, this one was conditional, containing statutes that had to be kept. If they were not kept—and time and again they were not—the covenant would be declared broken and would have to be renewed.

---

2. D. N. Freedman, "Divine Commitment and Human Obligation," *Int* 18 (1964): 419–31 (reprinted in Freedman, *Divine Commitment and Human Obligation*, 1:168–78).

The covenant with Israel was predicated on God's gracious election and deliverance of his people from Egyptian slavery. The "exodus," as it is called, is the central event of the Old Testament. "Salvation"—or "liberation," which also translates the Hebrew—in the exodus and in the Bible generally is not so much a granting of freedom as it is a change of masters.[3] Paul will talk later about having "freedom (in Christ)" (2 Cor. 3:17; Gal. 5:1, 13), but freedom is not the defining idea in either Old or New Testament salvation. Salvation in both is a "change of masters." In the Old Testament, Pharaoh is the old master, and the Lord God, after redeeming Israel, becomes the new. In the New Testament the old master is Satan and the power of sin; the new master is Jesus, who saves humankind from sin by his death on the cross.

The model for this theological concept comes from ancient Near Eastern law. If a person fell into slavery, which could happen easily in the ancient world, it was possible for a next of kin to pay the redemption price that the person himself could not pay. In such a case, the one redeemed would then serve the kin who paid the release. But the good news is that this servitude would be easier, because the kinsman would treat the redeemed person more kindly. (It is a bit like receiving a low-interest or no-interest loan from your parents or a generous uncle.) God, therefore, instructed Moses to tell Pharaoh: "Israel is my first-born son, and I say to you, 'Let my son go that he may serve me'" (Exod. 4:22-23 RSV). God did redeem Israel from slavery, and in so doing became the new master. Israel was thus obliged to serve God. The terms were laid out at Mount Sinai, where God gave Israel the Ten Commandments. These were introduced as follows:

---

3. David Daube, *The Exodus Pattern in the Bible* (London: Faber & Faber, 1963).

I am the Lord your God, who brought you out of the land of Egypt, out of the house of slavery; you shall have no other gods before me . . .

(Exod. 20:2-3; Deut. 5:6-7).

The Lord God could lay the law upon Israel because he is the one who liberated Israel. This law was not meant to be burdensome, although it later became so for the Jewish people, for Jesus, for Paul, for members of the Christian church, and for Gentiles wanting to join the church. But it was not meant to be burdensome, and the Israelite people at their best understood this. Psalm 119, the longest psalm in the Psalter, shows how Israel loved the Law. It begins:

> Happy are those whose way is blameless,
>   who walk in the law of the Lord.
> Happy are those who keep his decrees,
>   who seek him with their whole heart,
> who also do no wrong,
>   but walk in his ways. . . .
> I delight in the way of your decrees
>   as much as in all riches.
> I will meditate on your precepts,
>   and fix my eyes on your ways.
> I will delight in your statutes;
>   I will not forget your word.
> (Ps. 119:1-5, 14-16)

In Deuteronomy, Moses tells the Israelites before they cross the Jordan that they will have no difficulty carrying out God's Law. He says:

Surely, this commandment that I am commanding you today is not too hard for you, nor is it too far away. It is not in heaven, that you should say, "Who will go up to heaven for us, and get it for us so that we may hear it and observe it?" Neither is it beyond the sea, that you should say, "Who will cross to the other side of the sea for us and get it for us so that we may hear it and observe it?" No, the word is very near to you; it is in your mouth and in your heart for you to observe. (Deut. 30:11-14)

But this same Deuteronomy makes clearer than any other biblical book the conditional nature of the Horeb (= Sinai) covenant, fortifying it with blessings and curses (Deut. 11:26-32; 28). If Israel obeys the covenant, it will be blessed and will live long in the land the Lord has given it. But if it disobeys, the curses will fall, the most serious being Israel's loss of the land. Deuteronomy 28 does not make for pleasant reading, where the curses outnumber the blessings almost four to one.[4]

This covenant appropriates a treaty form well known in the ancient Near East, one drafted by powerful kings for kings subordinate to them. These treaties, which are covenants, basically, set forth the conditions (= law) of the relationship, after which come blessings and curses. If the subordinate king obeys the sovereign king, blessings will come upon him. If he disobeys, a litany of horrible curses will fall. The Hittite treaties keep the blessings and curses in balance,[5] but the Syrian and Assyrian treaties, like Deuteronomy 28, have considerably more curses than blessings. The Vassal Treaties of Esarhaddon (680–669 B.C.E.) have a multitude of curses and no blessings at all.[6]

---

4. Gerhard von Rad, *Deuteronomy: A Commentary* (OTL; London: SCM Press, 1966), 173.

5. See *Ancient Near Eastern Texts Relating to the Old Testament* (ed. James B. Pritchard; 3rd ed.; Princeton: Princeton University Press, 1969), 201, 205.

6. *ANET*[3], 538–41.

Covenant Breaking and Covenant Renewal

The story of the Old Testament is the story of covenant breaking. The seeds were sown early. Already in the wilderness, when Moses descended from Mount Sinai with the tablets of the Law, he found that the people in his absence—and with assistance from Aaron, his brother—had made a golden calf. Moses, in a blaze of anger, broke the stone tablets on which the Ten Commandments were inscribed. As a result, the commandments had to be rewritten on new tablets, after which the covenant was renewed (Exodus 24; 32–34).

More covenant renewals were required in the years that followed: under Moses, before his death and before Israel entered the promised land (Deut. 29:1); at Shechem before the death of Joshua (Josh. 24:25); and in Jerusalem under Kings Jehoiada (2 Kgs. 11:17), Hezekiah (2 Chron. 29:10), and Josiah (2 Kgs. 23:3). But a time came, finally, when the covenant had become so completely broken that renewal was no longer possible. Then fell the Deuteronomic curses with a terrible vengeance on the remnant of a once-great Israelite people, and the nation tumbled headlong into ruin in 586 B.C.E. This happened during the time of Jeremiah.

Jeremiah's Prophecy of a New Covenant

Just before Jerusalem fell to Nebuchadnezzar II and survivors began the long march into a Babylonian exile, Jeremiah—who understood himself to be "the prophet like Moses" of Deut. 18:18—announced a "new covenant" from his place of confinement in the court of the guard. This covenant, which is recorded in Jer. 31:31-34, and only there in the OT, is described as follows:

> Look, days are coming—oracle of Yahweh—when I will cut with the house of Israel and with the house of Judah a new covenant, not like the

33

covenant that I cut with their fathers in the day I took them by the hand to bring them out of the land of Egypt, my covenant that they, they broke, though I, I was their master—oracle of Yahweh.

But this is the covenant that I will cut with the house of Israel after those days—oracle of Yahweh: I will put my law in their inward parts, and upon their hearts I will write it. And I will be God to them, and they, they will be a people to me. And they shall not again instruct each person his fellow and each person his brother, saying, "Know Yahweh," for they, all of them, shall know me, from the least of them to the greatest of them—oracle of Yahweh—for I will forgive their iniquity, and their sin I will not remember again.
(Jer. 31:31-34 AB)

The "law" (Hebrew *torah*) will continue to exist in the new covenant, and an obligation to comply with its demands will still exist, but conditions will be vastly improved because God promises to write his *torah* on the human heart. Jeremiah does not specify what this (new) law will consist of, but it is reasonable to assume that it will be the law at the heart of the Sinai covenant, namely, the Ten Commandments. It will doubtless contain something more.

Scholars have considered two related questions when discussing the new covenant: (1) whether this covenant really is "new," and (2) whether the Sinai covenant over against which the new covenant stands continues to be viable. Some think that the new covenant will simply be a renewal of the Sinai covenant, and nothing more. Others believe that Jeremiah announces the end of the Sinai covenant and presents here a covenant that is really new. In my view, the new covenant has to be more than a renewed Sinai covenant, such as what took place on the plains of Moab, at Shechem, or in Jerusalem under three Judahite kings. Although this future covenant will admittedly have continuity with the Sinai covenant, it will nevertheless be a genuinely new covenant, one that marks a new beginning in the divine–human relationship. Why? Because (1) it is given without conditions; (2) it will be written on the hearts of people in a way the Sinai covenant was not (v. 33); and (3) it will be grounded in a wholly new act of divine grace, that is, the forgiveness of sins (v. 34).

Taking up these points in reverse order, we see first of all that in the Old Testament God certainly forgives sin; however, he also is not loath to punish the guilty. In a classic self-disclosure Yahweh describes himself as a

> God merciful and gracious, slow to anger, and abounding in steadfast love and faithfulness, keeping steadfast love for the thousandth generation, forgiving iniquity and transgression and sin, yet by no means clearing the guilty, but visiting the iniquity of the parents upon the children and the children's children, to the third and fourth generation. (Exod 34:6-7)

So God does forgive sin; nevertheless, forgiveness of sins is not what undergirds the Sinai covenant; in fact, forgiveness of sins does not figure at all in this covenant's formulation in Exodus and Deuteronomy (Exod. 32:32-34; Deut. 31:16-29). The act of divine grace undergirding the Sinai covenant, as was mentioned earlier, was the deliverance from Egypt (Exod. 20:2; Deut. 5:6). This early theology is best summed up in Joshua's words to the people at Shechem: If you disobey the covenant, Yahweh will *not* forgive your sins; instead he will punish you (Josh. 24:19-20).

Second, the new covenant of which Jeremiah speaks is written on the heart. The Sinai covenant was written on tablets of stone (Exod. 24:12; 31:18). It is true that this covenant was supposed to find its way into the human heart. Deuteronomy says as much (Deut. 6:6; 11:18; 30:14), and we learn this also from a verse many of us learned in childhood: "Thy word have I hid in my heart, that I might not sin against thee" (Ps. 119:11 KJV). Yet Deuteronomy knows—and Jeremiah knows—that the human heart is deceitful and layered with evil (Deut. 10:16; 11:16; Jer. 4:4). Jeremiah assesses the human condition more negatively, saying that the heart is evil, stubborn, and rebellious (5:23), that sin is "engraved" on the tablet of the heart (17:1), and that the heart "is deceitful above all things" (17:9). But now, however, with the new covenant in place, the law will penetrate the human heart because God will make it happen.

Third, we should note the unconditional and eternal nature of the new covenant. This covenant will be like the covenants God made with Noah, Abraham, David, and Phinehas. In fact, the future covenant is described in Jer. 32:40 and 50:5 as an "eternal covenant," a designation found elsewhere in the Old Testament (Ezek. 16:60; Isa. 55:3; 61:8). It is generally agreed that this "eternal covenant" is the same as the "new covenant" in Jer. 31:31-34, confirming that the new covenant will be everlasting. The Sinai covenant with its blessings and curses was never guaranteed to be everlasting. But this eternal covenant, in the words of James Muilenburg, will be a relationship of pure grace.[7]

Covenant in Later Judaism

In postexilic Judaism, with national life being reconstructed along the old lines, the Sinai covenant once again became central and the Law occupied a position of supremacy. At the same time, a new covenant was looked for in the future, at which time the messianic age would dawn. Among the Essene Jews at Qumran, the new covenant found fulfillment in a separated community that believed it was living in the "last days." Members of the community swore an oath to uphold a covenant variously described as a "covenant of God," an "eternal covenant," a "covenant of repentance," a "covenant of steadfast love," and a "new covenant."

7. James Muilenburg, "Isaiah," in *IB* 5:399.

The new covenant idea undergoes no further development in Judaism. The Midrashim contain merely a few citations of Jer. 31:33 for purposes of focusing on the old problem of remembering the Torah. There the Jeremiah verse is given a meaning close to the one it had originally: that forgetting the Torah can be expected in the present world, and only in the World to Come, when the Torah is (truly) written on the heart, will people no longer forget it (Midrashim: *Ecc. Rab.* 2:1; *Cant. Rab.* 1:2; *Pes. R.* 107a; *Yalqut* on Jer. 31:33). It may also be noted that in the modern *Encyclopaedia Judaica* (New York: Macmillan, 1971–73), which is the standard reference work among Jews, there are no articles on "new covenant" or "eternal covenant," and in the article on "covenant," neither of these covenants is mentioned.

New Covenant in Early Christianity

It was the Christian church that claimed Jeremiah's promise and understood itself to be the people of the new covenant. It thought of itself as a new people (1 Pet. 2:1-10)—Israel reborn, but a more inclusive Israel to which Gentiles now belong. Yet the term "new covenant" occurs in the Gospels only once, appearing on the lips of Jesus in the longer text of Luke 22:20, where, at the Last Supper, Jesus passes the wine and says, "This cup . . . is the new covenant in my blood."

Paul, the preeminent missionary and theologian of the early church, referred to himself and the Corinthian laity as "ministers of a new covenant" (2 Cor. 3:6); nevertheless, the new covenant was not prominent in his preaching. He might have said more about the new covenant were it not for his concern to establish a more ancient base than Jer. 31:31-34 for the new faith in Christ. The important promise for Paul was the one given to Abraham, that through him all the families of the earth would be blessed. Paul grounds the blessings through Christ in the Abrahamic covenant so they may apply equally to Jews and Gentiles (Gal. 3:14). His goal was to evangelize the Gentiles, but the Sinai covenant had been made only with Israel (Rom. 9:4; Eph. 2:11-13). Moreover, the Sinai covenant contained the law, which had now become a burden to everybody—Jew and Gentile alike. In Paul's view, the law only brings people under its curses. But Christ, by dying on the cross, becomes himself a curse redeeming those under the law who have faith in him (Gal. 3:10-14). The new covenant has only blessings, making it just like the Abrahamic covenant.

Paul does, however, give the Roman church a most extraordinary teaching on the new covenant, unlike any other in the New Testament and unlike any made subsequently by the Church Fathers. Elsewhere the new covenant is made to apply only to the church, which is the new Israel. But in Rom. 11:25-32 Paul applies the new covenant promise to the Israel that remains hardened to the gospel.[8] Paul says that at some future time, when the full number of Gentiles has come in, and the Parousia of Jesus occurs, *all* Israel will be saved. Isaiah 59:20 is quoted, and next comes the new covenant prophecy: "And this is my covenant with them, when I take away their sins" (Rom. 11:27). Here Paul gives the new covenant promise its most inclusive meaning: he believes this covenant really is for everyone. He concludes: "For the gifts and the calling of God are irrevocable" (Rom 11:29), by which he means not just the covenant promised to Abraham but also the new covenant. Both covenants are unconditional, eternal, and given for the salvation of all.

In the Letter to the Hebrews, the new covenant is given its most prominent place in the New Testament. Jeremiah's new covenant

---

8. C. H. Dodd, *The Epistle of Paul to the Romans* (London: Hodder & Stoughton, 1932), 182.

promise is quoted twice, once in its entirety (8:8-12) and once in abridged form (10:16-17). The Sinai covenant, here called the "first covenant," was shown to be faulty because the people under it were faulty (8:7-8a). Jeremiah's new covenant has better promises: it contains God's unconditional commitment to forgive sins; it is eternal (9:15; 13:20); and Jesus is the covenant's surety (7:22). According to Hebrews, Jeremiah in announcing this new covenant treats the Sinai covenant as obsolete. That obsolescence is just now being seen as the first covenant is ready to vanish away (8:13).

Jesus is the "mediator of the new covenant" (9:15; "better covenant" in 8:6; "fresh covenant" in 12:24; cf. 1 Tim. 2:5-6; Isa. 42:6; 49:8). In Judaism, the covenant mediator was Moses (cf. Gal. 3:19), and after his death the high priest. Jesus becomes the mediator of the new covenant by virtue of his death on the cross, which the author of Hebrews explains in priestly and sacrificial categories that were understood within Judaism (9:1-14).

In the abridged quotation of Jeremiah in Heb. 10:16-17, the accent is on the concluding words of the new covenant promise, which state that God will no longer remember the peoples' sins. Once forgiveness of sins is granted, there is no longer any sin offering that can be made (10:18, 26). This "once for all" view of Jesus' sacrifice is matched in Hebrews with a "once for all" view of repentance, enlightenment (baptism), and sanctification of the believer. If one deliberately sins after coming to a knowledge of the truth, that person profanes the blood of the new covenant and has only God's vengeance to look forward to (10:26-31). Christian sanctification, in the view of the author of Hebrews, has the effect of recasting the new covenant in terms of the old, and it qualifies the "blessings only" promise made to the church. Although curses are not explicitly made against individuals who lapse under the new covenant, they are implied (6:1-8; 10:26-31). The idea that deliberate sin makes a sin offering inefficacious is found also in Num. 15:30-31. But the author of Hebrews prays in a closing benediction that the Lord Jesus, "by the blood of the eternal covenant," will equip the elect to do God's will (13:20-21).

What about the Gospels? In Mark, thought by many to be the earliest Gospel, the new covenant idea is not present either explicitly or implicitly. In John, Jesus is presented as the "new Moses,"[9] but for this Gospel writer Jesus gives no new *torah*, unless one identifies such in the new commandment to "love one another" (3:34). Jesus himself is the *Logos*. John therefore makes a law-and-grace dichotomy similar to Paul's: "The law indeed was given through Moses; grace and truth came through Jesus Christ" (1:17). The Holy Spirit is John's answer to the new inner motivation required to know and do the *torah*. The Spirit dwells within the believer (14:17) and in Jesus' absence will bring his teachings (*torah*) to remembrance (14:26). The Spirit will also convince the rest of the world of sin, righteousness, and judgment (16:7-11).

In Luke, a clear echo of the covenant form in Deuteronomy occurs in Jesus' "Sermon on the Plain," given after the calling of the twelve apostles (Luke 6). In this sermon, Jesus presents the assembled crowd with four blessings and four woes:

> Blessed are you who are poor, for yours is the kingdom of God.
> Blessed are you who are hungry now, for you will be filled.
> Blessed are you who weep now, for you will laugh.
> Blessed are you when people hate you, and when they exclude you, revile you, and defame you on account of the Son of Man.
> Rejoice in that day and leap for joy, for surely your reward is great in heaven; for that is what their ancestors did to the prophets.

9. T. F. Glasson, *Moses in the Fourth Gospel* (Studies in Biblical Theology 10; Naperville, IL: Allenson, 1963).

But woe to you who are rich, for you have received your consolation.
Woe to you who are full now, for you will be hungry.
Woe to you who are laughing now, for you will mourn and weep.
Woe to you when all speak well of you, for that is what their ancestors
   did to the false prophets. (Luke 6:20-26)

New Covenant in Matthew

New covenant teaching is more prominent in Matthew, even though, as in the other Gospels, it is not here made explicit. The teaching is embodied in the writing and structuring of the Gospel. According to W. D. Davies, the Sermon on the Mount is a program for Matthew's church, which is located most likely in Syria (Antioch?) c. 85 c.e.[10] There is a stronger emphasis on the church in this Gospel than in any other. Greek ἐκκλησία, which translates as "church," appears in Matt. 16:18 and 18:17, and nowhere else in the Gospels. The Gospel of Matthew may have been used for teaching in the church, either for those desiring to join the church or for those newly joined once they had been baptized. According to Joachim Jeremias, Matthew is more teaching (διδαχή) than gospel proclamation (κήρυγμα),[11] where Jesus is being portrayed as the rabbi par excellence.[12] Yet the difference may not be that great; even today, preaching combines teaching with gospel proclamation.

Matthew, like Luke, presents Jesus as a "new Moses," but Matthew carries the typology further. He parallels the birth story of Jesus with the birth story of Moses, alluding in Herod's massacre of baby boys (Matt. 2:13-18) to Pharaoh's massacre of the same in Egypt (Exodus 1–2). Jesus is then brought out of Egypt, just as Moses was, leading

10. Davies, *Invitation to the New Testament*, 209–12.
11. Jeremias, *Sermon on the Mount*, 20–24.
12. See Jaroslav Pelikan, *Jesus through the Centuries: His Place in the History of Culture* (New Haven: Yale University Press, 1985), 9–20.

a "new exodus" and later giving his Torah on a "new Mount Sinai" in Galilee. The Sermon on the Mount is Jesus' "new Torah (Law)," which comes not to replace the old Torah, but to fulfill it (Matt. 5:17).[13]

We must look also to the structure of Matthew for theological ideas, which we can do if we hear the entire Gospel read aloud from beginning to end, something occurring rarely if at all in our own day, when only small portions of Scripture are read in public worship. Matthew's Gospel was intended to be read aloud in its entirety to a gathered assembly of early Christians, and when it was, the repetitions, contrasts, and other rhetorical features could be more easily heard. For people in the modern day, it is only concerts, movies, and other dramatic productions that occupy our attention for an hour or two. In ancient Israel, however, people gathered at the Feast of Booths every seven years to hear the entire Deuteronomic law proclaimed (Deut. 31:10-13). Early Christian communities listened similarly to all the Gospels and letters of Paul (Col. 4:16). Here in Matthew, the woes of chapter 23 would be heard especially as counterbalancing the blessings of chapter 5 (see chapter 1 above).

But some important differences exist between, on the one hand, Matthew's new covenant presentation and the blessings and curses of Deuteronomy and, on the other, those contained in treaties of the ancient Near East:

1. First, and most important, the blessings and woes in Matthew are spoken to different audiences—blessings proffered upon the new people of the kingdom (5:3-11), and "woes" proffered upon the old (23:13-36). In Deuteronomy, and in the international treaties, it is the same audience receiving both

13. W. D. Davies, *The Sermon on the Mount* (Cambridge: Cambridge University Press, 1969), 10–32.

blessings and curses. But in Matthew the new people of the kingdom receive neither woes nor curses, only blessings. Matthew believes there can be no abrogation of the new covenant and no destruction of the church (16:18). This is the new and eternal covenant announced by Jeremiah—God's pure and unconditional gift of grace to the church, against which the gates of hell cannot prevail.

2. The language in Matthew is also toned down. Greek μακάριοι ("blessed") and οὐαί ("woe") translate the Hebrew words אַשְׁרֵי and הוֹי, both milder terms than the Deuteronomic בָּרוּךְ ("blessed") and אָרוּר ("cursed"). Jesus does not go so far as to curse the scribes and Pharisees.

3. In Matthew the blessings and woes are simply announced. Neither is made conditional, which is to say, neither depends on obedience or disobedience to any legal demands. Blessings are unilaterally conferred on the new people of the kingdom, who receive them without price or obligation. The woes, likewise, are conferred in the same manner upon the scribes and Pharisees. Jesus is speaking here as a prophet, as he does throughout the Sermon on the Mount. He is not the Deuteronomic preacher, who simply lays before people the covenant obligations and warns them to be careful to do them. Jesus is a prophet, the likes of Jeremiah and others who spoke an authoritative word from the Lord.

4. Finally, the blessings of Matthew's new covenant come first, not last, as they do in Deuteronomy and in the international treaties. It is as if Jesus wants to get them out in front of everything else, not making his audience wait for something it might otherwise expect at the end.

3

At What Elevation Is Jesus' Sermon on the Mount?

The Sermon on the Mount as Transformational Preaching

Jesus' Sermon on the Mount has always held great fascination for me, and it continues to fascinate me, as it has countless Christians and non-Christians down through the ages. We live in a day when teachings embodied in this Sermon need much to be heard.

Our world today has trouble enough, and the Christian church is also in crisis. The daily newspapers and news on the television remind us without letup how impure the world and the church have become. What then should people do? Pray? Of course, but people need to do more than pray. Christians in other times like our own have returned to examine the foundations of their faith to see what they can learn, and I can think of no more foundational teaching in Christianity than Jesus' Sermon on the Mount. Matthew features it prominently at the beginning of his Gospel, where it appears to be nothing less than a "new covenant" presented to the nascent church.

The world many times has been transformed by this Sermon. It profoundly influenced Mohandas Gandhi and Martin Luther King Jr. in their efforts to achieve freedom and social justice. For them, Jesus' Sermon embodied not simply lofty ideals but teachings capable of being put into practice, and capable of bringing about substantive change. Gandhi was particularly impressed with the Sermon on the Mount, saying: "it went straight to my heart." Quoting Matt. 5:39-40 about not returning a strike on the cheek and giving up one's cloak along with one's tunic, he said that renunciation was the highest form of religion, for which reason Jesus' Sermon appealed to him greatly.[1] He went on to say: "The message of Jesus, as I understand it, is contained in the *Sermon on the Mount*. . . . It is that *Sermon* which has endeared Jesus to me." But, he added, "The message, to my mind, has suffered distortion in the West. . . . Much of what passes as Christianity is a negation of the *Sermon on the Mount*."[2] When Germany in the last century began experiencing deep crisis after Hitler came to power, one of its Lutheran pastors and theologians, Dietrich Bonhoeffer, wrote a book entitled *The Cost of Discipleship*, which was based on Jesus' Sermon on the Mount.[3] It was published in 1937, and had a great impact in its day as well as in the years subsequent to World War II.

No portion of Scripture was more frequently cited by the Church Fathers than the Sermon on the Mount.[4] Augustine of Hippo (354–430c.e.), not long after his conversion to Christianity, wrote a commentary on the Sermon, which was the first of its kind.[5] He

1. Mohandas K. Gandhi, *Gandhi's Autobiography* (trans. Mahadev Desai; Washington, DC: Public Affairs Press, 1960), 92; Gandhi, *What Jesus Means to Me* (ed. R. K. Prabhu; Ahmedabad: Navajivan Publishing House, 1959), 4.
2. Pinchas Lapide, *The Sermon on the Mount: Utopia or Program for Action?* (trans. Arlene Swidler; Maryknoll, NY: Orbis Books, 1986), 3; Gandhi, *What Jesus Means to Me*, 11.
3. Dietrich Bonhoeffer, *The Cost of Discipleship* (New York: Macmillan, 1963).
4. Warren S. Kissinger, *The Sermon on the Mount: A History of Interpretation and Bibliography* (Metuchen, NJ: Scarecrow, 1975), 6.

was also first to call this portion of Scripture *De sermone domini in monte* ("The Lord's Sermon on the Mount").[6] Martin Luther did not write a commentary on the Sermon, or on Matthew, but his *Weekly Sermons on Matthew 5–7*, which were preached at Wittenberg between October 1530 and April 1532, contain a treasure of insights into the Sermon, such as we have come to expect from this extraordinary man.[7]

The Sermon on the Mount as Preaching an Ideal

Beginning with Luther comes the idea that this Sermon preaches a way of life that is unattainable. Luther saw in the Sermon an impossible ethic designed to awaken us to our inadequacy and sinfulness, which would then drive us to seek God's mercy and help (Romans 5–7).[8] Luther is also recorded as saying that the Sermon on the Mount does not belong in city hall, for "one cannot govern" with it.[9]

Leo Tolstoy took the Sermon on the Mount very seriously, believing that these commands of Jesus had to be taken as obligatory in the most literal sense.[10] But he could not live by them and ended

---

5. H. D. Betz, *The Sermon on the Mount*, 11.

6. Saint Augustine, "Our Lord's Sermon on the Mount" (trans. William Findlay; rev. D. S. Schaff), in *Nicene and Post-Nicene Fathers of the Christian Church*, vol. 6, *Saint Augustin*, (ed. Philip Schaff; Grand Rapids: Wm. B. Eerdmans, 1980; originally 1887), 1–63; *The Preaching of Augustine* (ed. Jaroslav Pelikan; trans. Francine Cardman; Philadelphia: Fortress Press, 1973).

7. Betz, *Sermon on the Mount*, 15–16.

8. Jeremias, *Sermon on the Mount*, 11–13; Daniel J. Harrington, "The Sermon on the Mount: What Is It?" *The Bible Today* 36 (1998), 284.

9. Lapide, *Sermon on the Mount*, 4.

10. One sees this clearly in his novel *Resurrection* (trans. Rosemary Edmonds; London: Penguin Books, 1966), where his lead character, Nekhlyudov, begins reading the Sermon on the Mount and for the first time finds in it "not beautiful abstract thoughts, presenting for the most part exaggerated and impossible demands, but simple, clear, practical commandments, which if obeyed (and this was quite feasible) would establish a completely new order of human society" (pp. 565–66); cf. Amos N. Wilder, *Eschatology and Ethics in the Teaching of Jesus* (New York: Harper & Bros., 1939), ix.

his life tragically, abandoning his wife and children to die at the Astapovo railway station.[11] Fredrich Nietzsche was unimpressed with the Sermon, saying it taught a "slave morality." In its requirements of love and meekness he found a mood dangerous to the heroic temper.[12]

For many others—both believers and nonbelievers—the Sermon's teaching is too elevated. Robert Frost, in his poem "A Masque of Mercy" (1947),[13] includes a dialogue that takes place in a bookstore late at night after the doors have been closed among the Keeper, who is the owner of the store, his wife, and a fellow named Paul (apparently the apostle). The Keeper refers to "Paul's constant theme":

> . . . The Sermon on the Mount
>   Is just a frame-up to insure the failure
> Of all of us, so all of us will be
>   Thrown prostrate at the Mercy Seat for Mercy.

Paul asks the two what they make of the Sermon on the Mount. "The same old nothing," replies the wife. "A beautiful impossibility," responds the Keeper:

> An irresistible impossibility
>   A lofty beauty no one can live up to.
> Yet no one turn from trying to live up to . . .
>   Paul concurs.

Gerhard Kittel, in similar fashion, echoes the sentiments of Luther saying:

11. Henri Troyat, *Tolstoy* (trans. Nancy Amphoux; New York: Penguin Books, 1970), 923–63; Harvey K. McArthur, *Understanding the Sermon on the Mount* (New York: Harper & Bros., 1960), 107.

12. Wilder, *Eschatology and Ethics in the Teaching of Jesus,* ix.

13. Robert Frost, *Selected Poems* (Middlesex: Penguin Books, 1973), 268–69.

The meaning of the Sermon on the Mount is: Demolish! It can only tear down. In the long run it has only one purpose: to expose and exhibit the great poverty in empiric human beings.

Kittel continues:

This is what you ought to do, you wretched weakling, but you can't succeed, as you well know. That is why you need God's gracious love for everything you undertake.[14]

Karl Barth believed that constructing a picture of the Christian life from directives contained in the Sermon on the Mount has always proved impossible. He says, "It would be sheer folly to interpret the imperatives of the Sermon on the Mount as if we should bestir ourselves to actualize these pictures."[15] Reinhold Niebuhr agreed, saying, "The ethical demands made by Jesus are incapable of fulfillment."[16] And Krister Stendahl, Lutheran churchman and scholar, viewed the Sermon if not as utopian, at least as an unattainable ideal, putting him squarely in the tradition of Luther.

Some scholars have been content to say that Jesus' teachings are "exceptional." The great New Testament scholar Johannes Weiss, for example, said that the teachings on revenge and loving one's enemies constituted "exceptional legislation."[17] Albert Schweitzer believed that the Sermon on the Mount contained what he called an "interim ethic,"[18] for which reason it was on such a high level. Jesus' ethical proclamations were conditioned by an eschatological view of the world. The Sermon was to call people to repentance. When the end of the world is imminent, "unusual living" is called for. Paul's

---

14. Lapide, *Sermon on the Mount*, 5.

15. Lapide, *Sermon on the Mount,* 4.

16. Reinhold Niebuhr, *An Interpretation of Christian Ethics* (New York: Meridian Books, 1956), 59.

17. Jeremias, *Sermon on the Mount*, 13–14; Hans Windisch, *The Meaning of the Sermon on the Mount* (trans. S. MacLean Gilmour; Philadelphia: Westminster, 1951), 30.

18. Albert Schweitzer, *The Mystery of the Kingdom of God: The Secret of Jesus' Messiahship and Passion* (trans. Walter Lowrie; New York: Macmillan, 1950), 55.

teaching on marriage in 1 Cor. 7:25-31 builds on the same assumption.

Yet E. Stanley Jones said this:

> The Greatest need of modern Christianity is the re-discovery of the Sermon on the Mount as the only practical way to live. Now we have an undertone of doubt and fear that it is not workable. We feel that it is trying to give human nature a bent that it won't take."[19]

He went on:

> The Sermon on the Mount may seem impossible, but only in our worst moments. In our highest moments—that is, in our real moments—we feel that everything else is unbelievably impossible, an absurdity.[20]

At What Elevation Is the Sermon on the Mount?

The question I wish to ask, then, is, At what elevation is Jesus' Sermon on the Mount? How lofty is this sermon, anyway, and is there any hope at all of living by the teachings it contains? Some do not consider this an important question, but I believe it is of utmost importance. It is important if we are to take the Sermon seriously, and it is important once we have decided to take the Sermon seriously. After we have looked at what the Sermon itself says about attainability, I want to comment on a couple of difficult verses in the Sermon pertaining to attainability, and then go on to discuss three specific teachings in the Sermon that have been particularly troublesome—those on anger (5:21-26), nonretaliation toward evildoers (5:38-42), and judging others (7:1-5). I will interpret them as I think they were meant to be interpreted, making

19. E. Stanley Jones, *The Christ of the Mount* (London: Hodder & Stoughton, 1931), 13.
20. Jones, *Christ of the Mount*, 15.

them more serviceable to Christians and non-Christians in today's world. At the end, I will have a final word to say about the elevation of Jesus' Sermon on the Mount.

There is, as I have said, a widespread notion that this great compilation of Jesus' teaching is no more than an ideal, and that none of us—indeed no one, anywhere—can actually carry it out. We may get this idea from the Sermon itself. I think of verses such as 5:19, where one is warned about relaxing even the least of Jesus' commandments and teaching others to do the same; also the next verse, 5:20, where Jesus says that people's righteousness must exceed the righteousness of the scribes and Pharisees or they will never get into the kingdom of heaven; and finally, the word in 5:48 about the need for people to be perfect as their heavenly Father is perfect. Regarding this last verse, John Knox said, "If Jesus' words in Matthew 5:48, 'Be ye therefore perfect as your Father in heaven is perfect,' are taken at face value, they set a standard for our moral life which there is no possibility of our attaining."[21]

For many, the teachings on anger, nonretaliation, and judging others add to the perception that this Sermon sets forth a code of conduct by which one cannot possibly live, giving only an ideal that one can at best approximate. Even in that beautiful passage of 6:25-32, where Jesus says:

> Therefore I tell you, do not worry about your life, what you will eat or what you will drink, or about your body, what you will wear. Is not life more than food, and the body, more than clothing? Look at the birds of the air . . . (Matt. 6:25-26)

Here we have a teaching lifting up the lifestyle of an Elijah, or a John the Baptist, and how many of us want to give up the comforts we have—even if they are modest comforts—and live like ascetics in

---

21. John Knox, "Ethical Obligation in the Realm of Grace," *Shane Quarterly* 15 (1954): 55.

the desert? Just how simply is a follower of Jesus expected to live? Niebuhr says with reference to these verses, "No life can be lived in such *un*concern for the physical basis of life."[22] And yet the end of this passage says that if we seek *first* God's kingdom and his righteousness, all these things will be ours as well (Matt. 6:33). Maybe this is not a call to the ascetic life after all!

Now it must be admitted that there is something to be said in favor of idealistic teachings. It is laudable, is it not, to set high goals and strive to attain them. People who do this come out considerably better than those who set low goals, or who set no goals at all. But something else can and does happen when people—young and old—meet up with impossible ideals: They give up trying to attain them, knowing that in the end they will fall short. The great teachings are allowed to remain, enshrined in books such as the Bible, but people make no attempt to live by them. As a result, these great teachings are put "out of service." This is a problem lying at the very heart of Matthew's Gospel, and it is what brings forth the sharp censure of the scribes and Pharisees in chapter 23. Those sitting on Moses' seat expound great teachings, but they do not practice them (23:3).

I fear this is a problem with many today. It is always a lurking danger for preachers and teachers, but it affects parents and anyone else uttering lofty or censorious words on this subject or that, with reference to this person or that. People allow the Sermon on the Mount to remain a high ideal, meant perhaps for someone else but not for themselves, and they conveniently ignore it. And if we happen to be Lutherans, we are comforted by the certainty of our sinful state and God's infinite grace, believing that the latter together with a mustard-seed faith will save us in the end. In the 1930s,

---

22. Niebuhr, *Interpretation of Christian Ethics*, 47.

a Chinese philosopher is reported to have quoted to a Westerner visiting Peking this proverb: "A person's religion is not what they are, but what they are not; the lower a person is the higher his religion is likely to be to atone for his failure and lack."[23]

Some years ago when I was pastoring, I had a woman in my church who had a very high view of Scripture. She was a good woman, active in the church and an excellent director of our Christian education program. One day she came to talk to me in my office, and the discussion turned to the passage in Mark 10:11 where Jesus, in expanding his teaching on marriage to the disciples, said to them: "Whoever divorces his wife and marries another commits adultery against her." I explained that this teaching was probably aimed at the man who divorces his wife *in order to marry* another woman, where a "love triangle" had developed, and the man had decided to leave his wife for another woman in waiting.[24] Jesus was not referring to a divorced man who at some later time married another woman, someone who in no way was responsible for the breakup of the first marriage. But this woman, with her high view of Scripture, could not accept my interpretation. In her view, divorce and remarriage were wrong under any circumstances.

I was dumbfounded, since she herself had married a divorced man. This man's first marriage had failed some years earlier, and now rather recently he had met this woman in my church and the two had got married. No one saw anything wrong in the marriage. I certainly saw nothing wrong in it. I asked her, if Jesus' teaching was that marriage to a divorced person was unacceptable under any circumstances, how could she justify what she—and her husband—had done? Her answer was that God would understand their weaknesses. What had

---

23. Knox, "Ethical Obligation in the Realm of Grace," 73; cf. Edwin Rogers Embree, "A Conversation in Peking," *Atlantic Monthly* 146 (1930): 561–68.
24. Lundbom, "What about Divorce?" *Covenant Quarterly* 36, no. 4 (November 1978): 23.

happened, you see, was that a very elevated view of Scripture had led to Scripture no longer being an authority for her. So she had decided the difficult question of remarriage on her own, and then assumed that everything would be right in the end because of God's mercy and grace.

The Sermon itself has something quite different to say about attainability than what obtains in the common perception. At its close is a clear word about the expectation that Jesus—or Matthew—has that those hearing this sermon will, in fact, live in accordance with the teachings it sets forth. This is a very Jewish word, one that echoes Deuteronomy and the best of rabbinic teaching, viz., that one must *do* what God has commanded. Read again the closing words of the Sermon:

> Not everyone who says to me, 'Lord, Lord,' will enter the kingdom of heaven, but only the one who does the will of my Father in heaven. On that day many will say to me, 'Lord, Lord, did we not prophesy in your name, and cast out demons in your name, and do many deeds of power in your name?' Then I will declare to them, 'I never knew you; go away from me, you evildoers. (Matt. 7:21-23)

Then comes the parable of the two houses, which concludes the Sermon.

> Everyone then who hears these words of mine and acts on them will be like a wise man who built his house on rock. The rain fell, the floods came, and the winds blew and beat on that house, but it did not fall, because it had been founded on rock. And everyone who hears these words of mine and does not act on them will be like a foolish man who built his house on sand. The rain fell, and the floods came, and the winds blew and beat against that house, and it fell—and great was its fall! (Matt. 7:24-27).

These words coming at the climax of the Sermon could not be more clear. Those who hear Jesus' teaching are expected to do it.

His teaching is no unattainable ideal; it is a doable recipe for holy living.[25] A climactic passage in Deuteronomy says the same about Deuteronomic law:

> Surely, this commandment that I am commanding you today is not too hard for you, nor is it too far away. It is not in heaven, that you should say, "Who will go up to heaven for us, and get it for us so that we may hear it and observe it?" Neither is it beyond the sea, that you should say, "Who will cross to the other side of the sea for us, and get it for us so that we may hear it and observe it?" No, the word is very near to you; it is in your mouth and in your heart for you to observe. (Deut. 30:11-14)

The Deuteronomic preacher closes by saying that doing the commands is nothing less than walking the road to life; not doing them is walking the road to death (Deut. 30:15-19).

We have, then, in the Sermon no unattainable ideal but rather a doable recipe for holy living. Pious talk is not enough (7:21); mighty works are not enough (7:22-23); hearing God's word is not enough (7:26-27). The bottom line is hearing and *doing*, which in biblical thought is always the bottom line. The great Pharisee Gamaliel, who was Paul's teacher and is twice cited favorably in the book of Acts (5:33; 22:3), is reported to have said, "If a man's wisdom is greater than his deeds, his wisdom will be forgotten. But if his deeds are greater than his wisdom, then his wisdom will be remembered."[26] Dietrich Bonhoeffer cited these words, and the thrust of his *Cost of Discipleship* was that only the one who obeys can believe, a strident attack on the "cheap grace" that the German church was dispensing.

25. Frederick E. Schuele, "Living Up to Matthew's Sermon on the Mount: An Approach," in *Christian Biblical Ethics: From Biblical Revelation to Contemporary Christian Praxis* (ed. Robert J. Daly; New York: Paulist, 1984), 206.

26. In *Pirke Aboth* (*P. Ab.*) 3:12, the saying is attributed to Rabbi Hanina ben Dosa, and in 3:22 the comparison of one whose wisdom is greater than his deeds to the shrub in Jer. 17:6 is attributed to Rabbi Eleazar ben Azariah (c. 50 to 135 C.E.), who took the place of Gamaliel II after he was deposed from the presidency, but Eleazar continued to be associated with Gamaliel II in his office after the latter's restoration (see *APOT* 2:700, 702).

We need to give this Sermon another look, paying particular attention to verses that seem to support an unattainable ideal. The words in 5:19-20 can be dispensed with quickly:

> Therefore, whoever breaks one of the least of these commandments, and teaches others to do the same, will be called least in the kingdom of heaven; but whoever does them and teaches them will be called great in the kingdom of heaven. For I tell you, unless your righteousness exceeds that of the sdcribes and Pharisees, you will never enter the kingdom of heaven. (Matt. 5:19-20).

Here Jesus says that one must not relax even the least of his commands, nor teach others to do so. Rabbis of the New Testament period distinguished between "light" and "heavy" precepts. For example, honoring one's parents (Deut. 5:16)—the Fifth Commandment—was considered a heavy precept; taking the mother bird with her young (Deut. 22:6-7) was considered a light precept, an act that cost little and was easily violated (*m. Ḥul.* 12:5).

What the least of Jesus' commands might have been is not stated. If I were to choose, I would select the one about not swearing oaths (5:33-37), which could be a restatement of the Third Commandment about not taking the Lord's name in vain (Exod. 20:7; Deut. 5:11; cf. Lev. 19:12), otherwise, perhaps, an embellishment of the teaching regarding the taking of vows (Deut. 23:21-23). Swearing empty oaths, commonly taken to be a minor infraction, was nevertheless censured by Jeremiah (Jer. 4:2). It was considered to be a recurring problem by the rabbis, the Essenes (*CD* xv 1-5; cf. Josephus, *War* 2.135-36),[27] and preachers of Puritan New England, and it continues to be a problem today. Listen to the talk of people with whom you move about. Obviously, this teaching was and is easily broken. I am not referring here to the bearing of false witness (= perjury), which is

---

27. The Essenes avoided oaths, regarding them as worse than perjury.

the Ninth Commandment (Exod. 20:15; Deut. 5:20), and a different injunction entirely. I am referring to the use of God's name in an empty manner. Jesus says this command must be followed, and that it would be better if one does not utter an oath at all. He says, "Let what you say be simply 'Yes, Yes' or 'No, No.'"

In interpretation of the Decalogue, the least command was frequently taken to be the one about keeping the Sabbath day holy (Exod. 20:8-11; Deut. 5:12-15). According to the rabbis, this command had to be preached more than all the others because it was the easiest to break. Preachers in seventeenth-century New England harped continually on Sabbath breaking, for much the same reason. Today one hears few preachers inveighing against Sabbath violation, perhaps because they reckon it as being a command of lesser importance. But in Jesus' view, one does not keep only the more important commands; one keeps them all. Jeremiah took the same view, inveighing also against a violation of the commandment on Sabbath observance (Jer. 17:19-27).[28]

So far as the following word about exceeding the righteousness of the scribes and the Pharisees is concerned, we need only go to chapter 23 to see just how righteous these individuals were. The Pharisees had noble beginnings, but in Jesus' time their righteousness was hollow, for they expounded great principles but did not live by them. They were also overly legalistic and puffed up with self-righteousness, which is offensive to people in any age. God's new people, says Jesus, must seek a better righteousness. Jesus also wants this new people of God to attain a higher righteousness than the righteousness of the Gentiles, which doubtless left much to be desired (Matt. 5:46-47). Here Jesus' teaching is little different from the teachings of the Hebrew prophets, or the teachings of reformers in any age.

28. Lundbom, *Jeremiah 1–20*, 803.

Perhaps the preeminent verse supporting unattainability is 5:48, where Jesus says that we must be perfect as our heavenly Father is perfect. This is a more difficult verse, but the problem has largely to do with the English word *perfect*. The bar is raised here no higher than in the Old Testament, where Israelite people were told to be holy as the Lord their God was holy (Lev. 19:2; cf. Deut. 14:2, 21). 1 Peter 2:9 says that the church is a "chosen race, a royal priesthood, a holy nation, God's own people." In the verse here, the Greek word τέλειός means "perfect" in the sense of "whole, complete, fully constituted" (cf. LXX Deut. 18:13); it means essentially the same as Hebrew תמים, meaning "perfect, whole, complete, unblemished, blameless" (Deut. 32:4 in relation to God; Exod. 12:5 in relation to sacrificial lambs). Noah (Gen. 6:9), Abraham (Gen. 17:1), and Job (Job 1:1) were all "blameless," and Israel too was called to be "blameless" before God (Deut. 18:13; Josh. 24:14). None of these texts comes close to implying moral perfection, which would not have entered the mind of any ancient Israelite teacher, or any Jewish teacher of a later time.

Having discussed the question of elevation in the Sermon on the Mount more generally, I would now propose that we take another look at three of the most troublesome teachings in the Sermon on the Mount. They are grand teachings and, rightly understood and put into their proper context, are perfectly attainable. This is not to say that everyone can carry them out, or that any one person can carry them out all of the time. I am simply saying that these teachings are doable, giving credibility to Jesus' climactic words at the end of the Sermon.

(a) Anger (5:21-26)

5.[21]You have heard that it was said to those of ancient times, 'You shall not murder'; and whoever murders shall be liable to judgment.' [22]But I say to you that if you are angry with a brother or sister, you will be liable to judgment; and if you insult a brother or sister, you will be liable to the council; and if you say, 'You fool,' you will be liable to the hell of fire. [23]So when you are offering your gift at the altar, if you remember that your brother or sister has something against you, [24]leave your gift there before the altar and go; first be reconciled to your brother or sister, and then come and offer your gift. [25]Come to terms quickly with your accuser while you are on the way to court with him, or your accuser may hand you over to the judge, and the judge to the guard, and you will be thrown into prison. [26]Truly I tell you, you will never get out until you have paid the last penny.

This first antithesis in the Sermon weighs anger over against murder and says that it is not simply murder that makes one liable to judgment but also anger. Jesus wants to get behind this serious crime to the interior disposition causing it. He knows, and we know, that anger can and does lead to murder. It happened in the Cain and Abel story (Gen. 4:5-8) and threatened to be repeated with Jacob and Esau (Gen. 27:41-45).

When my wife and I were living in Beirut, now almost fifty years ago, an article in the *Daily Star* told about two men who met one morning in the restaurant for breakfast, and after an argument broke out, the one killed the other. They were said to be friends. What happened is that, after the two had finished eating, the one offered to pay for both breakfasts. The other man refused the offer and, slapping his lira on the table, said he would pay for them both. An argument ensued, in this case enflamed by affronts to each man's honor, which was no trifle. The first man responded to money now lying on the table by physically attacking the other man, who went tumbling to the floor. Not to be outdone, this man got up, went the short distance to his home, and returned with a pistol with which he shot his breakfast companion dead. Anger, combined here with an affront to honor, led to murder. The Lebanese court, it was later reported, attempted to enforce French law but was unable to prosecute the case because the assailant's honor had been impugned.

The words beginning v. 22 are particularly troublesome: "But I say to you that if you are angry with a brother or sister, you will be liable to judgment." Every time I have taught the Sermon on the Mount to adults there has been someone in the group who says that Christians should not get angry, and this half-verse is cited. But does Jesus really mean that all anger is wrong? If he did, no one could carry out his teaching, and everyone would be "liable to judgment." Incidentally, ἔνοχος ἔσται τῇ κρίσει ("liable he will be to judgment") means "judged guilty" or "condemned," not simply "be in danger of judgment." But does the angry person also stand condemned? If the angry person contemplates murder, yes, but is this true of every other anger?

The modern psychologist would be the first to tell us that a blanket prohibition against anger would surely be mistaken, whether against one's brother, sister, or anyone else. For a long time now we have been told that it is healthy to express anger. Anger expressed is tension relieved. In fact, anger may be the only proper response to injustice and wrongdoing. We have also learned a good deal in recent years about internalized anger. There are people who cannot or will not become openly angry but who harbor inner anger, which they may not consider to be anger, but is. And the psychologist knows, and we all know, that internalized anger is far more dangerous than anger expressed openly. In the biblical story, Cain's anger was internalized. The text says, "So Cain was very angry, and his countenance fell." Mayer Gruber has argued that the "fallen face" refers here to depression,[29] which probably means that Cain said nary a word to his brother. But the Lord knew that Cain was angry and told him so, warning him that "sin was lurking at the door" (Gen. 4:4-7). So beware! The person who says nothing at all may be more angry than the person who shouts. People who have not learned to express their anger properly will finally reach a point where "the lid will blow off," which is what happened with Cain, who went on to murder his brother.

The Bible recognizes that anger in and of itself is not wrong. The Psalmist says, "Be angry, but sin not" (Ps. 4:4 RSV), which is quoted and expanded upon in Eph. 4:26: "Be angry but do not sin; do not let the sun go down on your anger" (RSV). I was taught this latter verse by my grandmother, and I have tried to live by it. I remember as a young boy going into my mother's bedroom before I went to sleep to get things right with her.

Anger in the Bible is compared to fire, and we all know what happens if fire gets out of control. A large number of people must be pressed into service to put it out. Protracted anger is dangerous because it does more harm to the one harboring it than to the one against whom the anger is directed. But the Bible teaches nowhere that one cannot be angry.

What, then, is Jesus teaching here in the Sermon? Jesus seems to be concerned primarily with behavior that makes others angry. The Greek verb ὀργίζω in the active voice means "make angry, provoke to anger, irritate,"[30] and although a passive form appears in our present verse (Matt. 5:22, ὀργιζόμενος), the sense nevertheless requires "provoke to anger," rather than "become angry." I would translate v. 22a as "everyone who becomes provocative with his brother shall be liable to judgment." The danger is in making

29. M. Gruber, "The Tragedy of Cain and Abel: A Case of Depression," *JQR* 69 (1978): 89–97.
30. H. G. Liddell and R. Scott, *A Greek-English Lexicon* (Oxford: Clarendon, 1996), 1246, s.v. ὀργίζω.

someone else angry by provocative words or actions, which can easily escalate into something worse.

The Old Testament is far more concerned about "provocations to anger" than about "anger" itself. This is seen particularly on the theological level, where Israel is continually being censured for provoking Yahweh to anger. One finds this censure throughout Deuteronomy and Jeremiah (Deut. 4:25; 9:7-8, 18, 22; 32:15-22; Jer. 7:18-19; 25:6-7; 32:29-30, 32; 44:8).

In the New Testament, a good example of human provocation is found in Eph. 6:4, where a similar Greek verb, παροργίζω, carries this meaning:[31] "Fathers, *do not provoke* [μὴ παροργίζετε] your children *to anger*, but bring them up in the discipline and instruction of the Lord." Here it is not the anger of the children that is being censured but the provocation of the "fathers" (we might also add "mothers") causing the children's anger. Paul speaks a similar word in Col. 3:21: "Fathers, *do not provoke* [ἐρεθίζετε] your children, or they may lose heart."

The context in Matt. 5:21-26 confirms this interpretation. In the latter half of v. 22 the same thing is said only in different words: "if you insult a brother or sister you will be liable to the council." The Greek says, "if you say ῥακά to your brother (or sister) you will be liable to the Sanhedrin." The Greek word ῥακά is a word of supreme insult (= Aramaic ריקא, "empty"; Betz: "empty head!"), and the person using it knows that he or she is being provocative. The Sanhedrin was the supreme Jewish council of seventy-one members in Jerusalem, presided over by the high priest. The verse goes on to embellish the idea further, saying that if you address your brother with another contemptuous word, Μωρέ ("You Fool"), you will be liable to "the hell of fire" (RSV). The Greek has "Gehenna," that is,

---

31. Liddell and Scott, *Greek-English Lexicon*, 1343, s.v. παροργίζω.

the "Valley of Ben Hinnom" (Jer. 7:32; 19:6), which in the Second Temple period had become a place of punishment for the wicked in the afterlife, contrasted with the "paradise of delight" (4 Ezra 7:36; *2 Bar.* 59:10; 83:13). The judgment here may then be eschatological.[32]

Jesus does not have trivial offenses in mind but provocations likely to escalate into something worse. In such cases, the person responsible for the provocation is in the wrong.[33] The provocative individual will then be judged guilty, brought before the authorities, and punished, and his only recourse at this late stage is to settle things quickly—with or without a lawyer—before the heavy hand of judgment falls upon him. Jesus is not talking here about "righteous anger," or even the justified anger of someone wronged or oppressed. Nor is he saying that one must acquiesce in every conflict or settle every litigation out of court. He is talking to people who knowingly and wrongfully provoke others to anger, telling them that when things escalate, as they tend to do, they will be the ones held liable. Such people had better make things right with their brother or sister, and do it before bringing their gift to the Lord's altar. So interpreted, this teaching is one anyone can follow—and for their own good had better follow.

(b) Nonretaliation (5:38-42)

5.[38] You have heard that it was said, 'An eye for an eye and a tooth for a tooth.' [39]But I say to you, Do not resist an evildoer. But if anyone strikes you on the right cheek, turn the other also; [40]and if anyone wants to sue you and take your coat, give your cloak as well; [41]and if anyone forces you to go one mile, go also the second mile. [42]Give to everyone who

---

32. Betz, *Sermon on the Mount*, 221.

33. John L. McKenzie, "The Gospel According to Matthew," in *The Jerome Biblical Commentary II* (ed. Raymond E. Brown et al.; Englewood Cliffs, NJ: Prentice Hall, 1968), 71.

begs from you, and do not refuse anyone who wants to borrow from you.

Here we are dealing with a situation in which someone has done you an injustice, and Jesus begins by saying that you are not to apply the *lex talionis*. But let us look at the injustices. None is of great magnitude; as a matter of fact, all are relatively minor. None has to do with bodily injury, much less loss of life. The first is a slap on the right cheek, which, in the ancient world, would be reckoned as a case of "insult." Jesus says that when someone insults you, you are not to respond in kind; that is, you are not to slap him or her on the cheek. Yet ironically, he prescribes an action that will shame the other person, which is what turning the other cheek will do. One is to say, "Do it again! Here is my other cheek!"

The second indignity is also relatively minor. If someone takes not your coat, but your tunic (a shirt worn next to the skin), you are to offer him your cloak (outer garment) as well. Why is the person taking the shirt off your back? Probably because you have incurred a debt and it is being seized as a pledge.

Being forced to walk a mile was another indignity, this one having come with the Roman occupation of Palestine. Roman soldiers could compel a non-Roman subject to carry his equipment one mile.[34] Recall Simon, the man from Cyrene, who as a bystander along the road was compelled to carry Jesus' cross (Matt. 27:32). When such a thing happens, Jesus says you are to show your disdain for this loathsome practice by offering to do even more than what the person asks. I have done this often with overzealous border inspectors searching my luggage, helping them to see even more than what they are looking for. It has never failed to hasten the end of the indignity, but today, of course, you can no longer do this.

---

34. Krister Stendahl, "Matthew" in *Peake's Commentary on the Bible*, 777, ed. Matthew Black and H. H. Rowley (New York: Thomas Nelson and Sons, 1962).

Giving money to beggars and lending must also be understood as outlays on a very small scale. Beggars receive only crumbs or small change. Jesus is not talking about giving in to every request for money. He is simply telling his followers to be compassionate toward the poor. In Deuteronomy one is admonished continually to share their resources with the stranger, the orphan, and the widow, also with the Levite in town, who had no inheritance and, in the seventh century B.C.E., was out of a job because worship had been centralized in Jerusalem and the local sanctuaries were closed down (Deut. 12:12; 16:11, 14).

Luther said one must surely give to the poor, but one is not required to give whatever they ask for.[35] Calvin, too, said the following:

> None but a fool will stand upon the words, so as to maintain, that we must yield to our opponents what they demand, before coming into a court of law; for such compliance would more strongly inflame the minds of wicked men to robbery and extortion; and we know, that nothing was farther from the design of Christ.[36]

I have followed Luther's principle at times when I was pastor of a church, since the church, as every pastor knows, is often a magnet for panhandlers. And aggressive panhandling comes close to being robbery. One cannot be sure of motives or sincerity. I would typically not give someone the fifty dollars or more they were asking for but would offer to buy them food or fill up their car with gas. Sometimes my offers were refused. If the person accepted, I would take them to a nearby store or eatery and buy them a sandwich and something to drink, or take them to a filling station and have gas put in their car.

---

35. McArthur, *Understanding the Sermon on the Mount*, 108.
36. John Calvin, *Commentary on a Harmony of the Evangelists, Matthew, Mark, and Luke* I (trans. William Pringle; Grand Rapids: Baker Books, 2003), 299.

What is important about this teaching on nonretaliation is that it must not become a hard and fast principle made to apply to every conceivable indignity and violence done to one, to one's family, or to one's country, many of which are infinitely more grave. There are grievous evils in our world that one must resist and, in certain instances, fight against. Jesus is talking about not applying the law of retaliation to insult and other indignities one can handle, a teaching that is eminently doable.

We learn from the Roman historian Tacitus that even Roman leaders practiced the principle of nonretaliation in certain circumstances. Germanicus, the adopted son of the emperor Tiberius (14–37 C.E.), after being savagely attacked by his rival Piso, was said not to have returned in kind. Tacitus gives this report of Germanicus coming upon Piso on the island of Rhodes:

> The prince [Germanicus] was aware of the invectives with which he had been assailed, yet he behaved with such mildness that, when a rising storm swept Piso towards the rock-bound coast, and the destruction of his foe could have been referred to misadventure, he sent warships to help in extricating him from his predicament. (*An.* 2.55)[37]

It is true, of course, that the principle of nonretaliation (or nonviolence) here in the Sermon has been applied to large-scale injustices. I think, for example, of Gandhi's actions against the British, and Martin Luther King Jr.'s civil rights activity in our own country, both of which achieved extraordinary results. So one cannot and should not be dismissive regarding broader application of this principle. That having been said, one must beware of adversaries—great and small—who are bereft of any moral principles. Such people exist at all times and in all cultures, which means that this principle of nonretaliation cannot be made into a universal. And the

---

37. See *Tacitus II: The Annals: Books 1–3* (trans. John Jackson; LCL; Cambridge, MA: Harvard University Press, 1962).

principle as presented here in the Sermon clearly has smaller injustices in view and, as such, is doable by anyone at any time.

(c) Judging Others (7:1-5)

7 [1]"Do not judge, so that you may not be judged. [2]For with the judgment you make you will be judged, and the measure you give will be the measure you get. [3]Why do you see the speck in your neighbor's eye, but do not notice the log in your own eye? [4]Or how can you say to your neighbor, 'Let me take the speck out of your eye,' while the log is in your own eye? [5]You hypocrite, first take the log out of your own eye, and then you will see clearly to take the speck out of your neighbor's eye.

This teaching on judging other people has to be one of the most widely misunderstood and misquoted teachings of the Bible. I have discussed these verses often in adult study groups over the years, and almost every time there has been at least one person present who speaks up and reduces the saying to the first three words: "Do not judge," or else interprets v. 1 to mean, "Do not judge, and then you will not be judged." Jesus' words are thus interpreted to mean that Christians ought make no judgments at all, which is a gross misunderstanding of what the teaching is all about.

One must not simply reduce the teaching to the first three words, "Do not judge," or use the words in v. 1 to support the notion that judging people is something Christians must never do. Elton Trueblood, in his great little book of some years ago, *The Humor of Christ*,[38] got the teaching right. He recognized that everyone has to make judgments, and that human life loses its dignity if we cease to make judgments. What is more, judging is, in and of itself, not wrong. Life requires that we make judgments, not only upon evils

---

38. Elton Trueblood, *The Humor of Christ* (New York: Harper & Row, 1964), 60–61.

of various description but upon bad behavior and people who behave badly. There is the oft-quoted remark that "God hates the sin but loves the sinner." That may be true, but the New Testament—and even more the Church Fathers—repeatedly assert that God consigns not sin but people persisting in sin to hell.

The way one reads and interprets the Greek idiom in v. 1 makes all the difference between a teaching yielding good sense and one that does not. The verse should not be read, "Do not judge people, for then you yourself will not be judged," as if to say, the only way one can escape judgment is by not judging others, which is absurd. It means rather: "Do not judge in such a manner that your judgment ends up coming down upon you, instead of upon the person you are judging." Here again, the context makes everything clear. Jesus is talking about hypocrisy, which is spelled out in vv. 2-5 and is given larger treatment in chapter 23. He is talking about people who pounce upon others yet have in themselves the same or a similar problem that is infinitely greater. Here is where Trueblood sees humor in Jesus' teaching. In a fine example of oriental exaggeration, Jesus says that one must first take the log out of one's own eye before removing the speck from another's eye. In other words, "Get your own problem cleared up; then talk to other people about theirs!"

Much good work in the church and outside has been undone by self-righteous people who police everyone—family members, would-be friends, people they barely know—about one misstep or another, and then make exceptions for themselves. As a result, their judgments are not listened to, but we still have to put up with them. Hypocritical behavior causes entire churches to lose credibility. The prophet Hosea discovered to his sorrow that, because hypocrisy had permeated the whole of Israelite society, the Lord himself would have to step in and judge the people (Hos. 4:1-10).[39] All were corrupt—king, prophets, priests, and people. No one was capable of making judgments. Suspension of the law (*lex suspensus*) in the case of hypocritical behavior is a strong biblical theme. We encounter it in the story of Judah and Tamar (Genesis 38) and in the New Testament account of the woman caught in adultery (John 8:2-11). Jesus, then, is not telling people not to judge. Rather he is warning them to be ever so careful that the judgments they make do not end up coming down upon their own heads. The same applies to us, and this is thus another teaching we can and must follow.

The Sermon on the Mount Is A "Stretch"

How, then, shall we take the Sermon on the Mount? I have argued that the Sermon is doable. Yet I also want to retain some tension between what Jesus expects and what we often find ourselves doing. In my view, this Sermon is meant to stretch its hearers, and the tension it contains is only enough to make them into healthy, complete, and mature followers of Jesus Christ. J. Duncan M. Derrett says that Matthew's listeners were like athletes, 75 percent of whom were unfit.[40] He quotes Epictetus, who said that the true athlete is one who can meet the unusual tests and win. According to this analogy, Jesus is calling many of us to exercise class.

I prefer comparing Jesus to a doctor who tells you to do something you think you cannot do. I know the experience personally. Ten years ago I had both hips replaced. After the first surgery, on the same day, the doctor came into my room and told me he wanted me to get out of bed and stand on my feet. I said I could not possibly do that. But he and the nurse provided help, and with effort I did stand briefly on my two feet. During the next couple of days, I had to

39. Lundbom, "Contentious Priests and Contentious People," 52–70 (reprint, 216–31).
40. J. Duncan M. Derrett, *The Sermon on the Mount: A Manual for Living* (Northampton: Pilkington, 1994), 25.

walk to the door of my room, then a short distance down the hospital corridor, and later I had to do therapy exercises in a rehabilitation room. I remember wishing on some of those days that the nurses and therapists would forget to come and would leave me in my bed. Many times I thought I could not do what was being asked, but with effort, and with help from the therapist, I did do it. In each case it was a "stretch," but that is how I regained my health, was able to walk again, and become the whole person I so much wanted to be.

I remember two very elderly women in the therapy room who were also being exercised. One had to be ninety or older. She cried at her therapist, "I can't do it." I felt so sorry for her. The therapist was a compassionate man, but someone who in earlier days had trained the famed Romanian gymnasts. He remained firm, saying: "If you do not try, you will never walk again." The woman dried her tears and, with effort, took a few steps. As the days went on, she progressed, even as I progressed. I do not know how things finally turned out for her, but I imagine that she too was at last able to walk well enough to return home.

Jesus' Sermon on the Mount is meant to stretch us. Jesus asks us to do more than we think we can do, but nothing he asks is impossible. As a good teacher, and also the good physician that he was, he knew that his disciples must rise above mediocrity to become light and salt in the world. Our world today needs nothing less: teachers who stretch the minds of their students, and students who catch the vision and go on to do more than they ever thought they could do.

4

Imitatio Dei in the Sermon on the Mount

"Be Ye Therefore Perfect"

William Tyndale, preeminent translator of the New Testament into English, rendered Matt. 5:48 thus: "Ye shall therefore be perfect even as your father which is in heaven is perfect."[1] The King James Version of 1611 subsequently rendered the verse, "Be ye therefore perfect, even as your Father which is in heaven is perfect." The RSV and NRSV readings are similar. This English translation of a key verse in the Sermon on the Mount has been the source of difficulty for some, in that "perfect" can be taken to mean "absolutely flawless," or "without error," and with a comparison to God being made, a theological problem may arise, since Christian doctrine—likewise Jewish doctrine—nowhere affirms the idea that humans can become fully Godlike.

---

1. This translation of 1534 in modernized spelling occurs in David Daniell, ed., *Tyndale's New Testament* (New Haven: Yale University Press, 1989), 27.

Early on, Israel rejected ideas of divine kingship in Egypt and also any notion that human beings could become gods, as in Babylonian mythology. In the Babylonian creation story, Utnapishtim, survivor of the great flood, was welcomed with his wife into the assembly of the gods. Enlil boarded the ship and greeted him with the words: "Hitherto Utnapishtim has been but human. Henceforth Utnapishtim and his wife shall be like unto us gods."[2]

In the oldest biblical story of creation, the great sin of Adam and Eve in the Garden of Eden was eating forbidden fruit, which led to their having to die. But a wily serpent told them that eating would make them Godlike and they would not die. A half-truth. They did become Godlike, knowing good from evil, but the Lord God gave them a sentence of death and thrust them out of the Garden (Genesis 2–3). In the Priestly creation account, Genesis 1:1-2:4a, man and woman are made in the image of God and are given dominion over the earth (Gen. 1:27-28), but there is no talk of their becoming God. The Bible and subsequent Judeo-Christian thought affirm that God is entirely other than everything he has created.

Imitatio Christi in Christianity

In the Christian church, an emphasis on living a life after the manner of Jesus was there from the very beginning. We see it in Paul (2 Cor. 3:18; Phil. 3:12-15; Eph. 2:8-10; 4:22-24; Col. 3:1-17; 1 Thess. 4:1-8), and in other writings of the New Testament (Heb. 6:1-12; 1 Pet. 1:13-16; 4:1-6). Over the next millennium and a half, beginning with the hermits who retired to a life of solitude in the desert, the church witnessed a variety of monastic movements, which were attempts by Christians to flee this evil world and aspire to holy living.

---

2. ANET[3], 95.

In the fifteenth century, just before the Reformation, holiness reached a climax in the devotional classic, *The Imitation of Christ* (*Imitatio Christi*), by Thomas à Kempis (1380–1471).[3]

This little book, read widely within the Roman Catholic Church and without, is said to have attained a circulation exceeded only by the Bible. It is still read today. Thomas à Kempis is said to have written the work in 1418 but not put his name to it until 1441. Some maintain, however, that Thomas was only a copier of the work and that the real author was another, perhaps Gerhard Groote.[4] Nevertheless, tradition continues to regard Thomas à Kempis as the author.

Thomas was born c. 1380 in Kempen, Germany. At the age of twelve or thirteen he went to Deventer in Holland to be educated, and then in 1399, at nineteen, he entered the monastery of Mount St. Agnes at Zwolle, also in Holland, where his older brother John was prior. There he remained until his death on August 8, 1471, at ninety-one years of age. Thomas was a quiet monk, seeking to emulate the life and virtue of the first Christians, especially in the love of God and neighbor, and to live a life of simplicity, humility, and devotion. The bulk of his time was spent transcribing manuscripts.

The Imitation of Christ is a practical guide for holy living. The author begins by quoting from John 8:12 and saying:

> *He who follows Me will not walk in darkness*, says the Lord. These are the words of Christ by which He directs us to imitate His life and His ways, if we truly desire to be spiritually enlightened and free of all blindness of heart. Let it then be our main concern to meditate on the life of Jesus Christ. (I, 1:1)

---

3. Thomas à Kempis, *The Imitation of Christ* (trans. Joseph N. Tylenda; Wilmington, DE: Michael Glazier, 1984).
4. *The Imitation of Christ* (ed. and abridg. Paul Simpson McElroy; Mount Vernon, NY: Peter Pauper, 1965), 3–4.

He continues:

> This should be our chief employment: to strive to overcome ourselves and gain such a mastery that we daily grow stronger and better. (I, 3:3)

And again:

> If we eradicated one vice a year we should soon become perfect men. (I, 11:5)

Holiness was taken very seriously by this saint of the church.

Sanctification in the Reformers

Sanctification is present in the Reformers, although not particularly prominent in their thinking. Censuring justification by good works, as he did, Luther could hardly be much concerned with developing a doctrine of sanctification. Also, Luther distinguished between two kingdoms: the secular kingdom of this world, and the spiritual kingdom of Christ;[5] in the former, sanctified living was difficult, at best, and much of the time impossible. But in his *Larger Catechism*, when discussing the Third Article of the Creed, Luther did see sanctification as the work of the Holy Spirit in the believer:

> To this article, as I have said, I cannot give a better title than "Sanctification." In it is expressed and portrayed the Holy Spirit and his office, which is that he makes us holy. . . . But God's Spirit alone is called Holy Spirit, that is, he who has sanctified and still sanctifies us. As the Father is called Creator and the Son is called Redeemer, so on account of his work the Holy Spirit must be called Sanctifier, the one who makes holy.[6]

---

5. Robert A. Guelich, "Interpreting the Sermon on the Mount," *Int* 41 (1987), 119.
6. *The Book of Concord: The Confessions of the Evangelical Lutheran Church* (trans. and ed. Theodore G. Tappert; Philadelphia: Muhlenberg, 1959), 415.

How does this sanctifying take place? Answer: the Holy Spirit effects it through the community of saints, the church, for in the church is forgiveness of sins. Yet,

> forgiveness is needed constantly, for although God's grace has been won by Christ, and holiness has been wrought by the Holy Spirit through God's Word in the unity of the Christian church, yet because we are encumbered with our flesh we are never without sin.[7]

Lutheran tradition has usually been content simply to affirm that the Christian believer is *simul iustus et peccator* ("simultaneously righteous and sinner"). The Christian must trust in God's forgiveness, for becoming a saint in a sinful world is impossible.[8] One will therefore meet up with people today unable to countenance Paul's words in 2 Cor. 3:18,

> And all of us, with unveiled faces, seeing the glory of the Lord as though reflected in a mirror, are being transformed into the same image from one degree of glory to another; for this comes from the Lord, the Spirit"

Those words smack to some, especially those influenced by Luther's insistence on justification by grace alone, of an aspiration to self-achieved perfection. Yet in seventeenth-, eighteenth-, and nineteenth-century Pietism,[9] the Lutheran Church experienced a true transformation in the direction of holy living, as can be seen in the works of Johann Arndt (1555–1621),[10] Philip Jacob Spener (1635–1705),[11] August Hermann Francke (1663–1727),[12] Nicholaus

---

7. *Book of Concord*, 417–18.

8. So Martin Dibelius, expressing a Lutheran perspective, *The Sermon on the Mount* (New York: Charles Scribner's Sons, 1940), 111.

9. See Jaroslav Pelikan, "Pietism" in *Dictionary of the History of Ideas: Studies of Selected Pivotal Ideas* (ed. Philip P. Wiener; 5 vols.; New York: Charles Scribner's Sons, 1973–74), 3:493–95; Frederick Herzog, *European Pietism Reviewed* (Princeton Theological Monograph Series 50; San Jose, CA: Pickwick, 2003); Carter Lindberg, ed., *The Pietist Theologians: An Introduction to Theology in the Seventeenth and Eighteenth Centuries* (Oxford: Blackwell, 2005).

10. Johann Arndt, *True Christianity* (trans. Peter Erb; New York: Paulist, 1979); Johannes Wallmann, "Johann Arndt (1555–1621)," in Lindberg, *Pietist Theologians*, 21–37.

Ludwig von Zinzendorf (1700–1760),[13] Carl Olof Rosenius (1816–1868),[14] and others.

Calvin was more positive regarding sanctification than Luther, at least to the extent that he sought transformation of the world by controlling government and public life in Geneva.[15] In his *Institutes of the Christian Religion* (1536), he says that sanctification comes in being regenerated by God's Holy Spirit, making true holiness one's concern (3.14.1).[16] Regeneration comes in repentance, the sole end of which is to restore man and woman to the image of God that was lost in Adam's transgression (3.3.9).[17] Believers experience sanctification, but not sinless perfection in this life (3.3.10-15).[18] About outward and inward repentance, Calvin says:

> Now we can understand the nature of the fruits of repentance: the duties of piety toward God, of charity toward men, and in the whole of life holiness and purity. (3.3.16)[19]

But he goes on to say:

> I do not insist that the moral life of a Christian man breathes nothing but the very gospel, yet this ought to be desired, and we must strive toward it. But I do not so strictly demand evangelical perfection that I would

11. Philip Jacob Spener, *Pia Desideria* (trans. Theodore G. Tappert; Philadelphia: Fortress Press, 1964); K. James Stein, "Philipp Jakob Spener (1635–1705)," in Lindberg, *Pietist Theologians*, 84–99.

12. Gary R. Sattler, *God's Glory, Neighbor's Good: A Brief Introduction to the Life and Writings of August Hermann Francke* (Chicago: Covenant Press, 1982); Markus Matthias, "August Hermann Francke (1663–1727)" in Lindberg, *Pietist Theologians*, 100–114.

13. Karl A. Olsson, *By One Spirit* (Chicago: Covenant Press, 1962), 15–18; Peter Vogt, "Nicholas Ludwig von Zinzendorf (1700–1760)," in Lindberg, *Pietist Theologians*, 207–23.

14. Rosenius was a Swedish preacher and editor of *Pietisten* from 1842 to 1868; see Olsson, *By One Spirit*, 47–48.

15. Dibelius, *Sermon on the Mount*, 111; for a comparison of Luther and Calvin, see Guelich, "Interpreting the Sermon on the Mount," 119–20.

16. *Calvin's* Institutes *Abridged Edition* (ed. Donald K. McKim; Louisville: Westminster John Knox, 2001), 99.

17. *Calvin's* Institutes, 77–78.

18. *Calvin's* Institutes, 78.

19. *Calvin's* Institutes, 79.

not acknowledge as a Christian one who has not yet attained it. For thus all would be excluded from the church, since no one is found who is not far removed from it. . . . (3.6.5)[20]

In commenting on Eph. 5:25-27, Calvin says this about the church:

The church is holy, then, in the sense that it is daily advancing and is not yet perfect; it makes progress from day to day but has not yet reached its goal of holiness. (4.1.17)[21]

Wesley and Perfectionism

In the Protestant tradition, it was John Wesley (1703–1791) who developed fully a teaching on holy living, or Christian perfection.[22] Wesley found numerous New Testament passages supporting such a teaching (Matt. 5:48; Eph. 2:8; Phil. 3:12; Heb. 6:1; and others), and said it should be preached by all preachers and sought after by all believers in the church:

All our preachers should make a point of preaching perfection to believers constantly, strongly, and explicitly; and all believers should mind this one thing, and continually agonize for it.[23]

After his "heartwarming" experience at Aldersgate in 1738, Wesley began to preach and write extensively on Christian perfection. He preached nine times on Eph. 2:8 in 1738,[24] eight times on Matt. 5:48 between 1740 and 1785, and fifty times on Heb. 6:1 between 1739 and 1785.[25] His first tract on the subject of perfection was in 1739, entitled "The Character of a Methodist."[26] By 1741, another

---

20. *Calvin's* Institutes, 81.

21. *Calvin's* Institutes, 130.

22. See Mark K. Olson, *John Wesley's Theology of Christian Perfection: Developments in Doctrine and Theological System* (Fenwick, MI: Truth in Heart, 2007); for a comparison of Luther and Wesley on the Sermon on the Mount, see Tore Meistad, *Martin Luther and John Wesley on the Sermon on the Mount* (Lanham, MD: Scarecrow, 1999).

23. John Wesley, *A Plain Account of Christian Perfection* (Peabody, MA: Hendrickson, 2007), 119.

24. *The Works of John Wesley*, vol. 2, *Sermons II, 34–70* (ed. Albert C. Outler; Nashville: Abingdon, 1985), 155.

essay, "Christian Perfection," had been published, which was based on Phil. 3:12.[27] There was controversy enough on Wesley's teaching, so for the next twenty years the subject was discussed at conferences attended by Methodist clergy. At the first conference, convened on June 25, 1744, these questions on sanctification, or perfection, were raised and answered:[28]

Question: What is it to be *sancitified*?

Answer: To be renewed in the image of God, in righteousness and true holiness.

Question: What is implied in being a *perfect* Christian?

Answer: The loving God with all our heart, and mind, and soul (Deut. 6:5)

Question: Does this imply that *all inward sin* is taken away?

Answer: Undoubtedly; or how can we be said to be *saved from all our uncleanness?* (Ezek. 36:29).

At a second conference, on August 1, 1745, one question and answer was the following:[29]

Question: When does inward sanctification begin?

Answer: In the moment a man is justified. (Yet sin remains in him, yea, the seed of all sin, till he is *sanctified throughout*). From that time a believer gradually dies to sin, and grows in grace.

At yet another conference, these questions and answers received the focus of attention:[30]

25. *The Works of John Wesley,* vol. 3, *Sermons III, 71–114* (ed. Albert C. Outler; Nashville: Abingdon, 1986), 70.
26. Wesley, *Plain Account of Christian Perfection,* 16–19.
27. *Works of John Wesley,* vol. 2, *Sermons II, 34–70, 97–121.*
28. Wesley, *Plain Account of Christian Perfection,* 40.
29. Wesley, *Plain Account of Christian Perfection,* 41.
30. Wesley, *Plain Account of Christian Perfection,* 98–99.

Question:	Can those who are perfect grow in grace?
Answer:	Undoubtedly they can; and that not only while they are in the body, but to all eternity.
Question:	Can they fall from it?
Answer:	I am well assured they can; matter of fact puts this beyond doubt. Formerly we thought, one saved from sin could not fall; now we know the contrary. . . There is no such height or strength of holiness as it is impossible to fall from.
Question:	Can those who fall from this state recover it?
Answer:	Why not? We have many instances of this also. Nay, it is an exceeding common thing for persons to lose it more than once, before they are established therein.
Question:	What is the first advice that you would give them?
Answer:	Watch and pray continually against pride. If God has cast it out, see that it enter no more.

Wesley found it necessary to review the whole subject in 1764, and he summed up his views on Christian perfection in these propositions:[31]

1. There is such a thing as perfection; for it is again and again mentioned in Scripture.
2. It is not so early as justification; for justified persons are to "go on unto perfection," (Heb. 6:1).
3. It is not so late as death; for St. Paul speaks of living men that were perfect (Phil. 3:15).
4. It is not absolute. Absolute perfection belongs not to man, nor to angels, but to God alone.
5. It does not make a man infallible: None is infallible, while he remains in the body.

---

31. Wesley, *Plain Account of Christian Perfection,* 117–18.

6. Is it sinless? It is not worthwhile to contend for a term. It is "salvation from sin."

7. It is "perfect love" (1 John 4:18). This is the essence of it; its properties, or inseparable fruits, are, rejoicing evermore, praying without ceasing, and in everything giving thanks (1 Thess. 5:16, etc.).

8. It is improvable. It is so far from lying in an indivisible point, from being incapable of increase, that one perfected in love may grow in grace far swifter than he did before.

9. It is amissible, capable of being lost; of which we have numerous instances. But we were not thoroughly convinced of this, till five or six years ago.

10. It is constantly both preceded and followed by a gradual work.

11. But is it in itself instantaneous or not?

Wesley said that for some it is; for others it is not.

Wesley wrote two other essays, "The Scripture Way of Salvation," based on Eph. 2:8 (1765),[32] and "A Plain Account of Christian Perfection" (1767), which was another summary of his thinking.[33] We learn here that as a young man, before Aldersgate, Wesley had been influenced by the writings of others on Christian perfection. As early as 1725, when he was just twenty-three years of age, he had read Bishop Taylor's *Rule and Exercises of Holy Living and Dying*,[34] which he said began his formal interest in the reality of perfection. The year following he read Thomas à Kempis,[35] and soon afterwards two works by a Mr. Law: *Christian Perfection* and *Serious Call*.[36] Wesley's

32. *Works of John Wesley*, vol. 2, *Sermons II, 34–70*, 153–69.
33. For discussion on Wesley's "A Plain Account of Christian Perfection," see Olson, *John Wesley's Theology of Christian Perfection*, 308–25.
34. Wesley, *Plain Account of Christian Perfection*, 4.
35. Wesley, *Plain Account of Christian Perfection*, 5.
36. Wesley, *Plain Account of Christian Perfection*, 6.

final essay, "On Perfection," based on Heb. 6:1, was published in 1784.[37]

One sees an unmistakable influence of *Imitatio Christi*, doubtless as a result of Wesley's preaching and writing, in Anglo-American hymnody, where a fervent desire is expressed on the part of the Christian believer to live a life after the manner of Jesus. A holiness theme is present in the Afro-American Spiritual, "Lord, I Want to Be a Christian":

> Lord, I want to be a Christian in my heart, in my heart;
> Lord, I want to be a Christian in my heart.
> In my heart, in my heart,
> Lord, I want to be a Christian in my heart.
>
> Lord, I want to be more loving in my heart, in my heart;
> Lord, I want to be more loving in my heart.
> In my heart, in my heart,
> Lord, I want to be more loving in my heart.
>
> Lord, I want to be more holy in my heart, in my heart;
> Lord, I want to be more holy in my heart.
> In my heart, in my heart,
> Lord, I want to be more holy in my heart.
>
> Lord, I want to be like Jesus in my heart, in my heart;
> Lord, I want to be like Jesus in my heart.
> In my heart, in my heart,
> Lord, I want to be like Jesus in my heart. (*CovH* 1996 #345)

As young people we used to sing in Sunday School this hymn by James Rowe (1911):

---

37. *Works of John Wesley*, vol. 3, *Sermons III*, 71–114, 70–87.

Earthly pleasures vainly call me; I would be like Jesus;
Nothing worldly shall entrall me; I would be like Jesus.
Be like Jesus, this my song,
In the home and in the throng;
Be like Jesus all day long!
I would be like Jesus.

He has broken every fetter, I would be like Jesus;
That my soul may serve him better, I would be like Jesus.
Be like Jesus, this my song,
In the home and in the throng;
Be like Jesus all day long!
I would be like Jesus. (*CovH* 1931 #241)

There is also P. P. Bliss's "More Holiness Give Me" (1873):

More holiness give me, More striving within;
More patience in suff'ring, More sorrow for sin;
More faith in my Savior, More sense of His care;
More joy in His service, More purpose in prayer.

More purity give me, More strength to o'ercome;
More freedom from earth-stains, More longings for home;
More fit for the kingdom, More used would I be;
More blessed and holy, More, Savior, like Thee. (*CovH* 1950 #276)

And Christopher Wordsworth's great Epiphany hymn, "Songs of Thankfulness and Praise," contains these lines:

Grant us grace to see thee, Lord, Mirrored in thy holy word;
May we imitate thee now, And be pure, as pure art thou;
That we like to thee may be, At thy great Epiphany;

And may praise thee, ever blest, God in Man made manifest.
(*NEngH #56*)

There are many, many more such hymns.

Long before Wesley, it was St. Gregory of Nyssa (d. c. 385), one of the Cappadocian Fathers, who believed that it was entirely in the power of a human person to reach the goal of perfection.[38] Being influenced by Stoic philosophy, he placed much emphasis on human effort. In discussing the first Beatitude, "Blessed are the poor in spirit, for theirs is the kingdom of heaven," he said, "The end of the life of virtue is to become like to God."[39] He continued: "If it is impossible to imitate God, then beatitude is out of the reach of human life."[40]

Imitatio Dei in Judaism

In Judaism there has been an emphasis on the "imitation of God" (*imitatio Dei*) a "theological concept meaning man's obligation to imitate God in his actions." It is related to the *imago Dei* in Gen. 1:27[41] but is rooted in numerous other passages from the Old Testament.[42]

---

38. St. Gregory of Nyssa, *The Lord's Prayer. The Beatitudes* (trans. Hilda C. Graef; Ancient Christian Writers 18; Westminster, MD: Newman, 1954), 19.

39. Gregory of Nyssa, *Lord's Prayer. The Beatitudes,* 89.

40. Gregory of Nyssa, *Lord's Prayer. The Beatitudes,* 90.

41. Sidney Steiman, "Imitation of God (Imitatio Dei)," *EncJud* 8:1292–93.

42. For a discussion of the *imitatio Dei* in Judaism and its basis in texts of the Old Testament, see Solomon Schechter, "The Law of Holiness and the Law of Goodness," in his *Some Aspects of Rabbinic Theology* (London: Adam & Charles Black, 1909), 199–218; Israel Abrahams, "The Imitation of God," in his *Studies in Pharisaism and the Gospels* (Second series; Cambridge: Cambridge University Press, 1924), 138–54; George Foot Moore, *Judaism in the First Centuries of the Christian Era: The Age of the Tannaim* (2nd ed.; 2 vols.; Cambridge, MA: Harvard University Press, 1927), 2:109–11 (repr., New York Schocken, 1971); C. G. Montefiore, *Rabbinic Literature and Gospel Teachings* (London: Macmillan, 1930), 105; Steiman, "Imitation of God," 1292–93; Martin Buber, "Imitatio Dei," in his *Israel and the World: Essays in a Time of Crisis* (1948; repr., Syracuse, NY: Syracuse University Press, 1997), 66–77; John Barton, "Imitation of God in the Old Testament," in *The God of Israel* (ed. Robert P. Gordon; University of Cambridge Oriental Publications 64; Cambridge: Cambridge University Press, 2007), 35–46.

Humans are to be *like* God, not aspire to *be* God, which distinguishes biblical teaching from pagan ideas of being absorbed into the deity.[43]

According to Martin Buber, "The imitation of God, and of the real God, not the wishful creation; the imitation, not of a mediator in human form, but of God himself—this is the central paradox of Judaism."[44] It is a paradox "because God is of course infinitely greater than all human beings, so that to attempt to imitate him might seem like the ultimate blasphemy."[45]

Most important are two passages in Leviticus, where God tells the Israelites, "You shall be holy, for I the Lord your God am holy" (Lev. 19:2); "And be holy, for I am holy" (Lev 11:44); and "You shall be holy, for I am holy" (Lev. 11:45). Peter quotes the latter text in 1 Pet. 1:16. Paul, too, tells the Ephesian Christians, "Therefore be imitators of God, as beloved children" (Eph. 5:1).

Other Old Testament texts support the idea of the *imitatio Dei*: God tells Abraham, "Walk before me, and be blameless" (Gen. 17:1), and in Deuteronomy Moses tells all Israel, "You shall be blameless before the Lord your God" (Deut 18:13 RSV). Deuteronomy puts great emphasis on the holiness of Israel:[46]

Deut 7:6:	"For you are a people holy to the Lord your God"
Deut 14:2:	"For you are a people holy to the Lord your God"
Deut 14:21:	"For you are a people holy to the Lord your God"
Deut 26:19:	"and for you to be a people holy to the Lord your God"
Deut 28:9:	"The Lord will establish you as his holy people"

43. Steiman, "Imitation of God," 1292.
44. Buber, "Imitatio Dei," 71.
45. Barton, "Imitation of God in the Old Testament," 35.
46. Lundbom, *Deuteronomy: A Commentary*, 63.

What is more, Israel is to carry out benevolent activity because God does the same. People are to love the sojourner because God loves the sojourner (Deut. 10:18-19). Israelites are also to redeem slaves of their own people after six years, remembering that God redeemed them from slavery in Egypt (Deut. 15:12-15).

In the Covenant Code, Exodus 20-23, people are told in the Fourth Commandment to keep the Sabbath holy and not do any work on that day because the Lord rested on the seventh day after creating the world (Exod. 20:8-11).

The imitation of God continues in the rabbinic literature (*b. Sot.* 14a):[47]

a) Just as the Lord clothes the naked (Gen. 3:21), you should clothe the naked (cf. Matt. 25:36).

b) Just as the Lord comforts the bereaved, you shall comfort the bereaved.

c) Just as the Lord visits the sick, you shall visit the sick.

d) Just as the Lord buries the dead (Deut. 34:6), you shall bury the dead.

The rabbis admonished the Jewish people to imitate the qualities of divine mercy, forbearance, and kindness, but did not counsel imitating God in his attribute of stern justice.[48]

Imitatio Dei in the Sermon on the Mount

One should therefore take the verse in Matt. 5:48, "Be perfect, therefore, as your heavenly Father is perfect," as no more or less than

---

47. Steiman, "Imitation of God," 1292, where other rabbinic writings are cited.
48. For more discussion on the *imitatio Dei*, see the exegesis of Matt. 5:48 in chapter 14.

the admonition in Leviticus to be holy as the Lord God is holy. The problem just discussed has come largely from the use of the word "perfect" in our English Bibles, which does adequately translate the Greek, but carries with it more meaning than Jesus intended in his elevated word on right living in the Sermon on the Mount.

PART II

The Sermon on the Mount

5

Jesus on the Mountain (5:1-2)

We have seen that Matthew presents the Sermon on the Mount as Jesus' core teaching on the new covenant. This teaching is to be heard and put into practice by his disciples, and not only them, but all those aspiring to be his disciples. The Sermon begins on a very positive note. New covenant people are blessed, then said to be salt of the earth and light of the world. Jesus has come to fulfill the Law, not do away with it. New covenant people must therefore not relax even the least of his commands, but must aspire to a higher righteousness than that paraded by the scribes and Pharisees.

> 5 ¹*When Jesus saw the crowds, he went up the mountain; and after he sat down, his disciples came to him.* ²*Then he began to speak, and taught them, saying:*

1. *When Jesus saw the crowds, he went up the mountain; and after he sat down, his disciples came to him.* Crowds of people are present, and at the conclusion of the sermon they are seen to be a listening part of Jesus' audience (7:28), but Matthew keeps them in the background.

According to Matthew, crowds follow Jesus because of his preaching, teaching, and healings in Galilee. But here the disciples have the preferred position of sitting close to him. They will hear Jesus, but so will the crowds. Natural acoustics discovered at various locations in Palestine show that large crowds could hear a speaker distinctly if he was atop a mountain or on level ground below.[1]

he went up the mountain. The setting recalls Moses ascending the mountain to receive the tablets of Law that formed the core of the Sinai covenant (Exod. 19:3).[2] There, however, the people heard the divine voice "out of the fire, the cloud, and the thick darkness," in the valley below (Deut. 5:22). But now Matthew has Jesus giving the core teaching of the new covenant atop a Galilean mountain, with the people gathered somewhere below. Luther makes much of the public nature of Jesus' teaching, saying this is always how Christian preaching and teaching ought to be done. It should not be carried out, he says, off in some corner or even in private houses by self-authorized individuals who boast of being possessed by the Holy Spirit. Public utterances allow the speaker to be bold and prophetic; they also make possible broader scrutiny of what is being said. In the first century, rabbis commonly taught indoors, that is, in synagogues or in schools, although there were exceptions. If crowds became too great, they would go outside. Rabbi Johanan ben Zakkai is said to have taught all day outside on one occasion, lecturing to crowds on laws of the festivals.[3]

he sat down. The common practice in synagogues and in schools was for the rabbi to teach sitting down. The Talmud makes frequent

---

1. See B. Cobbey Crisler, "The Acoustics and Crowd Capacity of Natural Theaters in Palestine," *BA* 39 (1976): 128–41. Compare the biblical accounts of the speech of Jotham from the top of Mount Gerizim to the men of Shechem (Judg. 9:7–21), and an earlier covenant renewal ceremony at the same location after the Israelites had entered Canaan (Deut. 27:11–13).
2. C. G. Montefiore, *The Synoptic Gospels* (2nd rev. ed.; 2 vols.; London: Macmillan, 1927), 2:29.
3. Samuel T. Lachs, *A Rabbinic Commentary on the New Testament* (Hoboken, NJ: Ktav, 1987), 67.

use of the expression "he sat and discoursed." When Jesus visited the synagogue in his hometown of Nazareth, he stood up to read the Scripture but then sat down to give his interpretation (Luke 4:20). Jesus, therefore, is acting as a rabbi when he sits down to give his teaching.

his disciples came to him. The primary audience for this sermon is Jesus' disciples, which has led some to conclude that Jesus was directing his teaching toward those who had already made a commitment to follow him, not just anyone.[4] But what about the crowds who at the beginning are in the background and at the end register astonishment at what they have heard (7:28-29)? Jesus is surely addressing a mixed company: believers, seekers, and uncommitted onlookers. Matthew may be ambiguous in portraying the crowd, but he seems to be telling us that, though Jesus was speaking primarily to his disciples, a crowd was nevertheless present, listening in, and many in that crowd were deeply moved—some perhaps to faith in the teacher uttering these stirring words.

Leander Keck makes the point that, though Matthew is directing the Sermon on the Mount to the church, it is by no means restricted to the church, for at the conclusion of his Gospel Matthew specifies that a worldwide mission is to be undertaken so others will be brought into the discipline of the Sermon (Matt. 28:19-20). The Sermon, says Keck, is for all people, even though the Christian community is held accountable in a special way for what is being taught.[5] Christian preaching and teaching today are most often directed at those who have already had a prior Christian experience or made a prior Christian commitment; nevertheless, others wishing

---

4. Theodore H. Robinson, *The Gospel of Matthew* (Garden City, NY: Doubleday, Doran, 1928), 25–26.

5. Leander E. Keck, "The Sermon on the Mount," in *Jesus and Man's Hope* (ed. Donald G. Miller and Dikran Y. Hadidian; 2 vols.; Pittsburgh: Pittsburgh Theological Seminary, 1970–71), 2:315.

to listen in should be welcomed. If the preaching and teaching are truly God sent, some may very well be astonished enough to join the company of Christian believers.

2. *And he opened his mouth and he taught them, saying.* In this "sermon" Jesus is teaching, not evangelizing. The point is made again in 7:28, where the sermon is called *didachē* ("teaching"). In the early church, the sermon began worship and was *didachē*.[6] Some today say that sermons in Christian worship must always contain a proclamation of the gospel, others that it must always have an evangelistic thrust. Gospel proclamation, or *kērygma* in Greek, is of course essential to the mission of the church. But teaching is also essential to the church's mission. It would seem reasonable, then, that a sermon might be either *kērygma* or *didachē*, or a combination of both.

6. Jeremias, *Sermon on the Mount*, 21.

6

The Blessings (5:3-12)

^{3}*"Blessed are the poor in spirit,*
for theirs is the kingdom of heaven.
^{4}*"Blessed are those who mourn,*
for they will be comforted.
^{5}*"Blessed are the meek,*
for they will inherit the earth.
^{6}*"Blessed are those who hunger and thirst for righteousness,*
for they will be filled.
^{7}*"Blessed are the merciful,*
for they will receive mercy.
^{8}*"Blessed are the pure in heart,*
for they will see God.
^{9}*"Blessed are the peacemakers,*
for they will be called children of God.
^{10}*"Blessed are those who are persecuted for righteousness' sake,*
for theirs is the kingdom of heaven.

[11]*"Blessed are you when people revile you and persecute you and utter all kinds of evil against you falsely on my account. [12]Rejoice and be glad, for your reward is great in heaven, for in the same way they persecuted the prophets who were before you.*

The Sermon on the Mount begins not with commands, as in the Old Testament law code of Deuteronomy, but with blessings, which in Deuteronomy come last together with the curses (Deuteronomy 28). These blessings we call the "Beatitudes." Luther calls this "a fine, sweet, and friendly beginning." Here, without delay and with intentional directness, the blessings of the new covenant are pronounced on all who enter the kingdom Jesus is announcing, where "kingdom" refers to "the rule of God." A new people is being created, one that will later be known as the Christian Church. This community receives only blessings, no curses, for the covenant Jesus announces and later mediates is eternal and unconditional. Unlike the old covenant with Israel that was mediated through Moses, which was conditional and capable of being broken, this one cannot be broken. Matthew says as much later when he has Jesus telling Peter that against this new company of believers (= church) the gates of hell shall not prevail (Matt. 16:18). The woes Jesus announces in chapter 23 are directed against another audience entirely. Joachim Jeremias says the Beatitudes are something more: They are "concealed testimonies by Jesus to himself as the savior of the poor, the sorrowing, etc."[1]

3. *Blessed are the poor in spirit, for theirs is the kingdom of heaven.* Greek μακάριοι, commonly rendered "blessed" in English, translates the Hebrew אשרי (Pss. 1:1; 2:12; 32:1-2; 112:1; 144:15), which can also mean "happy." Some thirty sayings in the Old Testament begin

---

1. Jeremias, *Sermon on the Mount*, 24.

with "happy,"[2] and in Matthew μακάριοι occurs elsewhere in 11:6; 13:16; 16:17; and 24:46. To the poor in spirit Jesus gives happiness or blessing from God. E. Stanley Jones said that Aristotle used the Greek word for divine blessedness in contrast to human happiness,[3] but that distinction is too fine for the truth expressed here. In the economy of God, even human happiness can come to one who is crushed in spirit. Yes, the poor in spirit may at some point feel that they are anything but blessed, something that might equally be said about those who mourn or those who are persecuted for righteousness' sake (vv. 4, 10), but Jesus pronounces a blessing upon all of these, and it simply remains for those who believe to discover what exactly this means.

The expression "poor in spirit" is nevertheless difficult, for it appears nowhere in the Old Testament, the rabbinic literature, or elsewhere in the NT.[4] The expression has turned up, however, in the Qumran *War Scroll* (1QM 14:7: ובעניי רוח), which Jean Duhaime and the editors of 1QH in DJD translate as "humble spirit"[5] and T. H. Gaster as "lowly spirits."[6] In the Old Testament, Ps. 34:18 comes close: "The Lord is near to the brokenhearted, and saves the crushed in spirit."[7] See also Ps. 51:17 and Isa. 66:2. In Luke's Sermon on the Plain, blessing is bestowed simply on the "poor," over against whom stand the woe-stricken "rich" (Luke 6:20, 24). But the two terms, "poor" and "poor in spirit" would have had much

---

2. Gerald Friedlander, *The Jewish Sources of the Sermon on the Mount* (1911; repr., Library of Biblical Studies; New York: Ktav, 1969), 17.

3. Jones, *Christ of the Mount*, 43.

4. Betz (*Sermon on the Mount*, 111–12) says it occurs nowhere else in the Greek language.

5. Jean Duhaime, "War Scroll," in *The Dead Sea Scrolls: Hebrew, Aramaic, and Greek Texts with English Translations*, vol. 2, *Damascus Document, War Scroll, and Related Documents* (ed. James H. Charlesworth et al.; Princeton Theological Seminary Dead Sea Scrolls Project 2; Louisville: Westminster John Knox, 1995), 124–25; Hartmut Stegemann et al., eds., *Qumran Cave 1.III: 1QHodayota, with Incorporation of 4QHodayota-f and 1Q Hodayot b* (DJD 40; Oxford: Clarendon, 2009), 125.

6. T. H. Gaster, *The Dead Sea Scriptures* (rev. enl. ed.; Garden City, NY: Doubleday, 1964), 319. See also "stricken spirits" in 1QM 11:10; see Duhaime, "War Scroll," 118–19.

7. This verse is cited as a parallel by Friedlander, *Jewish Sources of the Sermon on the Mount*, 19.

the same connotation for a Hebrew- or Aramaic-speaking Jew.[8]
Hebrew עָנִי and עָנָו both denote someone who is economically poor,
but who is also "afflicted," "humble," or even "meek."[9] Jerome took
"poor in spirit" to mean a voluntary "humility in spirit" (Ps. 34:18),[10]
Augustine much the same: "humble and God-fearing, not having
a bloated spirit."[11] Chrysostom took it as "humble and contrite in
mind" (Ps. 51:17),[12] and Gregory of Nyssa as a "voluntary humility,"
by which he said we would be imitating God in Christ (2 Cor.
8:9; Phil. 2:5-7).[13] We might therefore regard Matthew's "poor in
spirit" as an attempt to render the fullness of either Hebrew word
into Greek. The "poor in spirit" are lowly people in society, poor,
yes, but at the same time dispirited, disheartened, and without much
hope. Such are typically exploited by the rich. In the thinking of
ancient people, economic poverty cannot be separated from the
psychological or spiritual condition that goes along with it.
Exploitation making one poor contributes to the weakened spirit of
that person. In the Psalms the exploited poor are frequently portrayed
as humble and God-fearing, leaving them open to God's mercy and
help, which they receive (Pss. 9:18; 12:5; 34:6; 40:17; etc.). Psalm 10
heaps scorn on the rich who arrogantly pursue the poor (עָנִי), saying

---

8. Lachs, *Rabbinic Commentary on the New Testament*, 70.

9. See R. H. Charles, "The Beatitudes," *ET* 28 (1916–17): 538–39; Ernest Best, "Matthew V. 3," *NTS* 7 (1960–61): 255–58.

10. St. Jerome, *Commentary on Matthew* (trans. Thomas P. Sheck; Fathers of the Church 117; Washington DC: Catholic University of America Press, 2008), 75.

11. St. Augustine, "Our Lord's Sermon on the Mount," in *Nicene and Post-Nicene Fathers of the Christian Church*, vol. 6, *Augustine: Semon on the Mount, Harmony of the Gospels, Homilies on the Gospels* (ed. Philip Schaff; 1887; repr., Grand Rapids: Eerdmans, 1980), 4; *The Preaching of Augustine: Our Lord's Sermon on the Mount* (trans. Francine Cardman; ed. Jaroslav Pelikan; Preacher's Paperback Library; Philadelphia: Fortress Press, 1973), 3.

12. John Chrysostom, *The Homilies of S. John Chrysostom, Archbishop of Constantinople, on the Gospel of Matthew* (3 vols.; Library of the Fathers of the Holy Catholic Church 11, 15, 34; Oxford: John Henry Parker, 1843–51), 1:199.

13. Gregory of Nyssa, *The Lord's Prayer. The Beatitudes*, 90–91.

they are greedy, wicked, and godless. Jesus heaps a similar scorn on the Pharisees and scribes in Matt. 23:4-14.

The idea that poverty is a good in itself, blessed by God, would be a departure from Jewish teaching. The Old Testament and rabbinic literature decry poverty, typically exhorting justice and mercy for the poor, the needy, and the afflicted (Ps. 82:3-4; Amos 2:6-8; Jer. 2:34; Isa. 49:13).[14] Almsgiving is said to be as weighty as all the other commandments.[15] The Messiah is one who will come to judge the poor in righteousness (Isa 11:4). The entire Old Testament—Law, Prophets, and Wisdom literature—teaches care of and benevolence toward the poor (Exod. 22:25-27; Deut. 15:1-11; 24:10-15; Lev. 25:35; Ps. 41:1-3; Prov. 19:7; Amos 8:4-7). Judaism knows no vow to adopt a life of poverty, such as what developed later in Christianity. The Talmud says that poverty in the house of a man is more distressful than fifty plagues (b. B. Bat. 116a). The Sermon on the Mount, therefore, does not regard the condition of poverty as a blessing. It is addressing the general condition of poverty, brokenness, and misery.[16]

In Jewish (as well as non-Jewish) thought we meet up with a wisdom standing diametrically opposite to conventional wisdom rooted in the popular mind.[17] According to conventional wisdom, blessing comes in such things as beauty, health, wealth, children, power, success, fame, a joyful life, and so on. Luther was quick to perceive conventional wisdom, saying it might well be put in the following terms: "Whoever is rich and powerful is completely blessed; on the other hand whoever is poor and miserable is rejected

14. Beryl D. Cohon, *Jacob's Well: Some Jewish Sources and Parallels to the Sermon on the Mount* (New York: Bookman Associates, 1956), 16.
15. B. Cohon, *Jacob's Well*, 18.
16. Betz, *Sermon on the Mount*, 114.
17. Hans Dieter Betz, *Essays on the Sermon on the Mount* (trans. L. L. Welborn; Philadelphia: Fortress Press, 1985), 30–33.

and condemned before God." This wisdom Luther finds well established among the Jews, and he says the book of Job is written to oppose it. Jesus in the present Beatitude draws upon anti-wisdom in order to surprise and awaken his audience—something that good teaching always does.

The key Old Testament passage serving as inspiration for this Beatitude and the one following on mourning is Isa. 61:1-3, which Jesus read in the Nazareth synagogue at the opening of his ministry (Luke 4:16) and which is paraphrased on another occasion when Jesus was asked by his disciples if he was the long-awaited Messiah or if they should await another (Matt. 11:5-6; Luke 7:22-23).[18] The passage reads:

> [1]The Spirit of the LORD God is upon me,
>> because the LORD has anointed me;
> he has sent me to bring good news to the oppressed (ענוים)
>> to bind up the brokenhearted,
> to proclaim liberty to the captives,
>> and release to the prisoners;
> [2]to proclaim the year of the LORD's favor,
>> and the day of vengeance of our God;
>> to comfort all who mourn;
> [3]to provide for those who mourn in Zion—
>> to give them a garland instead of ashes,
> the oil of gladness instead of mourning,
>> the mantle of praise instead of a faint spirit.
> They will be called oaks of righteousness,
>> the planting of the LORD, to display his glory.

18. Black, "Beatitudes," 125–26; see also D. Flusser, "Blessed Are the Poor in Spirit . . . ," *IEJ* 10 (1960): 9.

Mention here of people being given "the mantle of praise instead of a faint spirit" could stand behind the present Beatitude, but, if so, the accent would be on a future blessedness for those poor in spirit. But the usual interpretation is that the blessedness offered in this Beatitude and the others is not simply for the future, but something beginning right now in the present.

Matthew uses "kingdom of heaven" to mean "kingdom of God" (cf. Luke 6:20). Pious Jews substituted "heaven" for "God" in order to preserve the sanctity of the divine name,[19] and Matthew's Gospel is the most Jewish of the four Gospels. The "kingdom," for Matthew, is a central concept in Jesus' teaching, and at the center of his Gospel are placed the parables of the kingdom (chapter 13). Jesus' kingdom is a theocracy, designating the present and future authority of God over the lives of men and women (Josephus, *Apion* 2.165). It is the reign (or rule) of God on earth (Zech. 14:9).[20] The term is found also in Dan. 2:44; 7:13-14, where a future kingdom is promised at the coming of "a son of man," and saints of the Most High will inherit it (7:18).

We find out then why the poor in spirit are blessed: God's kingdom is theirs. Into the domain of God's rule the poor are given an immediate welcome. John the Baptist, and Jesus early on, preached, "Repent, for the kingdom of heaven has come near" (Matt. 3:2; 4:17). Dispirited souls weighed down by poverty and other woes are given a new lease on life. The kingdom begins now, and that is good news. But while the kingdom of heaven becomes immediate reality for all who seek entrance through Jesus (realized eschatology), there nevertheless remains a future kingdom in which what has presently been inaugurated will come in its fullness. The rabbis called

---

19. Joachim Jeremias, *New Testament Theology*, vol. 1 (trans. John Bowden; New Testament Library; London: SCM, 1971), 9. The term is common in the rabbinic and other Jewish literature, for example, *m. Ber.* 2:2; *Deut. Rab.* 2:31; *Sifre Deut.* 323; and so on.
20. B. Cohon, *Jacob's Well*, 22.

this the World to Come; Christians call it heaven. In either case, the blessings are understood as taking effect immediately, and they will be realized fully when the present world gives way to the next.

This theology is embodied in the hymnody of eighteenth- and nineteenth-century Swedish Pietism, which depicts life as a journey for the redeemed who yet know privation, trouble, and much suffering. Things will be infinitely better when the present world gives way to the next. One such hymn is Andreas Carl Rutström's "Chosen Seed and Zion's Children" (Lammets folk och Sions fränder):

Chosen seed and Zion's children, ransomed from eternal wrath,
Trav'ling to the heav'nly Canaan, on a rough and thorny path,
Church of God, in Christ elected, thou to God art reconciled,
But on earth thou art a stranger, persecuted and reviled.

Pleasantly thy lines have fallen, underneath the tree of life,
For the Lord is thy salvation, and thy shield in all thy strife.
Here the timid bird finds shelter, here the swallow finds a nest,
Trembling fugitive a refuge, and the weary pilgrim rest. (trans. Claude W. Foss; *CovH* 1950 #414)

Another is O. A. Ottander's "Trust in the Savior, O Precious Soul" (Håll dig vid klippan):

Trust in the Savior, O precious soul.
Let Him forever your life control.
Danger will threaten, threaten each day.
Trust in the Savior, He leads the way.

Anguish and sorrow, fears and distress,

Sins without number all must confess.
Bring them to Jesus, ask for release,
Trust in the Savior, He'll grant His peace.

Be not dismayed or troubled, my friend.
Soon in the homeland all grief will end.
There free from sorrow, sin, and distress,
We through the Savior find perfect rest.
(trans. A. Eldon Palmquist; *CovH* 1950 #342)

Another is Nils Frykman's "The Highest Joy That Can Be Known"
(Den högsta lycka), which contains these lines:

The Word doth give me wealth untold,
All good it has in store.
My deepest sorrows yield their hold
To joys forever more.

How often when in deep despair
My soul has been restored.
And when the tempter would ensnare
'Twould strength to stand afford.
(trans. Signe L. Bennett; *CovH* 1950 #220)

A favorite among the Swedish Pietists was Joel Blomqvist's
"Heavenly Spirit, Gentle Spirit" (Himladuva):

Heavenly Spirit, gentle Spirit,
O descend on us, we pray.

Come, console us, and control us,
Christ, most fair, to us portray

Hear us pleading, interceding,
Thou interpreter of love,
With thy fire, — us inspire
Holy flame from God above.,

Come to cheer us, be Thou near us
Kindle in us heaven's love.
Keep us burning, humble, yearning,
Dwell in us, O heavenly Dove.

Pilgrims, strangers, 'mid life's dangers,
We on Thee would e'er depend.
Spirit tender, our defender,
Guide us, keep us to the end.
(trans. Gerhard W. Palmgren; *CovH* 1950 #202)

Another was Jonas Stadling's "Are You Dismayed, Lonely, Afraid"
(Guds trofasthet):

Are you dismayed, lonely, afraid,
Thinking yourself forsaken?
God is your stay, trust him and pray,
New hope He will awaken

Friends may deceive, cause you to grieve,
God is your consolation.
Faithful and true, He is to you,
Comfort in tribulation.

Courage and might, guidance and light,
God will in mercy render.
In every pain, conflict and strain,
He is your true defender.
(trans. E. Gustav Johnson; *CovH* 1950 #73)

4. *Blessed are those who mourn, for they will be comforted.* This
second Beatitude also develops out of Isa. 61:1-3, specifically vv.
2-3. Mourning is deep sadness over the loss of things people hold
dear—other people, first of all, but also possessions, a job, honor, or
whatever else makes life rich and joyful. Mourning usually includes
weeping, but Matthew once again is less concrete, preferring the
more general "mourning" of his Isaiah text. Luke 6:25b has
"mourning and weeping." Mourning is never a welcome guest, yet it
visits everyone.

Can those who mourn be blessed? Gregory of Nyssa says,

> If one looks at it from the point of view of the world, he will certainly
> say that the words are ridiculous, and argue like this: If one calls blessed
> those people whose life is spent enduring all manner of misfortune, it
> follows that those who live without sorrow or care must be miserable.[21]

But Jesus says "Yes," continuing to turn conventional wisdom on its
head by pronouncing a blessing on individuals who might otherwise
think they had escaped the blessing of God, for mourning has to do
with loss, and blessings are measured in terms of what one has gained.
Perhaps interpretation should be broadened to include mourning for
the desperate plight of others or a situation in the world deeply tragic.
E. Stanley Jones says that this Beatitude "means an active sharing and
bearing of the world's hurt and sin in order to cure it. . . . [I]t means

---

21. Gregory of Nyssa, *The Lord's Prayer. The Beatitudes*, 106.

the kind of mourning that Jesus manifested when he wept over the city of Jerusalem."[22]

Comfort is the proper end to mourning. When the loss is still recent, our comfort is likely to be a quiet rest or peace. But over time comfort will witness the return of joy (Isa. 61:3; 66:10). Prisoners wrongly interned express unbridled joy upon being released. The present verse implies that God is the comforter, where in the Old Testament God is the supreme comforter of Israel (Isa. 40:1; 57:18-21; 66:13-14) and the comforter of the Psalmist in Ps. 23:4.[23] Divine oracles juxtaposed in the book of Jeremiah promise God's comfort to a weeping Rachel (Jer. 31:15-17):

[15]Thus said Yahweh:
The voice of lament is heard in Ramah
    bitterest weeping
Rachel is weeping over her sons
    she refuses to be comforted over her sons
        because they are not.

[16]Thus said Yahweh:
Restrain your voice from weeping
    and your eyes from tears
For there is a reward for your labor
    —oracle of Yahweh—
    and they shall return from the land of the enemy

[17]And there is hope for your future
    —oracle of Yahweh—
    and sons shall return to their territory (AB).

22. E. Stanley Jones, *Christ of the Mount*, 51.
23. B. Cohon, *Jacob's Well*, 24–25.

The Talmud carries the promise of God's comfort a step further. It says, "The Holy One, blessed be He, comforted mourners . . . so you shall comfort mourners" (*b. Sot.* 14a). It also states that "Comforter" (*Menahem*) shall be one of the names of the Messiah" (*b. Sanh.* 98b).

Can we say more about what Jesus means in this Beatitude? What sort of mourning leaves people blessed, or does blessing come only after one has been comforted? The Greek future passive, παρακληθήσονται, which is translated "they shall be comforted," has prompted many to conclude that Jesus is talking about a present condition that is bad, but which will be reversed by a future condition that is good. That is, people who mourn *now* will be comforted later. Luther noted that, in Luke, Jesus pronounces a woe on those who laugh now but in the future will mourn and weep (Luke 6:25). This same idea is illustrated in Luke's parable of the rich man and Lazarus (Luke 16:19-31), where the poor Lazarus is brought to the bosom of Abraham, and Abraham is heard telling the rich man languishing in the fire, "but now he [that is, Lazarus] is comforted here, and you are in anguish" (Luke 16:25). We might also cite Ps. 126:5-6, which says:

> May those who sow in tears
> > reap with shouts of joy.
> Those who go out weeping,
> > bearing the seed for sowing,
> shall come home with shouts of joy,
> > carrying their sheaves. (Ps. 126:5-6)

However, it has been pointed out that the future passive here and elsewhere in the Sermon is a Jewish device to avoid using the name of God.[24] Jesus is talking first and foremost about God's comfort, although that will not preclude comfort given to mourners by other people.

There are good reasons for not pressing a future state of comfort to the point of excluding a present comfort that Jesus may have in mind for those who have been mourning for centuries. In Isa. 61:1-4, the long-awaited consolation of Israel is promised (cf. Isa. 25:8; 60:20; 66:10-11; Sir. 48:24). Now Jesus is bringing in the kingdom of heaven, which means that comfort is offered right away for people who have waited long for it. Jesus says in Matt. 9:15 that the people cannot mourn when the bridegroom (that is, he himself) is still with them. Luther is thus correct in saying that this Beatitude refers both to the now and to the hereafter. What is more, the Christian experience—because God has broken into community and individual life with his new rule—commonly knows joy amid sorrow.

Pietistic hymnody is filled with songs about joy amid sorrow, and mourning that one day will give way to an even greater joy in Heaven. John Brun's "In Heaven All Is Gladness" (Hos Gud är idel glädje) expresses both joys:

In heaven all is gladness—Here troubles press, and fears.
Here often bowed and sighing, I eat "the bread of tears."
Here joy and sorrow mingle for Christ's beloved bride,
But 'tis not so up yonder, for there doth joy abide.

Would I exchange conditions with one, whose all's below?
Nay, rather I'd be sowing good seed tho' tears may flow.
If at the close of journey I but in joy may reap,
When worldlings' joys are over, and they, too late, must weep.

24. Jeremias, *New Testament Theology*, 1:9–14; Betz, *Sermon on the Mount*, 124.

My hope for life eternal rests on foundation sure.
My cross I therefore gladly will yet awhile endure.
Soon there shall be no sorrows, no plaints, nor sighs for me,
When, with uncovered vision, my Savior I shall see.
(trans. Composite; *CovH* 1950 #510)

A future joy that will replace the present mourning is well expressed in A. L. Skoog's "We Wait for a Great and Glorious Day" (Snart randas en dag):

We wait for a great and glorious day,
As many as love the Lord,
When shadows shall flee, and clouds pass away,
And weeping no more be heard.
O wonderful day that soon may be here,
O beautiful hope the pilgrim to cheer,
Thy coming we hail in tuneful accord,
Thou glorious day of Christ, our Lord.

For crosses we've borne then crowns will be giv'n,
For tempests eternal calm,
For pathways of thorns, rich mansions in heaven,
For warfare the victor's palm.
(trans. A. L. Skoog; *CovH* 1950 #181)

Another such witness to the life of the Christian pilgrim is C. A. Stenholm's communion hymn, "Springs of Grace Are Streaming" (Hälsokällan), which contains these lines:

Soothing balm is pouring into hearts that grieve,
Joy and hope restoring, when earth's comforts leave.

When my heart is sinking, 'neath the load of care,
At this fountain drinking Heaven's strength I share.
(trans. E. Gustav Johnson, *CovH* 1950 #434)

Those who know this joy can be joyful at funerals; they can be joyful in the midst of financial reversals; they can be joyful when they are out of a job or have entered retirement (which for many is a mourning); they can be joyful when people dishonor them; and so on. This joy is not a superficial joy that hides sorrow; it is a joy coexisting with sorrow, and one that triumphs over sorrow. It is a present joy experienced by the Christian believer. Much to be pitied is the person who cannot be comforted. Luther says that no one can stand continued mourning. It is unnatural, and yet there are people for whom continued morning is true. Of these we can only say that they know not the blessing made available in this Beatitude. Mourning is to be followed—immediately or soon after—by God's gift of comfort.

There is also something terribly wrong with people who do not mourn when they should. Amos talks about the rich in Samaria who lie on beds of ivory, eat lamb and veal, sing, drink wine in bowls, and anoint themselves with the finest oils, *but are not grieved over the ruin of Joseph* (Amos 6:4-6). These are the people who will mourn later (v. 7; cf. Luke 6:25b). I knew a prominent religious leader who would respond to the mention of a grievous wrong, even within the church, with only a nervous smile. He should rather have shown signs of mourning. Do we mourn over the violence in our cities, the immorality in our country, and the enormous injustices in our world? Do believers mourn over foolishness going on in the church, and in the lives of people who call themselves by the name of Christ? They should. Here it should also be added that there is a mourning deeper than weeping or audible fright, one so great that the person is unable to cry or complain to anyone (Luther). But in this Beatitude Jesus is saying that even these people will be comforted.

5. *Blessed are the meek, for they will inherit the earth.* This Beatitude appears to echo Ps. 37:11, which says that the meek will inherit/ possess the earth, but there, אֶרֶץ is usually translated "land" (NRSV), where reference would be to land in Palestine. See also Ps. 25:13.[25] The meek (οἱ πραεῖς) are humble folk,[26] similar to the "poor in spirit." They are not proud and not given to violence. The NEB translates "gentle spirit." The Targum to Ps. 37:11 translates, "But the humble shall possess the land."

Perhaps due to the similarity between "meek" and "poor in spirit," certain ancient manuscripts—also Clement and Origen—place the present Beatitude second instead of third (so JB), which puts "poor and spirit" and "meek" in parallel.[27] The juxtaposition of these two ideas appears to occur in a reconstructed Qumran document, the *Thanksgiving Hymns* (1QH 18:14-15/23:15-16),[28] only with the difference that the "meek" segment comes first and "contrite in spirit" second. The two are nevertheless juxtaposed. Third comes the "mourn" segment. The Qumran text as translated by David Flusser compares with Matt. 5:3-5 as follows:[29]

---

25. Stendahl ("Matthew," 775) cites the Qumran *pesher* on this psalm.
26. Johnson, "Matthew," 282.
27. Betz, *Sermon on the Mount*, 119 n. 207, 125.
28. Flusser ("Blessed Are the Poor in Spirit," 1–13) cites the passage as 1QH 18:14-15, but in DJD 40 it is listed as 23:15-16 (pp. 276–81).
29. Flusser, "Blessed Are the Poor in Spirit," 3–4. For another translation of 1QH 18:14-15, see Menahem Mansoor, *The Thanksgiving Hymns* (Studies on the Texts of the Desert of Judah 3; Leiden: Brill, 1961).

1QH 18:14–15/23:15–16	Matthew 5:3–5
[I thank you, God, for havingappointed] me in Thy truth a messenger[of the peace] of Thy goodness,	
to proclaim to *the meek* the multitude of Thine mercies, and to let them *that are of contrite spirit* he[ar salvation] from [everlasting] source and to *them that mourn* everlasting joy.	[3]Blessed are *the poor in spirit*, for theirs is the kingdom of heaven. [5]Blessed are *the meek* for they will inherit the earth. [4]Blessed are *those who mourn* for they will be comforted.

Both documents, as Flusser points out, lift up expressions occurring in Isa. 61:1–2 and 66:2b.

Moses is the meek person par excellence in the Old Testament (Num 12:3). He was certainly not a weak person, but he was meek.[30] Jesus too was meek, according to the description in Matt. 11:29. Greek πραεῖς means "gentle, humble, meek, not being over impressed by a sense of one's self importance." Aristotle used the term to describe a man who is master of himself, who has self-control.[31] Betz says that meekness is not a given condition but an ethical attitude to be acquired.[32]

Isaiah 60:20–22, speaking of the future glory of Zion, says:

> Your sun shall no more go down,
>> or your moon withdraw itself;
> for the LORD will be your everlasting light,
>> and your days of mourning shall be ended.
> Your people shall all be righteous;
>> they shall possess the land [inherit the earth] forever,

---

30. On the inadequacy of "meek" as a proper translation of Hebrew ענו and Greek πραεῖς, see W. E. P. Cotter, "The Meek," *ET* 33 (1921–22): 280.

31. Aristotle, *Nic. Eth.* iv 5:3: "Now we praise a man who feels anger on the right grounds and against the right persons, and also in the right manner and at the right moment and for the right length of time. He may then be called gentle-tempered." See Cotter, "Meek," 280.

32. Betz, *Sermon on the Mount*," 126.

They are the shoot that I planted, the work of my hands,
    so that I might be glorified.
The least of them shall become a clan,
    and the smallest one a mighty nation;
I am the LORD;
    in its time I will accomplish it quickly. (Isa 60:20-22)

The expression "inherit the earth" is said to be synonymous with "theirs is the kingdom," with Samuel Lachs going on to say that this Beatitude supports the idea that all Israelites have a share in the World to Come.[33] If so, Jesus is saying that the meek are destined to inherit the kingdom he is inaugurating.

Is it true that the meek will inherit the earth? One would suspect that it is rather the proud and the violent. Common wisdom says that it is the strong and self-assertive who inherit the earth.[34] But Deut. 8:17-20 warns Israel that pride and arrogance will result in a loss of the wealth of the land given to the nation by God, which is eventually what happened. In 586 B.C.E., when Nebuchadnezzar put an end to Israelite nationhood, something remarkable happened: the meek inherited the earth (Jer. 39:10). That is, the bulk of Judah's survivors were carted off into exile, but Nebuzaradan, an officer of Nebuchadnezzar, is said to have left behind "poor people who owned nothing" and given them vineyards and fields. The meek inherited the earth. This same Nebuzaradan, who released the persecuted prophet Jeremiah from his chains, gave him the option of going to Babylon, where he would be well cared for, or staying in the land. The Babylonian officer said, "See, the whole land is before you; wherever it seems good and right in your eyes to go, go!" (Jer. 40:4

---

33. Lachs, *Rabbinic Commentary on the New Testament*, 74.
34. Cotter, "Meek," 280.

AB). Jeremiah chose to stay in the land. The meek again inherited the earth.

In discussing this Beatitude, Luther focuses on the control that individuals seek over land. He correctly observes that there is often much arguing among family members and neighbors over property and land. Here again it happens that the proud lose and the meek inherit. How often have we seen families destroyed over arguments about inheriting land? And how often have we seen friendships end forever because of arguments about property and property lines?

6. *Blessed are those who hunger and thirst for righteousness, for they will be filled.* Luke simply has "hunger" in his Beatitude (Luke 6:21), but Matthew expands to "hunger and thirst for righteousness." Here again, Matthew is oriented toward ethics, for, as Betz says, hunger and thirst by themselves have no ethical value.[35] "Righteousness" (Gk. δικαιοσύνη) is a favorite term of Matthew, appearing again in vv. 10 and 20. In v. 20 Jesus says his followers must strive for a righteousness better than that of the scribes and Pharisees. They must also rise above attitudes and behavior of the best of the Gentiles (5:46-48; 6:7, 32). The idea is well rooted in the Old Testament. The Psalmist says, "My soul thirsts for God, for the living God" (Ps. 42:2). And the messianic king, says Jeremiah, will be a righteous Branch of David, one who will execute justice and righteousness in the land (Jer. 23:5-6). According to Daniel's view of the end-times, those awakening to everlasting life, who have turned many to righteousness, will shine like the stars forever and ever (Dan. 12:2-3). Righteousness was also highly prized in the classical world. When Socrates had died, Plato said of his friend, "Of all those of his

---

35. Betz, *Sermon on the Mount*, 129. The point was made earlier by C. H. Dodd, "The Beatitudes," in *Melanges bibliques rédigés en l'honneur de André Robert* (Travaux de l'Institut Catholique de Paris 4; Paris: Bloud & Gay, 1957), 409.

time whom we have known, [he was] the best and wisest and most righteous man" (*Phae.* 118).

What is "righteousness"? It can mean "what is right" (JB), "to do what is right," or "to see right prevail" (NEB). The Hebrew behind the Greek term is צְדָקָה, which also carries meanings of "vindication" and "salvation" (Isa. 62:1-2). The persistent widow in the parable of Luke 18:1-8 hungers for righteousness, that is, vindication, from a judge who is unrighteous. Matthew Black says that δικαιοσύνη "is the vindication of the cause of the afflicted saints, the fulfillment of Isa. 61:1,"[36] which brings us once again to the passage that lay behind the first two Beatitudes.

Those who hunger and thirst for righteousness may have to wait for satisfaction, as the persistent widow did. But Luther emphasizes that satisfaction comes in the here and now, and even more in the hereafter. In the Jewish apocalyptic literature, for example, *2 Bar.* 48:48-50, the persecuted righteous are promised a reward in the World to Come.[37] In the Jewish anticipation of the messianic banquet, too, there was (and still is) a hunger and thirst waiting to be satisfied—one having much to do with righteousness.[38] Do Christians think of their hunger and thirst for righteousness when they approach the Lord's table, which is a foretaste of the heavenly banquet? Believers are admonished to undertake self-examination before coming to the table, so as to avoid divine judgment (1 Cor. 11:28-32). Listen again to the words of invitation:

> All that humbly put their trust in Christ and desire his help *that they may lead a holy life*; all that are truly penitent for their sins and would be delivered from them; all that walk in love with their neighbors and

36. Black, "Beatitudes," 125–26.
37. Betz, *Sermon on the Mount*, 144.
38. Lachs, *Rabbinic Commentary on the New Testament*, 74; The Essenes, too, in their common meal anticipated the messianic banquet; see Frank Moore Cross, *The Ancient Library of Qumran and Modern Biblical Studies* (1958; rev. 3rd ed.; Sheffield: Sheffield Academic Press, 1995), 77.

intend to live a new life, following the commandment of God and walking henceforth in his holy ways, are invited to draw near with faith and to take this holy sacrament. (*BWCC*, 71–72)

But then follows a warning:

Come to this sacred table, not because you must, but because you may; *come to testify not that you are righteous,* but that you sincerely love our Lord Jesus Christ, and desire to be his true disciples. (*BWCC*, 72; cf. Matt. 9:13).

Righteousness is a tricky term: on the one hand, we are told to hunger and thirst for it, but, on the other, we should not claim to possess it. There is a righteousness we must avoid, one described by Jesus in his parable about the Pharisee and the tax collector (Luke 18:9-14). Here Jesus is calling people to a better righteousness, one of deeds not words of self-praise. In discussing this Beatitude, Luther expressed concern about "counterfeit saints," an example of which he saw in the monks.

7. *Blessed are the merciful, for they will receive mercy.* In the classic self-disclosure of Exod. 34:6, God identifies himself as "The LORD, the LORD, a God merciful and gracious," where the two divine attributes of "mercy" and "grace" come close together in meaning, denoting "unmerited favor." Both are free gifts and can be neither demanded nor presumed upon. Psalm 103:1-5 blesses God for all his benefits: forgiveness, healing, redemption, steadfast love, mercy, and everlasting goodness. In the Old Testament, see also Deut. 4:31; Pss. 86:15; 103:8; 111:4; and so on. Luke, after his Sermon on the Plain, reports Jesus as saying, "Be merciful, just as your Father is merciful" (Luke 6:36).

Mercy is expected of God's people; the prophet Micah says that God desires it more than sacrifice (Micah 6:8; Matt. 12:7). Mercy is seen in acts of mercy, that is, compassion toward the poor, the suffering, and the needy. This is graphically described in Jesus' parable of the Good Samaritan, showing that mercy is a virtue to be found in all people (Luke 10:29-37). But it is lacking, says Jesus, in the scribes and Pharisees (Matt. 23:23). In the Old Testament, mercy is shown even to the non-Israelite population of Nineveh that repents of its wickedness (Jonah 4). Almsgiving is an act of mercy, and Jesus teaches the proper attitude in almsgiving later in the Sermon (6:2-4).

It follows that those who show mercy will receive mercy from God. The future passive in Greek is once again a circumlocution to avoid mention of the name of God.[39] Thus, to the merciful God will be merciful. In the Talmud it says, "He who is merciful to others, mercy is shown to him by Heaven (God), while he who is not merciful to others, mercy is not shown to him by Heaven (God) (*b. Shab.* 151b). Jesus' parable about the unmerciful servant (Matt. 18:23-35) makes much the same point. See also James 2:13. Mercy is also related to justice and punishment. St. Gregory said that true justice embodies an element of mercy, a time-honored principle followed even in our own day. Mercy may suspend judgment, but if it does not, it should at least temper the judgment.

8. *Blessed are the pure in heart, for they will see God.* Purity in the Bible often means "cleanness" or "without blemish," for example, in ceremonial usages in Exodus and Leviticus, but it can also mean "not mixed with anything," as, for example, when we speak today of pure maple syrup, pure chocolate, pure gold, and the like. To be "pure in heart" might then refer to having a clean heart, which would be a new inner disposition after repentance (Ps. 51:10), or possibly a "righteous character," that is, one in which is no deceit, no evil motives, no bad intentions. Psalm 73:1 says, "Truly God is good to the upright, to those who are pure in heart." Jesus registered

---

39. Betz, *Sermon on the Mount*, 134.

shock when he saw Nathanael coming toward him; Jesus said, "Here is truly an Israelite in whom there is no deceit" (John 1:47). The man had purity of heart and became Jesus' disciple. But "purity of heart" could also mean "singleness of heart," which in the Bible is contrasted with "double-mindedness" (James 1:5-8; 4:8). The latter is the duplicity spoken of in Matthew 23, the chapter that contains the woes that balance the present Beatitudes. The *Didache* (2:4) says, "Do not be of two minds or speak from both sides of your mouth, for speaking from both sides of your mouth is a deadly trap." The heart in ancient thought was the center of the will, which we moderns tend to locate in the mind (as "to set one's mind to do something"). Augustine said that "purity of heart" was "singleness of heart," and Søren Kierkegaard's famous dictum was: "purity of heart is to will one thing."

People with pure hearts are permitted entrance into the presence of God, that is, into God holy sanctuary. Psalm 24:3-6 provides the background for this Beatitude, speaking about the person who is rightly prepared for the worship of God:

> ³Who shall ascend the hill of the LORD?
>> and who shall stand in his holy place?
> ⁴Those who have clean hands and pure hearts,
>> who do not lift up their souls to what is false,
>> and do not swear deceitfully.
>
> Then comes the blessing:
> ⁵They will receive blessing from the LORD,
>> and vindication from the God of their salvation.
>
> Finally a mention of "seeing" the God of Jacob:
> ⁶Such is the company of those who seek him,
>> who seek the face of the God of Jacob. (Ps. 24:3-6)

Psalm 73:1 says:

> Truly God is good to the upright,
> to those who are pure in heart.

Here, as elsewhere in the Bible, "seeing God" is not to be taken literally, for no one can actually see God (Exod. 33:20; John 1:18—which excepts the Son; 1 John 4:12). "Seeing (the face of) God" has no visual dimension in the Bible; it means being in God's presence—or better, experiencing God's presence (Pss. 11:7; 42:2; Heb. 12:14). In the case of Moses, "face to face" means "mouth to mouth" (Num. 12:8), where reference is to hearing and speaking (Exod. 33:11). The rabbis taught that to see God was to see his "glory,"[40] but not even Moses could see God's glory (Exod. 33:18-23). Later rabbinic scribes also altered the phrase "to see God" to the passive "to be seen by God" to avoid a theological difficulty.[41]

9. *Blessed are the peacemakers, for they will be called children of God.* Peacemakers are those who succeed in preserving (a genuine) peace or who restore a peace that has been destroyed by friction and strife.[42] In this latter role, peacemakers are agents of reconciliation, people who bring individuals, families, communities, and even nations back to a state of harmony and well-being. Peacemakers also make peace between individuals and God. Peace is highly prized in the Old Testament and in Jewish tradition generally (Ps. 34:14; Isa. 52:7; Zech. 8:16). Hillel taught, "love peace, pursue peace, and love mankind" (*m. Ab.* 1:12), and *Slavonic Enoch* 52:11-12 says:

> Happy is he who establishes peace;
> Cursed is he who strikes down those who are at peace.

40. Lachs, *Rabbinic Commentary on the New Testament*, 76.
41. B. Cohon, *Jacob's Well*, 32.
42. Filson, *Matthew*, 78.

The Aaronic benediction of the Old Testament ends: "The LORD lift up his countenance upon you, and give you peace" (Num. 6:26), to which the Talmud adds, "This is to tell you that blessings are of no avail unless peace goes with them" (*Num. Rab.* 11:7). The writer of Hebrews connects peacemaking with the prior blessing. He says, "Pursue peace with everyone, and the holiness without which no one will see the Lord" (Heb. 12:14).

What is peace? Behind the Greek εἰρήνη (from which our word "irenic" comes) stands the Hebrew word *shalom* (שׁלום), which is particularly rich. *Shalom* means more than "absence of conflict," carrying with it the positive meanings of "harmony, prosperity, happiness, wholeness, and well-being." *Shalom* is sound health, sought after and highly valued by individuals, families, communities, and nations everywhere. Jewish people greet one another with *shalom*, which is a wish on the part of the greeter that all is well with you and those dear to you. It sends forth a blessing. The Pauline letters begin with the greeting "Grace to you and peace . . ." (Rom. 1:7; 1 Cor. 1:3; 2 Cor. 1:2; Gal. 1:3; etc.).

A distinction, nevertheless, needs to be made between "peacemakers" and "peacekeepers" so-called, for between the two is a world of difference. Peacekeepers—at least some of them—let problems alone, in the interest, they say, of "keeping peace." But in so doing they end up causing more trouble by allowing threatening or dangerous situations to develop.[43] True peacemakers do not evade divisive issues. Proverbs 10:10 (LXX only) says, "Whoever winks the eye causes trouble, but the one who rebukes boldly makes peace." The *Didache* (4:3) says: "Do not create a schism, but bring peace to those who are at odds." Peacemakers are thus constructive agents of tranquillity, people who have a part in God's creative work.[44]

---

43. Herman Hendrickx, *The Sermon on the Mount* (rev. ed.; London: Geoffrey Chapman, 1984), 32.
44. Francis Greenwood Peabody, "The Peace-Makers," *HTR* 12 (1919): 51–66.

Whether one is attempting to preserve a genuine peace or working to restore it, he or she must face issues and expend whatever energy is necessary to get those issues resolved. And they should be resolved, as Philo says, "without a single spark to be rekindled" (*Spec. leg.* 192). This can be difficult, which explains, perhaps, why real peacemakers are so few, and why the same receive a blessing from Jesus. Those who aspire to peacemaking who let old problems lie are an unblessed lot. Jeremiah comes down hard on those who preach peace when there is no peace, that is, when injustice, greed, and falsehood are running rampant in the land (Jer. 6:13-14 = 8:10b-11). Psalm 72:1-7 says that peace has to be balanced off with righteousness, an idea that finds expression also in Isaiah (32:17). For the wicked, says Second Isaiah, there is no peace (Isa 57:21). That peacemaking is a direct consequence of righteousness can be seen also in Heb. 12:14 and James 3:18.[45]

In the Old Testament, Isaiah was the great prophet of peace. For him the end-time would be a return to the beginning time, which was the peace prevailing in the Garden of Eden. Isaiah says, "the wolf shall live with the lamb, the leopard shall lie down with the kid, the calf and the lion and the fatling together, and a little child shall lead them" (Isa. 11:6). The thought therefore developed that peace would characterize messianic times. The Messiah would be called "Prince of Peace," and under his authority "there would be endless peace" (Isa. 9:6-7). See also Isa. 2:2-4 (Micah 4:1-3); 32:15-20.[46] And yet Jesus did *not* always bring peace, at least not initially, but rather a sword (Matt. 10:34-39).[47] But in John's Gospel, Jesus' parting words to the disciples are, "Peace I leave with you; my peace I give to you; I do not give to you as the world gives" (John 14:27).

---

45. Betz, *Sermon on the Mount*, 138.
46. Jack R. Lundbom, *The Hebrew Prophets* (Minneapolis: Fortress Press, 2010), 68–70.
47. Peabody, "Peace-Makers," 54.

Christians are called to be peacemakers. When one is not part of the dispute, peacemaking today is called mediation or arbitration. Mediators and arbitrators are pressed into service to help settle management and labor disputes, also problems in international relations. These individuals must be able to discern root causes, must get to the bottom of things, and above all must be seekers after the truth. It is not enough simply to counsel opposing parties to be nice to one another, to show love, and to forget all former grievances. Proper attitude is important, and there is much to be said for the need of both sides to show charity—without which real peace cannot be established. Luther gave this advice to peacemakers: "Carry the best to both sides." He learned this from St. Augustine, who had observed how his mother went about settling disputes. It is a good rule to follow. Luther also said that if it becomes necessary to talk about an evil deed, one should go directly to the person, as specified in Matt. 18:15, not unburden oneself to others.

Peacemakers will be called "sons of God."[48] The expression "son of . . ." is a Hebraism meaning "having the nature and showing the spirit of" someone[49]—that someone, most likely, being one's father. Augustine assumed that sons share the nature of their fathers, as had Paul before in comments to the church at Corinth (1 Cor. 4:14-16). One can also be a son (or daughter) in a more general sense. Abraham's sons—that is, the Pharisees—are expected to do what Abraham did (John 8:39). Instead, Jesus says they have become "descendants of those who murdered the prophets" (Matt. 23:31).

Expressions such as the present one are said to exist in Hebrew because the language is deficient in adjectives.[50] Barnabas is a "son of encouragement" (Acts 4:36), which is to say he is an encouraging

48. On "sons of God," see Betz, *Essays on the Sermon on the Mount*, 122–23.
49. Filson, *Matthew*, 78.
50. William Barclay, *The Beatitudes and the Lord's Prayer for Everyman* (New York and Evanston: Harper & Row, 1968), 99.

sort of person, one who lifts the spirits of those weighed down by despondency. James and John are "Sons of Thunder" (Mark 3:17), that is, "thunderous characters." Thus, to be a "son of God" is to be someone showing the nature of God, the spirit of God, someone "God-like" who, in the present case, is working for peace. This Beatitude might then be rephrased, "Blessed are the peacemakers, for they are Godlike." In Wis. 2:13, 18, the righteous are called "sons of God."[51]

Philo called God the Prince of Peace (*Decal.* 178), and because God is about the work of peace, the New Testament refers to God as "God of peace" (Rom. 16:20; 2 Cor. 13:11; Phil. 4:9; Heb. 13:20).[52] God is the great reconciler, having given up his son to death in order that he might reconcile the world to himself (2 Cor. 5:19). Jesus is the perfect peacemaker, the Gospels calling him "Son of God" (Mark 15:39; Luke 1:35; John 1:34; 3:16-18; 11:27; etc.). Jesus mediated a new covenant (Heb. 9:15; 12:24), which reconciled to God even the Gentiles who were alienated from him, thus becoming for both Jews and Gentiles, says Paul, "our peace" (Eph. 2:13-18). Followers of Jesus are to be reconcilers in the world. Later in the Sermon Jesus says that by loving our enemies we become "sons of (our) Father who is in heaven" (Matt. 5:45, RSV). Jesus wants us to be imitators of God (5:48; 6:12, 14-15; 7:10-11), who is the ultimate peacemaker.[53]

10. *Blessed are those who are persecuted for righteousness' sake, for theirs is the kingdom of heaven.* Jesus gives this blessing on those who meet with persecution, perhaps some who are being persecuted at the present time. Luke is more concrete in his Sermon on the Plain, where Jesus blesses those who are hated, excluded, reviled, and given an evil name, all of which come "on account of the Son

---

51. See also *P. Ab.* 3:19 (= *m. Ab.* 3:14).
52. On God as the principal peacemaker, see Betz, *Sermon on the Mount,* 138.
53. Betz, *Sermon on the Mount,* 138.

of Man" (Luke 6:22). Matthew has the persecution occurring "for righteousness' sake," which again employs "righteousness" as a key term in his Gospel and a fundamental concept in all the Beatitudes.[54] Matthew will be concrete in the next Beatitude, which is his last (v. 11). In the present Beatitude persecution comes to one who has taken a stand for "the cause of right" (NEB; JB), although Matthew knows too that it is on account of the "Son of Man," whom Pilate called "a righteous man" (Matt. 27:19 RSV). The persecution is not for behavior deserving of punishment, which is another thing entirely (1 Pet. 4:15-16).

To be "persecuted" is to be "pursued" or "chased (after)," which is more vivid since the hostility is seen to have taken on legs. One normally experiences persecution from strangers or enemies at a distance, but it happens that family members and friends will sometimes take up the chase. Jeremiah discovered that his "friends of *shalom*" were his persecutors (Jer. 20:10-11). In ancient Israel, the prophets became the persecuted lot, although from the Psalms we learn that David knew persecution firsthand. The suffering of the righteous is a recurring motif in the Psalms (Pss. 7:1-17; 31:15-18; 69:1-28; 109:1-31; 119:73-88; etc.) and it comes to classic expression in the book of Job.[55] Jesus cites the persecution of the prophets in v. 12, expanding on the same idea in concluding his litany of woes in 23:29-38. Wisdom of Solomon 2:10-12 knows individuals living their lives to the full and crushing those whose lives reprove their own. They say:

> Let us oppress the righteous poor man;
>   let us not spare the widow
>   or regard the gray hairs of the aged.

54. Betz, *Sermon on the Mount*, 142.
55. Betz, *Sermon on the Mount*, 144.

> But let our might be our law of right,
>> for what is weak proves itself to be useless.
> Let us lie in wait for the righteous man,
>> because he is inconvenient to us
>>> and opposes our actions . . . (Wis. 2:10-12 RSV)

1 Enoch 95:7 says that such people will receive their just reward:

> Woe to you sinners, for you persecute the righteous!
> For you shall be handed over and be persecuted through oppression.
> Its yoke shall be heavy upon you.

This blessing concludes with the same words as the first: "for theirs is the kingdom of heaven." This might be viewed as an *inclusio* tying together eight original Beatitudes,[56] but there are good reasons for including in Matthew's structure vv. 11-12, as we shall see in a moment. The "kingdom of heaven" means the same thing as it does in v. 3: the rule of God brought with the coming of Jesus.

What are we to say about this blessing, which St. John Chrysostom called the "golden chain" of the persecuted?[57] Some in Jesus' audience would doubtless have registered surprise when they heard that the persecuted are to be numbered among the blessed. T. H. Robinson calls it a paradox.[58] According to the usual wisdom, the persecuted were a cursed lot (Deut. 28:45). One is blessed only after being delivered from persecution. In Psalm 23, when the Lord had delivered David from his enemies, David looked ahead with confidence to the future, saying, "surely goodness and mercy will follow me all the

56. Betz, *Sermon on the Mount*, 142, 146.
57. Quoted in Alan M'Neile, *The Gospel according to St. Matthew* (London: Macmillan, 1952), 53.
58. Robinson, *Gospel of Matthew*, 32.

days of my life" (v. 6), where "follow" is literally "pursue"). Jeremiah, too, sings in a loud voice only after he has been delivered from his persecutors (Jer. 20:11-13). But Jesus pronounces a blessing on people who are presently being persecuted and will in the future be persecuted (Matt. 10:16-42). At the end of the passage where he sends out the Twelve, Jesus says that his disciples will receive a "prophet's reward" or a "the reward of the righteous" (v. 41), which is commentary enough on the present Beatitude. It should be pointed out also that the rabbis in their teachings held martyrs in high regard.[59]

For early Christians, the world was a battleground and discipleship was costly. Evidence of this appears often in the pages of the New Testament (Matt. 10:16-42; John 15:20; 2 Cor. 11: 23-27; 2 Tim. 3:10-12; James 1:12; 1 Pet. 3:13-17; 4:12-14). Christians were persecuted because they were different,[60] and their being different had much to do with the teaching given here in the Sermon on the Mount. Persecution results when one lives a better righteousness, when one is faithful to the call of Jesus. Surrender to Christ, said Luther, means being willing to suffer persecution in the world.

11. *Blessed are you when people revile you and persecute you and utter all kinds of evil against you falsely on my account.* This Beatitude is both climactic and transitional. It is about twice as long as the previous Beatitudes, and a transition is indicated by the shift to the second person "you." This second person continues into the next section on salt and light, and it will dominate all the way to the parable of the two houses and the Sermon's conclusion in 7:24-29, where there is a shift back to the third person.

Because of the increased length of this Beatitude and the transition to the second person, some have argued that vv. 11-12 are a later

---

59. So Johnson, "Matthew," 287.
60. Barclay, *Beatitudes and the Lord's Prayer for Everyman*, 101–24.

expansion to an original eight Beatutudes. But this is unlikely, because both features in a series are well known moves in Hebrew rhetoric.[61] The shift to the second person "you" makes the teaching more direct. Augustine says the shift to "you" allows the Sermon to speak to those who are absent and those who afterwards will come into existence.[62] That is to say, this Sermon continues to speak to audiences in the future.

In this Beatitude, Matthew becomes concrete in describing the persecution, as Luke does in Luke 6:22, and Matthew parallels the Lukan blessing by saying that the persecution will come "on my account." Luke says it will come "on account of the Son of Man." Christians will be made to suffer slander, defamation, and disgrace (Luther). Persecution, then, will not consist simply in being "chased (after)," but will be withstanding verbal onslaughts that are patently false. Luke puts the accent on words that are spoken—both evil words and words deceptively friendly (Luke 6:22, 26). Luke also includes exclusion, which may refer to persecutions at the hands of Jews when Christians—who were also Jews—were excluded from the synagogue.[63] It is unclear whether such persecutions are in Matthew's mind.

Some ancient manuscripts in the Western tradition omit "falsely," which may be a gloss[64] since the word is not needed. Originally, "on my account" was qualifier enough. Those suffering for the sake

---

61. For expansion coming at the end of a series and a shift also to the second person, see Daube, "Three Questions of Form in Matthew V," 21–23; Daube, *New Testament and Rabbinic Judaism*, 196–201. Daube illustrates with two examples from Simeon Singer's *Authorized Daily Prayer Book of the United Hebrew Congregations of the British Empire* (9th ed.; London: Eyre & Spottiswoode, 1912), 16–17, 167 [1992 ed.: 38, 414]), one very similar to the Beatitudes. On the shift to the second person pronoun for directness in the poetry of Jeremiah, for example, in Jer. 5:7, see Lundbom, *Jeremiah: A Study in Ancient Hebrew Rhetoric*, 77 (1997: 103).

62. Augustine, "Our Lord's Sermon on the Mount," 6; *Preaching of Augustine*, 7.

63. Georg Strecker, *The Sermon on the Mount* (trans. O. C. Dean Jr.; Nashville: Abingdon, 1988), 43.

64. M'Neile, *Gospel according to St. Matthew*, 53.

of Jesus can be expected to be righteous individuals (so v. 10), in which case disparaging remarks made against them will at least be unjust, if not altogether false. But Augustine knows people who glory wrongly in their persecutions and their base reputations.[65] Hurtful remarks, after all, may be true! Augustine is thinking mainly about heretics and schismatics in the church, but the same could be said of any wrongdoers getting their due, for example, murderers, thiefs, mischief makers, and so on (1 Pet. 4:15).

12. *Rejoice and be glad, for your reward is great in heaven, for in the same way they persecuted the prophets who were before you.* These "sweet and comforting words," as Luther calls them, conclude the Beatitudes. The Lukan blessings likewise conclude on an upbeat note (Luke 6:23). This is probably no accident, since we know that the rabbis later avoided downbeat conclusions to Scripture read in the synagogue. When the passage ended harshly, or with a word of judgment, for example, Isa. 66:24 and Mal. 4:6, the penultimate verse of a more positive nature would be reread as the final conclusion,[66] ensuring a "happy ending." Here the upbeat ending also gives emphasis to the incongruity in the blessings, many of which might otherwise be taken as curses. Although the Old Testament knew of "persecution for righteousness' sake," for example, the Suffering Servant in Isa. 42:1-8, it—and Judaism generally—never taught that one should rejoice in persecution.[67] Christians later developed a passion and even an exultation in martyrdom, but this was not present in Judaism, where it was a sad necessity.[68]

---

65. Augustine, "Our Lord's Sermon on the Mount," 8; *Preaching of Augustine*, 15.

66. Leon Liebreich, "The Compilation of the Book of Isaiah," *JQR* 46 (1956): 277.

67. B. Cohon (*Jacob's Well*, 34) says, "It has never [been] taught [in Judaism] that we should rejoice in being persecuted for the sake of any prophet or leader."

68. B. Cohon, *Jacob's Well*, 37.

Early Christians were admonished to rejoice in their sufferings, and they did (Acts 5:41). The teaching is given clear exposition in 1 Pet. 4:13-14:

> But rejoice in so far as you share Christ's sufferings, that you may also rejoice and be glad when his glory is revealed. If you are reproached for the name of Christ, you are blessed, because the spirit of glory and of God rests upon you. (RSV)

Peter goes on to tell Christians not to be ashamed (v. 16). If they take this to heart, whatever shame has been heaped upon them will be transformed into inner peace and joy. Peter's forward glance to when Christ's glory will be revealed compares with the forward glance here: "for your reward is great in heaven." Since persecution often resulted in death, one had to look beyond this life for vindication. And Christians did look beyond this life, even though some rewards, of course, did accrue on earth. The kingdom of heaven begins now and rewards begin now (Augustine).[69]

Jesus, like the rabbis, did not hesitate in speaking about rewards, although when quantifying rewards Jesus consistently made the point that they were "out of all proportion to the service rendered" (Matt. 19:29; 25:21, 23).[70] Rewards were God's free gift. The Mishnah also contains a teaching on "your reward is great" in connection with light and grave precepts (*m. Ab.* 1:3; 2:1; 4:2).

At the end, the prophets are cited as individuals whom Christians might well emulate. The prophets "who were before you" are the older prophets, such as Elijah, Amos, Jeremiah, and Zechariah. John the Baptist, who suffered death at the hands of Herod (Matt. 14:3-12), would also be on any list. Jesus held him to be the greatest of the

---

69. See Johnson, "Matthew," 288.
70. Johnson, "Matthew," 288.

prophets (Matt. 11:7-15). Persecution of prophets was well known in New Testament times (Matt. 23:29-37; Acts 7:52; Heb. 11:32-38).

7

Be Salt and Light in the World (5:13-16)

¹³*"You are the salt of the earth; but if salt has lost its taste, how can its saltiness be restored? It is no longer good for anything, but is thrown out and trampled under foot.* ¹⁴*You are the light of the world. A city built on a hill cannot be hid.* ¹⁵*No one after lighting a lamp puts it under the bushel basket, but on the lampstand, and it gives light to all in the house.* ¹⁶*In the same way, let your light shine before others, so that they may see your good works and give glory to your Father in heaven.*

The Sermon continues on a positive note. Jesus is now speaking directly to his audience, shifting to metaphors that illustrate what discipleship should consist of. Disciples should be salt and light in the world. The saying about salt occurs slightly revised in Mark 9:50 and Luke 14:34–35.

13. *You are the salt of the earth.* "Earth" here means "people of earth" (Augustine) or "world," not earth in the sense of "ground." "Earth" balances "world" in the teaching about light. Salt has no value for

the ground; in fact, it destroys the ground (Deut. 29:23; Ps. 107:34). It was common in antiquity to punish a defeated enemy by sowing salt in their land. Salt has positive associations in the Old Testament, where, as a necessary ingredient in sacrifices, it symbolizes the durative nature of the covenant (Exod. 30:35; Lev. 2:13; Num. 18:19; 2 Chron. 13:5).[1]

What does Jesus mean when he says his disciples are to be salt of the world—better yet, salt *in* the world? First of all, we need to know something more about salt and how it is used. In ancient times, just as today, salt was considered a staple. The Talmud says, "The world cannot exist without salt."[2] Salt performs two important functions: (1) it seasons food; and (2) it is a preservative for food. In the days before refrigerators and freezers, salt kept meat and other foods from spoiling. Quite naturally, then, metaphorical usages have had to do with seasoning and preservation. For example, it has been said that, without people such as those described here, "human life would be both insipid and corrupt."[3] The idea that the world would quickly come to destruction if Christians were not present finds eloquent expression in the *Epistle to Diognetus*, chapters 5–6.[4] Even in the Old Testament, God says that ten righteous men would have saved wicked Sodom and Gomorrah (Gen. 18:32).[5] Here in the Sermon, disciples of Jesus must be salt if they are essential for the well-being of the world, a world otherwise bent on destruction. Salt has also been taken to mean "distinctiveness"; that is, Christians are to be distinctive among other people in the world. Pliny says, "for the whole body nothing is more beneficial than salt and sun" (*Nat. Hist.* 31.45), and he

---

1. W. J. Dumbrell, "The Logic of the Role of the Law in Matthew V 1-20," *NovT* 23 (1981): 12.
2. Lachs, *Rabbinic Commentary on the New Testament*, 82.
3. M'Neile, *Gospel according to St. Matthew*, 55.
4. Johnson, "Matthew," 288–89.
5. W. S. Wood, "The Salt of the Earth," *JThS* 25 (1923–24): 170.

goes on to discuss the various uses of salt to preserve from corruption and for medicine.

Luther considered salt to be the "bite" expected of a preacher when preaching Christ and the Word. His focus was more on the church than on the world, or perhaps we should say on a church ever in danger of being infiltrated by the world. In any case, the Christian preacher needs to be prophetic—denouncing scandals and speaking out against other forms of godlessness. If the preacher does not do this but tells people that they are doing just fine, the preacher is like salt that has lost its taste and is therefore worthless.

We must still ask what is required of Christians to be good seasoning in the world and to aid in preserving the world from destruction. Luther singled out prophetic preaching, but surely "salty living" consists of more than this. Luther did recognize broader implications in Jesus' words when he pointed out that being salt means being everything Jesus described in the blessings: rejoicing when one is poor in spirit and is persecuted for righteousness' sake, allowing oneself to mourn, being meek, seeking righteousness with persistence, showing mercy, and making peace. A core list for identifying "salty Christians." We may note also Jesus' words to his disciples in Mark 9:50: "Have salt in yourselves," followed by "Be at peace with one another," which includes Matthew's seventh Beatitude on peacemakers.

but if salt has lost its taste, how can its saltiness be restored? This question has been much discussed, because it is widely recognized—and can now be stated with scientific certainty—that pure salt cannot lose its saltiness. It is said that salt deposits, such as those near the Dead Sea, lose their saltiness after having been drenched by rain,[6] which can happen to salt that is not pure salt, that

---

6. Filson, *Matthew*, 80.

is, salt mixed with other substances.[7] Salt of this nature would appear to lose its taste. Nevertheless, it remains the case that pure salt cannot deteriorate.

The protasis of Jesus' argument appears, then, to be hypothetical, the apodosis being a rhetorical question to which the answer was, "It cannot!" The whole idea is an absurdity, like suggesting that water might be able to lose its wetness.[8] Rabbi Joshua ben Hananya (80–120 C.E.) was asked, "When salt becomes unsavory, wherewith is it to be salted?" to which he replied "With the afterbirth of a mule!" Question: "Is there an afterbirth of a mule?" Answer: "Can salt become unsavory?"[9] Jesus may then be proposing—with full awareness—something contrary to fact. This happens more or less in his following statement about setting a lamp under a bushel. Everyone knows this would never be done. It is unthinkable, for under a bushel a lamp goes out. But the proposal is made all the same to make a point. The same is true with the set-up question about salt. But there is nothing hypothetical or contrary to fact in the application. Disciples could lose their saltiness, and this is something that must not happen.

It is no longer good for anything, but is thrown out and trampled under foot. If salt were to lose its saltiness, it would be worthless. This is what will happen to disciples who lose their saltiness: They will become worthless, be discarded, and beaten into the ground by others passing by. We must not imagine that just because Jesus uses a hypothetical argument a real problem is not being addressed. Quite the contrary. Jesus knows his followers could lose their distinctive character. Their lives could become a "throw-away." Luther believed that people

---

7. See discussion in Eugene P. Deatrick, "Salt, Soil, Savior," *BA* 25 (1962): 41–48.

8. Betz, *Sermon on the Mount*, 159.

9. Wolfgang Nauck, "Salt as a Metaphor in Instructions for Discipleship," *Studia Theologica* 6 (1952): 174; Lachs, *Rabbinic Commentary on the New Testament*, 82.

in the church could lose their saltiness, and thus render themselves worthless. But it must not happen.

14. *You are the light of the world.* If salt is essential to the world, so is light. God's first act of creation was to bring light (Gen. 1:3), and the created order could not have continued without it. Light is an important metaphor throughout the Bible and in the rabbinic writings. It is used of God. The Psalmist says, "The LORD is my light and my salvation" (Ps. 27:1; cf. Isa. 60:19-20; 1 John 1:5). God's word is light: "Your word is a lamp to my feet, and a light to my path" (Ps. 119:105). King David was said to be the lamp of Israel (2 Sam. 21:17; 1 Kgs. 11:36). And John in his Gospel calls Jesus "the light of the world" (John 1:4-14; 8:12). Joachim Jeremias says this teaching in John presupposes the words here in the Sermon on the Mount for the early church,[10] although Hans Dieter Betz points out that the Sermon does not otherwise refer to Jesus himself being the light.[11] The rabbis named Adam "Lamp of the World," and they applied the epithet "lamp" even to themselves. For example, when Johanan ben Zakkai's disciples visited him during his illness, they addressed him as "Lamp of Israel," or according to some readings, "Lamp of the World."[12] The metaphor had even wider application in New Testament times: Jerusalem was the Light of the World (cf. Isa. 60:3), and the olive oil in the Temple was said to be the Light of the World.[13] But, according to the New Testament book of Revelation, the New Jerusalem will have no need of sun or moon, for the glory of God will be its light and the Lamb (Jesus) its lamp (Rev. 21:23; 22:5).

The most important background for this teaching is the idea in Second Isaiah that Israel was called by God to be "a light to the

---

10. Jeremias, *Sermon on the Mount*, 25.
11. Betz, *Sermon on the Mount*, 163.
12. Abrahams, *Studies in Pharisaism and the Gospels*, 16; Lachs, *Rabbinic Commentary on the New Testament*, 83.
13. Abrahams, *Studies in Pharisaism and the Gospels*, 16.

nations/Gentiles" (Isa. 42:6-7; 49:6; 60:1-3; cf. Acts 13:47; Rom. 2:19). Now Jesus tells his disciples—who constitute a new Israel—"You are the light of the world."

What does it mean to be "the light of the world"? The most basic concept associated with light is righteousness (Prov. 4:18). People seeking to be a light must be righteous and must perform acts of righteousness (v. 16: "good works"). The connection between light and acts of righteousness is made in a Midrash on "Let there be light" in Gen. 1:3 (*Gen. Rab.* 2). Another Jewish writing says that Israel can be a light to the Gentiles/nations only if it keeps from sin (*T. Levi* 14:3-4). Paul tells the Christians at Philippi that they must be unblemished children of God in the midst of a wicked and perverse generation, among whom they shine "as lights of the world" (Phil. 2:15 RSV).

So being the light of the world has everything to do with righteousness, which, as was said earlier, is a key term in the Sermon and in Matthew. But as was the case with salt, here too we must seek a broader interpretation. It would seem that Jesus is again asking that his disciples adopt the modes of behavior he has just blessed; that is, his word on light harks back to the Beatitudes. Those people are the ones—perhaps the only ones—who can lighten a dark world.

A city built on a hill cannot be hid. This could well be a proverb,[14] to which most would give ready assent. Because we are talking about light, it has been suggested that the image is of a city at night. Ancient cities, of course, were not lit up in the way modern cities are, but at sundown surely, when the last rays of the sun were still casting their soft glow, the city would be easily visible from a distance. Jesus, however, may have been thinking about cities in broad daylight. In bright sunlight cities set on a hill are especially

---

14. Betz, *Sermon on the Mount*, 161.

prominent. Whether in daylight or at night, it remains true that a city on a hill cannot be hid. Jesus could be talking about his home village of Nazareth, which is a city set on a hill. Or he could be referring to Jerusalem, which, as we mentioned, was called the Light of the World. Jerusalem would be more appropriate because of its symbolic significance for Judaism.[15] But the remark may simply be a proverb, something generally agreed to be true. What Jesus wants to impress upon his disciples is that prominent, righteous living is the best witness to a holy and righteous God.

15. *No one after lighting a lamp puts it under the bushel basket.* This is another statement contrary to fact, or in this case to experience, absurd enough to be humorous. Perhaps it is another proverb.[16] A lamp placed under a bushel basket soon goes out, at which point it becomes useless. A similar teaching turns up in Mark and Luke: Mark 4:21 adds "or under a bed," and Luke 11:33 "left to burn in the cellar," both equally ludicrous.

There is no need, with Augustine, to give allegorical significance to the "bushel basket." It is enough to draw the conclusion that disciples should not conceal their light—a real possibility, once we recall what "light-giving" behavior Jesus has in mind when he blesses the poor in spirit, those who mourn, those suffering persecution, and so on. People in each of these conditions will want to keep quiet, to keep their experiences private, and perhaps will feel shame even if they have no guilt. But Jesus is telling his disciples to bring out into the open what they may prefer to hide under a bushel.

but on the lampstand. That a lamp should be placed on a lampstand is obvious. But that the behavior called blessed by Jesus should be

---

15. Lachs, *Rabbinic Commentary on the New Testament*, 83; see also Dumbrell, "Logic of the Role of the Law, " 14–16. Betz (*Sermon on the Mount*, 161) also thinks that the reference has to be to Jerusalem.

16. Betz, *Sermon on the Mount*, 161–62.

brought unashamedly into the open is not the least bit obvious. Yet a witness of precisely this nature is seen in 2 Cor. 11:16—12:13, where Paul boasts of all the shameful things that have befallen him. On other occasions, too, Paul does not hesitate to magnify weaknesses, as, for example, when he tells Festus in the presence of King Agrippa that none of the things that happened to him were "done in a corner" (Acts 26:26). We are talking about things that make a person look bad or, if not bad, at least weak and powerless. But Paul tells the Corinthians more than once that weakness in God's economy becomes strength (1 Cor. 1:25-28; 9:22-23; 2 Cor. 11:29-33; 12:5-10; 13:4). How much of this witnessing goes on today in our churches? Christians prefer to hide their weaknesses and troubles, even if they know some good might come of it.

and it gives light to all in the house. In a one-room Palestinian house, a single lamp on a lampstand lights the whole room. Importance is sometimes placed on the words "all in the house," which differs from Luke's "those who enter (the house)" (Luke 8:16; 11:33). Those *in* the house could be taken to be Jews,[17] in which case those *entering* the house would be Gentiles. Matthew may then have in mind disciples who are expected to be lights to fellow Jews (cf. Matt. 10:6; 15:24). While it is true that the better righteousness of the present chapter is set over against *both* Jewish and Gentile righteousness, the beginning of the chapter seems to focus more on the scribes and Pharisees (5:20). Paul in Romans chided his fellow Jews for thinking of themselves as "light," when they should in fact be teaching themselves about being that light (Rom. 2:17-24).

16. *let your light shine before others, so that they may see your good works and give glory to your Father in heaven.* The section ends with

---

17. Nauck ("Salt as a Metaphor in Instructions for Discipleship," 177) says that Jesus' words about salt and light, indeed his entire Sermon on the Mount, must be understood in light of a strong opposition in Matthew to the Scribes and Pharisees.

Jesus exhorting the assembled that they be the lights they are supposed to be. The term "good works" occurs only here in the New Testament. Protestants have had difficulty affirming the need for good works in the Christian life, influenced as they are by Paul and Luther who put the accent on divine grace and human faith for salvation in Christ. Yet both Peter and Paul recognize that good works are important (1 Pet. 2:12; Rom. 2:6-11), and Luther, too, when commenting on this verse, leaves no doubt that good works are much needed from Christians. Augustine says the same, and Origen testified that it was the lives lived by the early Christians that were their invincible witnesses.[18] The New Testament is filled with exhortations to good works (Rom. 9:12-21; 2 Cor. 6:1-10; Gal. 5:16-26; Eph. 4:1-2; Col. 3:12-17; 1 Thess. 5:12-21; etc.), many of which are listed in the Beatitudes and other teachings of the Sermon on the Mount. Here in the Sermon, the light—which the good works reflect—is to be directed to people in the outside world.[19]

The final word is climactic,[20] and most important. The true end of all good works is that God be glorified. The rabbis knew this,[21] and so did Augustine, who said that hypocrites seek praise for themselves (cf. Matt. 6:1-18; Gal. 1:10). "Father who is in heaven" and "heavenly Father" are pious substitutes for God (5:16, 45, 48; 6:1, 14, 26, 32; 7:11, 21), circumlocutions well attested in rabbinic writings and appearing at the beginning the Lord's Prayer (see note for 6:9 below).

18. Johnson, "Matthew," 290.
19. Betz, Sermon on the Mount, 163.
20. Strecker, Sermon on the Mount, 51–52.
21. Lachs, Rabbinic Commentary on the New Testament, 85.

8

A Better Righteousness (5:17-20)

[17]*"Do not think that I have come to abolish the law or the prophets; I have come not to abolish but to fulfill.* [18]*For truly I tell you, until heaven and earth pass away, not one letter, not one stroke of a letter, will pass from the law until all is accomplished.* [19]*Therefore, whoever breaks one of the least of these commandments, and teaches others to do the same, will be called least in the kingdom of heaven; but whoever does them and teaches them will be called great in the kingdom of heaven.* [20]*For I tell you, unless your righteousness exceeds that of the scribes and Pharisees, you will never enter the kingdom of heaven.*

With the mention of "good works" in v. 16, it will come as no surprise in vv. 21-48 to hear Jesus talking about specific demands—some would say commands—that give substance to the new covenant.[1] But before presenting these demands, Jesus wants to

---

1. Strecker, *Sermon on the Mount*, 53; Davies, "Matthew 5, 17-18" in *Mélanges bibliques rédigés en l'honneur de André Robert* (Travaux de l'Institut Catholique de Paris 4; Paris: Bloud & Gay, 1957), 430.

clarify his stance toward the Hebrew Scriptures, which developed from the core law of the old covenant: the Ten Commandments. Some general statements are in order. Hans Dieter Betz calls these "hermeneutical principles,"[2] which are principles of interpretation, and they appear here now in vv. 17-20.

The teachings on salt and light are said to look *back* on the prior blessings. The general principles, however, appear to look *ahead* to the demands that follow, suggesting that vv. 17-20 are a watershed of sorts for the chapter. But it may not be that simple. Both Augustine and Luther see in the demands—also in the general principles—specific teaching on what being salt and light in the world really amounts to.[3] If this is true, then the teachings on salt and light are the watershed, pointing back to the blessings and ahead to demands of the new covenant. However we decide this structural issue, it is clear that the principles now being stated introduce and put in perspective the demands coming next. Jesus' core teaching of the new covenant will not replace or render invalid teachings in Hebrew Scripture. They come in order to fulfill them.

17. *Do not think that I have come to abolish the law or the prophets.* Jesus wants to be clear that he has no desire to abolish the law *and* the prophets (RSV). Some take the expression "law and the prophets" as a pleonasm for the law itself.[4] But the Law and the Prophets are canonized Jewish Scripture of the time, the third collection of sacred texts, the Writings, not yet having been canonized. Some think that the Writings gained canonical status at the Council of Jamnia, held by the Jews in 95 c.e., but, according to another view, canonization of the Writings was a process that began in 65 c.e. and was not

2. Betz, *Essays on the Sermon on the Mount*, 37–53.
3. So also Robinson, *Gospel of Matthew*, 34.
4. Davies, "Matthew 5, 17-18," 430.

completed until 140 c.e..[5] In any case, the Hebrew Scriptures at the time consisted only of the Law and the Prophets.

Since Jesus is about to present teachings of the new covenant, his listeners might conclude that he wants to do away with the old covenant and law associated with it, also preaching of the prophets that called people back to covenant obedience. The Greek word "abolish" (καταλῦσαι) is strong, meaning "completely do away with" (cf. 2 Macc. 2:22; 4:11), and probably indicates that Jesus is making a disclaimer to the most radical charge that could be leveled against him. It goes without saying that he will interpret Scripture differently and in some cases render old commands obsolete. Other Jewish teachers did the same. But abolish Scripture he will not.

Jesus is emphatic in his denial. The aorist subjunctive, "Do not think" means "Do not even begin to think." Jesus is saying, "Don't even let it enter your mind that I have come to abolish the law and the prophets." Jewish tradition affirmed the ongoing validity of Mosaic Law,[6] and the Bible, too, warns not to add or subtract from an inspired word committed to writing (Deut. 4:1-2; Rev. 22:18-19). Things, of course, become more complicated when one takes into account the oral tradition of the Pharisees, which Jesus did not entirely follow (Matt. 15:1-20). But here Jesus is making reference to a written law (v. 18).[7] According to the Talmud, Moses gave Israel 613 precepts, 365 of them negative (corresponding to the number of days in a solar year), and 248 positive (the number of joints or bones in a man's body). David reduced the number to eleven, Isaiah to six, Micah to three, Isaiah again to two, and Amos and Habakkuk to only one: "Seek me and live" (Amos 5:4); "but the righteous live by their faith" (Hab. 2:4) (*b. Mak.* 24a).

---

5. Lachs, *Rabbinic Commentary on the New Testament*, 87, who cites the views of Solomon Zeitlin.
6. B. Cohon, *Jacob's Well*, 45.
7. Betz, *Sermon on the Mount*, 182.

I have come not to abolish but to fulfill. We may get some help in interpreting these words by citing a Hebrew idiom to which the name "exaggerated contrast" has been given.[8] This idiom, found in Arabic as well as in modern English, juxtaposes two antithetical statements for the sole purpose of emphasizing the one appearing second. The first statement, were it to appear alone, would be false, but in the idiom it sets up the second statement taken to be more important than the first. The Hebrew language is not well suited to express relativity, that is, "more than," "less than," "rather than," and so on, which helps explain the use of this idiom. One example is in Deut. 5:3:

> Not with our ancestors did the LORD make this covenant,
> but with us, who all of us here alive this day.

Did the LORD make his covenant with the Sinai generation? Of course! But the Deuteronomic preacher wants to emphasize that the covenant is also being made with the generation now assembled years later in the plains of Moab. For other examples of the idiom in the Old Testament, see Amos 7:14; Jer. 7:22-23; 22:10.[9] In modern English we have the greeting card written for someone growing older that reads:

> You're not getting older
> You're getting better!

Is the person getting older? Of course, but the well-wisher wants to convey a gentler and more important message: "You're getting better." In the New Testament we find this exaggerated contrast: Jesus says, "I have come to call not the righteous, but sinners" (Mark

8. James G. Carleton, "The Idiom of Exaggerated Contrast," *The Expositor* Series 4, no. 6 (1892): 365–72.
9. See discussion in Lundbom, *Jeremiah 1–20*, 488–89.

2:17). Does Jesus mean that he is not calling righteous souls to follow him? Not at all. He is happy when the righteous Nathaniel answers the call to discipleship (John 1:47), but here he simply wants to emphasize that he was sent *more* to call sinners than to call the righteous. In John 3:17 is another use of this idiom: "Indeed, God did not send the Son into the world to condemn the world, but in order that the world might be saved through him" (John 3:17). Did Jesus' coming into the world condemn the world? You bet it did. But God's infinitely *more important* purpose—or one might even say God's *real* purpose—was to save the world.

Here in the Sermon Jesus is being very straightforward when he says that he does not want to "abolish" the Law and the Prophets, but what he wants to emphasize is that his real purpose is to bring the Law and the Prophets to fulfillment. We said earlier that the word "abolish" was strong, but some in Jesus' audience may take any challenge to the Law as a move in the direction of abolishment. The exaggerated contrast takes care of this problem. We see something of the same in the apostle Paul, who has great difficulty in explaining his relation to the Law. He says, "Christ is the end of the law" (Rom. 10:4), and "the law was our disciplinarian until Christ came" (Gal. 3:24), yet he calls the Law holy (Rom. 7:12) and claims to uphold it (Rom. 3:31). Every Bible reader recognizes some tension between the older Law and the teachings of Jesus, or between the Old Testament and the New Testament.[10] In some cases Jesus sets aside demands of the Law, and at other times he upholds them. Jews and Christians do the same today, yet neither wants to abolish the Law and the Prophets. The idiom used by Jesus handles this nicely: "I have come not to abolish but to fulfill."

---

10. Johnson, "Matthew," 291.

18. *For truly, I tell you, until heaven and earth pass away, not one letter,* *not one stroke of a letter, will pass from the law until all is accomplished.* This refers to the Jewish doctrine of the ongoing validity of the written Law.[11] A Midrash says: "Our sages said: No letter shall ever be abolished from the Torah. . . . the smallest tittle will not be erased from thee" (*Exod. Rab.* 6:1).[12] Philo, too, said this:

> But Moses is alone in this, that his laws, firm, unshaken, immovable, stamped, as it were, with the seals of nature itself, remain secure from the day when they were first enacted until now, and we may hope that they will remain for all future ages as though immortal, so long as the sun and moon and the whole heaven and universe exist. Thus though the nation has undergone so many changes, both to increased prosperity and the reverse, nothing—not even the smallest part of the ordinances—has been disturbed, because all have clearly paid high honour to their venerable and godlike character. (*Vit. Mos.* 2.14-15)

truly. This corresponds to Hebrew *'āmēn*, which Jesus puts at the beginning of his saying to emphasize its truth and importance. This occurs nowhere in the rabbinic literature.[13] In the Bible, *'āmēn*, occurs at the end of a text (Pss. 41:13; 72:19; Rom. 16:27; Heb. 13:25; 2 Pet. 3:18; Rev. 22:20-21). But see 1 Kgs. 1:36 and Jer. 28:6. A positive affirmation here counterbalances the negative statement in v. 17.

until heaven and earth pass away. "Heaven and earth" express permanence and are often applied to the Law.[14] The Law is valid to the end of the world.

not one letter, not one stroke of a letter KJV: "(not) one jot or one tittle." The Greek has ἰῶτα and κεραία. The *iota* is the smallest letter of the Greek alphabet and is generally taken to represent the Hebrew *yod*, which in the square (Aramaic) script of the first century C.E.

11. Davies, "Matthew 5, 17-18," 432.
12. *See* Lachs, *Rabbinic Commentary on the New Testament*, 88. On the tittle, see also *Cant. Rab.* 5:11.
13. Daube, "Three Questions of Form in Matthew V," 27–31.
14. Lachs, *Rabbinic Commentary on the New Testament*, 88.

(also in modern Hebrew script) is the smallest letter. Greek κεραία is a projection, hook, or stroke of the letter,[15] possibly translating the Aramaic *tāgā'*,[16] which refers to the "crown" (three dots) over certain Hebrew letters,[17] and maybe also the tiny extension or serif distinguishing Hebrew "b" (ב, *bet*) from "k" (כ, *kaph*), and "d" (ד, *dalet*) from "r" (ר, *resh*).[18]

19. *Therefore, whoever breaks one of the least of these commandments, and teaches others to do the same, will be called least in the kingdom of heaven; but whoever does them and teaches them will be called great in the kingdom of heaven.* Jewish tradition distinguished between "light" and "heavy" precepts. For example, honoring one's parents (Deut. 5:16) was considered a heavy precept; taking the mother bird with her young (Deut. 22:6-7) was considered a light precept (*m. Ḥul.* 12:5),[19] an act that cost little and was easily done. The point being made here is that one does not disregard lesser commands but obeys all of them. The Mishnah says, "Be as heedful of a light precept as a grave one, for you know not the reward of each" (*m. Ab.* 2:1; 4:2).

20. *For I tell you, unless your righteousness exceeds that of the scribes and Pharisees, you will never enter the kingdom of heaven.* This is the climactic verse of the unit and the theme of the entire Sermon, serving also to introduces the antitheses that follow.[20] Scribes were the theological teachers of Judaism, and Pharisees were pious laymen from every part of the community: traders, craftsmen, and professional men.[21]

---

15. Lachs, *Rabbinic Commentary on the New Testament,* 88.
16. E. F. Sutcliffe, "One Jot or Tittle, Mt. 5.18," *Biblica* 9 (1928): 458–60.
17. *Dict Talm,* 1646; cf. *b. Shab.* 104a; *b. Men.* 29b.
18. According to David Noel Freedman (personal communication), the tittle referred to the small extension in the Hebrew and Aramaic letters *bet* and *dalet.*
19. See Davies, "Matthew, 5, 17–18," 432; Lachs, *Rabbinic Commentary on the New Testament,* 88–89.
20. Neil J. McEleny, "The Principles of the Sermon on the Mount," *CBQ* 41 (1979): 552–53; Daube, *New Testament and Rabbinic Judaism,* 55.
21. Jeremias, *Sermon on the Mount,* 23.

9

_____

What about Anger? (5:21-26)

²¹*"You have heard that it was said to those of ancient times, 'You shall not murder'; and 'whoever murders shall be liable to judgment.' ²²But I say to you that if you are angry with a brother or sister, you will be liable to judgment; and if you insult a brother or sister, you will be liable to the council; and if you say, 'You fool,' you will be liable to the hell of fire. ²³So when you are offering your gift at the altar, if you remember that your brother or sister has something against you, leave your gift there before the altar and go; first be reconciled to your brother or sister, and then come and offer your gift. ²⁵Come to terms quickly with your accuser while you are on the way to court with him, or your accuser may hand you over to the judge, and the judge to the guard, and you will be thrown into prison. ²⁶Truly I tell you, you will never get out until you have paid the last penny.*

21-22. *You have heard that it was said . . . But I say to you.* This antithesis modifies a form used by the rabbis of Jesus' time.[1] They would present a statute of law, and then say:

> You might understand (these words to mean) . . .
> But you must say instead . . .

So, in an exposition of the Fifth Commandment, it would go as follows:

> "Honor your father and your mother." You might understand "Honor them with words only." But you must say instead, "Parents are to be honored not only with speech, but by deeds as well."

Jesus modifies the form by substituting the authoritative "But I say to you," which has more the ring of the prophet.[2] The rabbinic form is academic and more argumentative.[3] Here there is no argument, simply a proclamation. Jerome says Jesus is replacing the prophetic, "Thus said the Lord."[4] The crowd correctly perceived this claim of authority at the end of the Sermon (7:28-29). David Daube points out that the antithesis as a whole in vv. 21-26, as well as the other antitheses in vv. 27-48, follow a common Jewish form where a general principle is proclaimed, and then this is followed by a series of illustrations. It occurs in Eccles. 3:1-8 and often in the rabbinic literature.[5]

21. *You have heard that it was said to those of ancient times, 'You shall not murder'; and 'whoever murders shall be liable to judgment.'*

---

1. Daube, *New Testament and Rabbinic Judaism*, 55–62; Bennett H. Branscomb, *Jesus and the Law of Moses* (New York: Richard R. Smith, 1930), 239–40. See earlier Solomon Schechter, "Some Rabbinic Parallels to the New Testament," *JQR* O.S. 12 (1899–1900): 427–28; and Samuel S. Cohon, "The Place of Jesus in the Religious Life of His Day," *JBL* 48 (1929): 95–96.
2. Amos N. Wilder says, "The larger part of Jesus' ethical teaching falls in the category of prophetic injunction" ("The Teaching of Jesus II: The Sermon on the Mount," in *IB* 7: 163).
3. Daube, *New Testament and Rabbinic Judaism*, 55–62.
4. B. Cohon, *Jacob's Well*, 46.
5. Daube, "Three Questions of Form in Matthew V," 24–27.

Jesus' teaching begins with a reference to the Sixth Commandment (Exod. 20:13; Deut. 5:17), which is better translated, "You shall not murder," rather than "You shall not kill" "Those of ancient times" (τοῖς ἀρχαίοις) are authorities of the distant past.[6]

22. But I say to you that if you are angry with a brother or sister, you will be liable to judgment; and if you insult a brother or sister, you will be liable to the council; and if you say, 'You fool,' you will be liable to the hell of fire. The teaching is actually about anger, an inner disposition that can lead to murder. It did so in story of Cain and Abel (Gen. 4:5-8) and probably would have been repeated in the case of Jacob and Esau (Gen. 27:41-45), except that their mother intervened. It has happened countless times since. In fact, most if not all murders are preceded by anger. Sirach 28:10-11 says, "strife kindles fire, and a hasty quarrel leads to bloodshed." The Talmud contains this word: "He who publicly shames his neighbor is as though he shed blood"(*B. Meṣ.* 58b). *Sifre Deuteronomy*, commenting on Deut. 19:11, says that the Sages taught that if one transgresses a minor commandment he will eventually transgress a major commandment, and in the end shed blood (186/7). Early Christians receive this warning in the *Didache* (3:2): "Do not be prone to anger, for anger leads to murder; nor be zealous, contentious, or irascible. For from all these are born acts of murder." Greek "brother" (so RSV), which the NRSV expands to "brother or sister," usually means "fellow Israelite" in the Old Testament (Deut. 15:2; Lev. 19:17); here it means "fellow disciple."[7]

If you are angry with a brother or sister. This is a phrase on which the whole teaching turns, and it is difficult. Some draw the hasty conclusion that to become angry is wrong and that anyone who gets

---

6. Betz, *Sermon on the Mount*, 215.
7. Lachs, *Rabbinic Commentary on the New Testament*, 92. This is also the view of Krister Stendahl, who notes, nevertheless, that Jesus did break through the barrier of particularism. He cites in this connection Matt. 18:15-20 ("Matthew, 776 ").

angry is in the wrong. But, reading on in the verse, we see that Jesus has a certain type of anger in mind. He is not referring to every expression of anger, which is no surprise since the Bible makes it clear that anger in and of itself is not wrong. The Psalmist says, "Be angry, but sin not" (Ps. 4:4 RSV), a passage that is quoted and expanded upon in Eph. 4:26: "Be angry but do not sin; do not let the sun go down on your anger" (RSV).

The Bible contains three important teachings about anger: (1) that one must be *slow* to anger (Prov. 14:29; 15:18; 16:32; 19:11; Eccles. 7:9; James 1:19); (2) that anger must *not get out of control* (Prov. 29:11; Ps. 37:8: "Refrain from [passionate] anger"); and (3) that anger must be *short-lived* (Eph. 4:26). Aristotle agreed that anger must not come too quickly or last too long, saying simply that it must be carried out in the right way, at the right time, and with the right persons (*Nic. Eth.* iv 5). In the Bible, God is slow to anger (Exod. 34:6) and does not keep his anger forever (Pss. 30:5; 103:9); but, unlike in human beings, God's anger can burn with great intensity (Deut. 32:22; 2 Kgs. 22:17; Jer. 7:20; 15:14; 17:4; 21:12). But the Bible nowhere teaches that one must not be angry. There is also such a thing as "righteous anger." The prophets were angry (Jer. 6:11; 15:17); Jesus was angry (Mark 3:5); Paul was angry (Acts 17:16); and we are all angry at one time or another.

Besides giving an implied warning about anger that could lead to murder—an anger that must be disallowed in any and every case—Jesus is concerned primarily with behavior making other people angry. The Greek verb ὀργίζω in the active voice means "make angry, provoke to anger, irritate,"[8] and although a passive form occurs in our present verse, ὀργιζόμενος, the sense—and also the context—requires "become provocative" rather than "become

8. Liddell and Scott, *Greek-English Lexicon*, 1246, s.v. ὀργίζω.

angry." I would therefore translate v. 22a: "everyone who becomes provocative with another shall be liable to judgment." The wrongdoing is making someone angry by provocative words or actions, which can escalate into something worse. Jesus says one must refrain from this type of anger. Some ancient manuscripts add "without cause" (εἰκῇ), giving the reading, "if you are angry with a brother or sister without cause, you will be liable to judgment." This is generally judged to be a secondary reading; nevertheless, it qualifies the anger and brings the interpretation in line with what the larger context requires.[9]

Provocative anger is spoken about also in Eph 6:4, where the similar Greek verb παροργίζω, carries this meaning:[10] "And fathers, *do not provoke* (μὴ παροργίζετε) your children *to anger*, but bring them up in the discipline and instruction of the Lord." Paul speaks a similar word in Col 3:21: "Fathers, do not provoke (ἐρεθίζετε) your children, or they may lose heart."

shall be liable to judgment. The provocative individual will be brought before authorities of the local court[11] and punished. The Greek assumes that such a one is "judged guilty," or "condemned." The person is not simply in danger of judgment, which is clarified by the usage in v. 21, where the one who murders stands condemned. Krister Stendahl says the other person in vv. 23-24 has a (just) claim,[12] which means that the person responsible for the provocation is in the wrong.[13]

9. See P. Wernberg-Møller, "A Semitic Idiom in Matt. V. 22," *NTS* 3 (1956–57): 71–73.
10. Liddell and Scott, *Greek-English Lexicon*, 1343, s.v. παροργίζω.
11. David Smith ("Raka!" *ET* 15 [1903–4]: 236) says the "Judgment" was the local court in every provincial town that tried all offenses committed within its jurisdiction. This interpretation is accepted by Kemper Fullerton, "Raka," *ET* 15 (1903–4), 429; also Robert A. Guelich, "Mt 5:22: Its Meaning and Integrity," *ZNW* 64 (1973): 39–52.
12. Stendahl, "Matthew," 776.
13. McKenzie, "Matthew," 71.

and if you insult a brother or sister, you will be liable to the council.
That is, whoever says *Raka* to his brother or sister. Greek ῥακά is
equivalent to Aramaic ריקא, "empty," or "empty head," which was
a term of contemptuous address. It appears frequently in the rabbinic
literature, and the person uttering it knows he is leveling a supreme
insult. The Talmud records an incident where a rabbi met an ugly
man on a journey and returned his polite greeting with a "Raca!"
But then he realized that he had done wrong, and asked the man's
forgiveness (*b. Ta'an.* 20ab).[14]

Here Jesus envisions a more severe punishment. The Greek reads,
"Whoever says ῥακά to his fellow shall be liable to the Sanhedrin,"
which was the supreme Jewish council of seventy-one members in
Jerusalem, presided over by the high priest. The initial provocation
has led to something more serious. The Sanhedrin would not likely
hear a case simply involving one's use of ῥακά, but it would hear a
more serious case that began with the insult ῥακά.

And if you say, 'You fool,' you will be liable to the hell of fire.
Greek Μωρέ is another contemptuous word of insult, meaning "You
fool!" A serious offense beginning with this word against a brother
(or sister) will land a person in *Gehenna*. Gehenna reproduces the
Hebrew for "Valley of Hinnom" (Jer. 7:32; 19:6). The Valley of
Ben Hinnom (Josh. 15:8) was west and south of Jerusalem, and later
Jewish apocalyptic writings transformed the picture of it into a hell
of fire (*1 Enoch* 54:1-2). Gehenna, or Gehinnom, became a pit of
torment for the wicked in the afterlife, contrasted with the "paradise
of delight," a place of refreshment where the righteous would find
themselves (*4 Ezra* 7:36; *2 Bar.* 59:8-10; 83:13). In the Talmud,
Gehinnom was contrasted with Gan Eden (the Garden of Eden),
which is paradise (*b. Yom.* 87a). The Talmud says that Gehinnom

14. B. Cohon, *Jacob's Well*, 48.

will be punishment for (1) one who commits adultery; (2) one who publicly shames his neighbor; and (3) one who fastens an evil epithet upon his neighbor (*b. B. Meṣ.* 58b).

23-24. *So when you are offering your gift at the altar, if you remember that your brother or sister has something against you, leave your gift there before the altar and go; first be reconciled to your brother or sister, and then come and offer your gift..* The brother or sister has a legitimate claim against you, so before you make your offering to God, it is necessary first to be reconciled to that person. The Mishnah says that the Day of Atonement does not atone for offenses against one's neighbor unless one is reconciled with him (*m. Yom.* 8:9; cf. Matt. 3:7-10). The rabbis surrounded the Torah with cautionary rules, which, like danger signals, were to stop a person before he gets within breaking distance of the Law (*m. Ab.* 1:1: "Make a fence around the Torah: Be reconciled to your brother").[15] Jesus, too, built a fence around the Law by outlawing inclinations as well as deeds.

25. *Come to terms quickly with your accuser while you are on the way to court with him, or your accuser may hand you over to the judge, and the judge to the guard, and you will be thrown into prison.* Once again, the accuser taking you to court has a legitimate claim against you. The thing to do, then, is to be reconciled quickly before the heavy hand of judgment falls upon you (cf. Luke 12:57-59).

26. *Truly I tell you, you will never get out until you have paid the last penny.* No mercy here. The "penny" (κοδράντης) is the smallest coin of Roman currency.

---

15. See also *m. Ab.* 3:13 (*P. Ab.* 3:18): "Tradition is a fence for the Torah."

10

Beware of Lust (5:27-30)

27"You have heard that it was said, 'You shall not commit adultery.' 28But I say to you that everyone who looks at a woman with lust has already committed adultery with her in his heart. 29If your right eye causes you to sin, tear it out and throw it away; it is better for you to lose one of your members than for your whole body to be thrown into hell. 30And if your right hand causes you to sin, cut it off and throw it away; it is better for you to lose one of your members than for your whole body to go into hell.

27. You have heard that it was said, 'You shall not commit adultery.' Jesus' second teaching builds on the Seventh Commandment prohibiting adultery (Exod. 20:14; Deut. 5:18). According to the Old Testament, adultery was committed when a man—married or single—had sexual relations with another man's wife. It was the marital status of the woman—and only the woman—that made it adultery. If she was not married, it was "harlotry" or the like, an indiscretion on the part of the man to be sure, but not adultery. Adultery was a particularly serious crime because the offender could bring into the woman's family a child the husband did not want. Yes, adultery was a violation against the woman, whether or not she complied willingly, but it was primarily a crime against her husband. In the New Testament period, adultery seems to have been expanded to include sexual relations between a married man and any woman, married or unmarried, taken thus to be a violation of the commitment a man made to his own wife. This is the view of adultery today. In *American Jurisprudence*, a legal encyclopedia, it is said: "Modern-day statutes variously define adultery as: any sexual intercourse by a married person other than with that person's spouse," adding other like liaisons. It continues: "in modern parlance, adultery, by definition, is sexual intercourse between a married man and a woman not his wife, or between a married woman and a man not her husband."[1]

28. *But I say to you that everyone who looks at a woman with lust has already committed adultery with her in his heart.* Once again, Jesus goes behind the deed to the inner disposition leading up to the deed, which is a common theme in the rabbinic literature. In the Mishnah, Rabbi Eliezer Haqqappar is reported as having said, "Jealousy, lust, and ambition drive a person out of this world" (*m. Ab.* 4:21). The Talmud maintains that unchaste imagination is more injurious than the sin itself (*b. Yom.* 29a). The *Apocalypse of Moses*, in discussing Eve's transgression in Genesis 3, says, "the serpent poured upon the fruit the poison of his wickedness, which is lust, the root and beginning of every sin" (19:3). Philo, too, said that "desire, from which flow the most iniquitous actions . . . is like a flame in the forest; it spreads abroad and consumes and destroys everything" (*Decal.* 173). And in the Midrashic literature: "The moment a man contemplates sinning it is as though he has committed a trespass against the Omnipresent" (*Num. Rab.* 8:5).

---

1. *American Jurisprudence* (2nd ed.; Rochester, NY: Lawyers' Co-operative, 1962–), 1149. I am indebted to Attorney James T. Ryan, of Woodbury, Connecticut, for providing me with this reference (letter dated April 20, 2006).

It could be that reference is being made here to the Tenth Commandment on not coveting (Exod. 20:17; Deut. 5:21), which has been much discussed in connection with the problem of liability for "intention" in Jewish law and law elsewhere in the Greco-Roman world.[2] Among the things not to covet is a neighbor's wife. This commandment differs from the other Decalogue prohibitions in that it cannot be quantified and is therefore not punishable in a human court. Coveting takes place in the heart, and there is no way to prove that someone is guilty of it. Only when coveting leads to murder, adultery, stealing, or some other verifiable wrong can punishment be meted out. But the idea did exist in the ancient world that merely to intend a wrong was itself a wrong, and this principle obtained in justice meted out by God.[3] The heavenly Father sees the hidden recesses of the heart (1 Sam. 16:7; Ps. 44:21; Jer. 17:10; Rev. 2:23) and will punish. Jesus knows that coveting a neighbor's wife is wrong, and the present teaching may develop from this commandment.

Does Jesus mean that adultery in the heart is as bad as adultery in the flesh? Not at all. No husband whose wife is given a lustful look by another man would say that. The Talmud says that God will judge an evil intention if it bears fruit, that is, if it is followed by a deed. If the evil intention does not bear fruit, that is, is not followed by a deed, God will not judge it (*b. Qid.* 40a). The same idea exists in the Midrash (*Midr. Ps.* 30).[4] Lust must have in view the committing of the deed,[5] which is what Luther taught. For Luther it boiled down to a matter of the will; where the will was lacking, adultery was lacking. Jerome had earlier made a distinction between "pre-passion," which

---

2. See Bernard S. Jackson, "Liability for Mere Intention in Early Jewish Law," *HUCA* 42 (1971): 197–225.

3. Jackson, "Liability for Mere Intention," 207.

4. See William G. Braude, *The Midrash on Psalms* (New Haven: Yale University Press, 1959), 388–389.

5. S. G. Green, *Notes on the Sermon on the Mount* (London: Sunday School Union, 1879), 13.

was not a sin, and "passion," which was. Only if a man consents and makes an affection out of a thought has he gone from pre-passion to passion; if he is disposed to act, he has committed adultery in his heart.[6]

The question, then, is how serious must the inner disposition be before it becomes adultery, or do all impure thoughts that men have about women amount to the same thing? Should we understand Jesus' teaching to include "male fantasies," which have no end in view and generally go nowhere?

Some years ago I was speaking on this passage to a ministerial group, and in the discussion afterwards one of the senior ministers said he had been in the hospital recently, and while there he became tired of all the religious greeting cards that were being sent to him, offering prayers on his behalf and wishing him—with an appropriate Scripture verse—a speedy recovery. He would much rather have had a copy of *Esquire* magazine, which was noted for its pictures of scantily attired women. He wanted to know if I thought this desire was a violation of Jesus' command. I said it was highly doubtful, citing Luther's comment that one had to possess a genuine desire to carry out an adulterous affair to be guilty of "adultery in the heart." Was my friend wanting to engage in a bit of "male fantasy"? Perhaps. Was he guilty of adultery in the heart? Assuredly no. Male fantasies should be evaluated for what they are—gross exaggerations of male prowess or one's irresistibility to women or one woman in particular—which pass quickly and leave all but the most depraved of men wishing they had not entertained such thoughts in the first place.

29. *If your right eye causes you to sin, tear it out and throw it away; it is better for you to lose one of your members than for your whole body to be thrown into hell.* Hyperbole, but a good warning, all the same,

6. Jerome, *Commentary on Matthew*, 81–82.

to a man with strong, lustful urges (cf. Matt. 18:8-9; Mark 9:43-48). There are similar expressions in the Talmud about cutting out/off the eye, nose, mouth, and other parts of the body (see *b. Shab.* 108a). It has been suggested that for people in antiquity the right eye was the more valuable of the two (1 Sam. 11:2), but this is open to question.[7] In the Bible and in the rabbinic literature, the eye is the bodily member most often blamed for leading men astray, especially to sexual sin.[8] The *Didache* (3:3) warns too about lust leading to adultery.

causes you to sin. Greek σκανδαλίζω means "cause to stumble." From this word we get the English "scandalize" and "scandal." Here the Swedish Bible reads, "If your right eye leads you to seduction (*förförelse*)," the same word that is used with reference to the "right hand" in v. 30.

30. *And if your right hand causes you to sin, cut it off and throw it away; it is better for you to lose one of your members than for your whole body to go into hell.* Jesus knows that the hand, too, gets a man into trouble. The suggestion has been made that "hand" may refer euphemistically to the penis, which seems to be the meaning of *yad* in Isa. 57:8-10 (2x), and also possibly in Cant. 5:4. The euphemism is now confirmed in Ugaritic and appears in the Qumran *Manual of Discipline* (1QS 7:13-14), where a thirty-day penalty is imposed on the man who puts out his "hand" from beneath his clothing, or whose clothing is torn so as to reveal his nakedness.[9] Jesus knows men who

---

7. Lachs, *Rabbinic Commentary on the New Testament,* 97
8. See Num. 15:39; Ezek. 6:9; 18:6; *T. Ben.* 8:2; *b. Sanh.* 45a; *b. Sot.* 8a; *Lev. Rab.* 23:12; *Num. Rab.* 9:1; 17:6.
9. Elisha Qimron and James H. Charlesworth, "Rule of the Community," in *The Dead Sea Scrolls: Hebrew, Aramaic, and Greek Texts with English Translations,* vol. 1, *Rule of the Community and Related Documents* (ed. James H. Charlesworth et al.; Princeton Theological Seminary Dead Sea Scrolls Project 1; Louisville: Westminster John Knox, 1994), 32-33; A. Dupont-Sommer, *The Essene Writings from Qumran* (trans. G. Vermes; Oxford: Basil Blackwell, 1961), 89; Marvin H. Pope, *Song of Songs: A New Translation with Introduction and Commentary* (AB 7C; Garden City, NY: Doubleday, 1977), 517.

have been made eunuchs, and some even who have made themselves eunuchs for the kingdom of heaven (Matt. 19:12). But the literal "hand" makes perfectly good sense in the present verse, where also "right hand" balances off "right eye" in v. 29, making a euphemistic interpretation of "hand" less likely. At most Jesus could be making an indirect allusion to the *membrum virile*. Either is better cut off if it causes a man to sin.

11

What about Divorce? (5:31-32)

31"It was also said, 'Whoever divorces his wife, let him give her a certificate of divorce.' 32But I say to you that anyone who divorces his wife, except on the ground of unchastity, causes her to commit adultery; and whoever marries a divorced woman commits adultery.

31-32a. It was also said, 'Whoever divorces his wife, let him give her a certificate of divorce.' But I say to you that anyone who divorces his wife, except on the ground of unchastity, causes her to commit adultery. This teaching has no antithesis beginning, only "It was also said," making it sound like an addition to the solemn warning against lust, which could lead to a divorce. Shorter than the other antitheses, it is also without amplification. It may be a doublet of Matt. 19:9, although the wording is different. Nevertheless, this is a bona fide antithesis containing a teaching consistent with Matthew's Gospel. Compare the marriage and divorce teachings in Mark 10:11-12 and Luke 16:18.

In the background is the divorce and remarriage law of Deut. 24:1-4. Verse 1 can stand alone (KJV following the Targums and Luther), and if so, it becomes Moses' allowance of divorce, but the prevailing opinion now is that the verse is a dependent clause taking divorce for granted, with the law then going on in vv. 2-4 to regulate remarriage (RSV, NRSV, also Calvin). We can assume that a law permitting divorce did exist; it simply is not given in Deut 24:1, nor anywhere else in the Old Testament. But the Old Testament takes divorce for granted (Lev. 21:7, 14; 22:13; Num. 30:9; Deut. 22:19, 29). Jesus, in any case, is citing a long-standing Jewish tradition permitting divorce, which obtained in New Testament times and continues up to the present day. Jewish law has always allowed divorce, and in certain situations even required it.[1] But divorce was accepted reluctantly. The Talmud says that when a man divorces his wife "even the altar sheds tears" (cf. Mal 2:13) (b. Git. 90a; b. Sanh. 22a). The prophet Malachi spoke this word from the Lord: "I hate divorce" (Mal. 2:16).

Jesus' words are again directed to the man, who in biblical times controlled the marriage and was the only one—at least among Jews living in Palestine—who could issue a bill of divorce (m. Yeb. 14:1).[2] This situation obtained until the twelfth century c.e., at which time the consent of the wife became a necessary condition for divorce.[3] In New Testament times, the only legal recourse a woman had was that she could sue for divorce if (1) the husband had objectionable physical characteristics (boils; was a coppersmith or a tanner); or (2) his conduct toward her was reprehensible. If the court ruled in her favor, the husband would be required to give her a bill of divorce.[4]

---

1. M. Ket. 7:1-5, 9-10; m. Yeb. 2:8; b. Yeb. 63b (citing Prov. 22:10).
2. David Daube, "The New Testament Terms for Divorce," Theology 47 (1944): 65.
3. Reuven Yaron, "The Restoration of Marriage," JJS 17 (1966): 1.
4. Moore, Judaism, 2:125; Daube, "New Testament Terms for Divorce," 65; Ben Zion (Benno) Schereschewsky, "Divorce (In Later Jewish Law), EncJud 6:126.

But it was still the husband who issued the divorce. Jewish women residing in outlying areas, where Gentile influence was greater, had more rights and could legally divorce their husbands.[5] This seems to be the situation presupposed in Mark 10:12, which David Daube says sounds very "un-Jewish."[6] Roman divorce law was liberal. We know that c. 100 B.C.E. the Romans allowed termination of a marriage for no reason at all—by either party. All the husband or wife had to say was "That's it!" and walk out the door. It was not even necessary to register the divorce with the authorities.[7]

By the New Testament period Jews had long been debating the grounds for divorce. The school of Hillel (Hillel lived c. 60 B.C.E. to 20 C.E.) was more liberal, allowing divorce not only for sexual immorality but for other reasons, such as burning the husband's food.[8] The rival school of Shammai (Shammai lived in the first century B.C.E.) allowed for divorce only in cases of sexual immorality (*m. Git.* 9:10).[9] Both schools based their interpretation on Deut. 24:1. The Pharisees, then, when questioning Jesus about divorce in Matt. 19:3-9 and Mark 10:2-9, were anxious to know whether he would allow divorce "for any cause." Jesus did not answer them directly, giving them instead a statement on the permanence of marriage, which he based in Gen. 2:24. Later, when speaking privately with his disciples, he went on to say according to the Markan account, "Whoever divorces his wife and marries another commits adultery against her, and if she divorces her husband and marries another,

---

5. In the Jewish colony at Elephantine, each spouse had the power to dissolve the marriage without establishing any grounds of "matrimonial offences"; see David L. Lieber, "Divorce (In the Bible)" in *EncJud* 6:124.

6. Daube, "New Testament Terms for Divorce," 66; Filson, *Matthew*, 87.

7. David Daube, in a lecture given to my class in Christian Origins at the University of California, Berkeley (March 8, 1977). See also Daube, "New Testament Terms for Divorce," 65; and Alfredo Mordechai Rabello, "Divorce of Jews in the Roman Empire," in *The Jewish Law Annual IV* (ed. Bernard S. Jackson; Leiden: Brill, 1981), 79–102.

8. On a bad wife who prepares food her husband does not want, see *b. Yeb.* 63ab.

9. Moore, *Judaism*, 2:123–24.

she commits adultery" (Mark 10:11-12). Luke differs from Mark only in that he omits the case of a woman divorcing her husband. The teaching here—without any context— reads: "Anyone who divorces his wife and marries another commits adultery, and whoever marries a woman divorced from her husband commits adultery" (Luke 16:18). In Matthew, Jesus says, "Whoever divorces his wife, except for unchastity, and marries another commits adultery" (Matt. 19:9). Other ancient manuscripts contain additions bringing the teaching in line with Matt. 5:32, either adding after "unchastity" the words "causes her to commit adultery, " or at the end of the verse adding "and he who marries a divorced woman commits adultery" (NRSV footnote).

This teaching on marriage and divorce in all three Gospels is difficult and has evoked much discussion. In my view, two things must be kept in mind in any attempt to come up with a proper interpretation: (1) Jesus is directing his words not to women but to men, who were the ones controlling marriage and divorce; and (2) Jesus has situations in mind where there is a third party—sometimes a woman, sometimes a man—waiting in the background to destroy the marriage. This second point is hardly ever discussed by commentators, but it is one of the chief problems in any marriage breakup, as all legal experts know.

What is Jesus' view of marriage, divorce, and remarriage? We can begin with Jesus' words in Mark 10:9: "Therefore what God has joined together, let no one separate." Jesus believes that marriage is to last. Period. Let there be no misunderstanding about this. But who is the "man" in his statement? It could be the husband, who by law has simply to write his wife a certificate of divorce (*get*)[10] and send her out of his house. If the "man" is the husband, then Jesus is making

---

10. On the *get*, see *m. Git.* 2:5.

a very strong—perhaps absolute—statement against divorce, although he may simply be saying that this is how it should be and may not be precluding instances where the marriage, for one reason or other, has failed and is better dissolved. But most take this as an absolute statement disallowing all divorce.

The "man" could also be someone other than the husband, an intruder who wants the marriage dissolved so he can have the woman for himself. If Jesus has this scenario in mind, then an absolute word disallowing divorce is the only one making any sense. Jesus does not want *any man* breaking up another man's (and woman's) marriage, made as it is in accordance with God's plan.

Jesus, then, may not be precluding all cases of divorce, only those where there is third-party involvement and someone is "in waiting" once the marriage is dissolved. That someone wants to marry the divorcee. Jesus believes divorce should not happen, but he knows—as we all know—that divorces can and do occur. And if they do occur, so long as there is no third-party involvement, he may reluctantly accept divorce, even though he wishes things were otherwise. Clergy today worthy of their office teach that marriage is to be permanent, and they conduct marriage ceremonies in which it is explicitly affirmed in the vows taken by the bride and groom. But usually clergy will, at a later time or in another situation, reluctantly accept divorce if a marriage was ill-advised or simply did not work. It would be strange indeed if Jesus departed from Jewish tradition and disallowed divorce under any circumstances, even though many commentators, church theologians, and Christian believers believe that this is precisely what he did. But the New Testament, upon closer examination, does not appear to have Jesus giving absolute teachings on divorce and remarriage, neither in Mark nor in Luke, and especially not in Matthew.

The passage in Mark 10:11-12 can be dealt with most readily. There Jesus has apparently successfully answered the Pharisees who wanted to know his view on divorce. He begins by putting the divorce question to them, and they say that Moses allowed a man to divorce his wife. True, but Jesus says this was because of the people's hardness of heart, and that from the beginning it was not to be. A man shall leave father and mother and be joined to his wife, and the two shall become one. True. The Pharisees would doubtless have agreed with this. But then Jesus says that no one should rend asunder what God has joined together, would they agree here? Probably they would, for the rabbis also taught that marriages were made in heaven.[11] Mark reports nothing more about the public give and take. Presumably Jesus' answer settled the matter, at least for the time being.

Only afterwards do the disciples want to know more about Jesus' words to the Pharisees. His amplification has been widely taken as an absolute statement precluding divorce and remarriage. But I suggested some years ago in an earlier work that what Jesus is really saying to the disciples is that one must not divorce his or her spouse (in outlying regions wives could divorce husbands) *in order to* marry another person "in waiting," where a so-called "love triangle" has developed, and a divorce and remarriage would be the result. The husband may already have had sexual relations with the other woman. We do not know, and actually it does not matter. At the very least the man wants to have sexual relations with the woman, which, according to Jesus' prior teaching in the Sermon, is "adultery in the heart" (Matt. 5:28). In such a case, a man's divorce of his wife and remarriage to the woman in waiting is deemed unacceptable. It is adultery. In Mark, the same applies to the wife. If she has

---

11. B. Cohon, *Jacob's Well*, 51.

eyes for another man in waiting, her divorce too is adultery. Jesus is not making an absolute statement against divorce, for there are many cases—as we all know—where third-party involvement is not an issue. A marriage has simply (and tragically) failed, and it was dissolved. Sometime later the man or woman may wish to remarry, and Jesus' words do not preclude this from happening. Jesus does not address such a situation in his words to the disciples.

The teaching in Luke 16:18 should be interpreted similarly, only here no mention is made of a woman divorcing her husband. Precluded in this teaching are only (1) a man from divorcing his wife in order to marry another woman in waiting; and (2) a man from marrying a divorced woman if he has intruded into her marriage and caused a divorce. What has actually taken place, God only knows. Something has happened that should not have happened. It is more than a simple (but tragic) case of divorce and remarriage. In both Lukan examples, third-party involvement has to be assumed, and Jesus once again takes the subsequent divorce and remarriage to be adultery.

The report in Matt. 19:3-9 is similar to the report in Mark 10:2-12, only here we have the "exception clause" that occurs also in the Sermon (Matt. 5:31-32). In addition is the statement in Matt. 5:32, and in some textual witnesses of Matt. 19:9, that the man, by issuing his wife a divorce, has "caused her (ποιεῖ αὐτήν) to commit adultery." What does this mean? The husband issuing the divorce is being judged guilty, but how does the divorce make his former wife an adulteress? The phrase is difficult, although it has Matthew more in line with Jewish teaching in reporting Jesus as saying that a man *can* divorce his wife if she is guilty of "unchastity" (πορνεία). Greek πορνεία can mean adultery, but it is a broader term that can refer to a range of indecent acts. Deuteronomy 24:1 permits a man to divorce his wife for an "unseemly thing" (Heb. '*erwat dābār*, lit., "a naked thing"), which the LXX translates as "a shameful thing" (ἄσχημον πρᾶγμα). Some commentators take πορνεία in Matt. 5:32 and 19:9 as a translate of the Hebrew of Deut. 24:1, which is generally—but not always—taken to be some sort of sexual indiscretion.[12] It cannot be adultery, for then the woman would be put to death and obviously precluded from marrying again, which is what Deut. 24:1-4 is seeking to regulate.

Here in the Sermon, Jesus may be telling men that when they divorce their wives for petty reasons, self-serving purposes, or for no reason at all, they *make* the woman an adulteress. Or they make the woman *as if she were an adulteress*, even though she may not be. How so? Well, for one thing, they give the woman a bad name, and some will think—rightly or wrongly—that the woman is guilty of some sort of sexual indiscretion. It could be simply immodesty, but in matters of this sort, who can really know what has actually happened? It is scarcely different today, where family members and friends hear only snippets about a marital breakup and try to piece things together—and then often after speaking to only one party of the dispute. Another possibility is that the husband may be dismissing his wife without giving her a bill of divorce; then, if the woman has sexual relations with another man, or marries another man, she will be guilty of adultery in the legal sense. On the face of it, Jesus seems clearly to allow for divorce if the grounds are legitimate, objecting only to Hillel's divorce allowance for frivolous infelicities. Jesus is expressing compassion for women who have been victimized by this "easy divorce" law.

32b. *and whoever marries a divorced woman commits adultery.* This phrase is not difficult once we assume third-party involvement and see in it another stern warning to men, this time not only husbands

---

12. Hillel took the term to mean any kind of obnoxious behavior or mannerism, not necessarily something sexual (*b. Git.* 90a; cf. Deut. 23:15); Lieber, "Divorce (In the Bible)" in *EncJud* 6:124.

but also men eager to see a woman divorced so they can have her. The intruder may have already have committed adultery with the man's wife, or he may be guilty of "adultery in the heart" (5:28). Either way, he commits adultery by marrying another man's wife whom he made every effort to get. Jesus is not addressing a situation in which a man marries a divorced woman with whom he had no part in causing the divorce.

12

Better Not to Use Oaths (5:33-37)

> ³³"*Again, you have heard that it was said to those of ancient times, 'You shall not swear falsely, but carry out the vows you have made to the Lord.' ³⁴But I say to you, Do not swear at all, either by heaven, for it is the throne of God, ³⁵or by the earth, for it is his footstool, or by Jerusalem, for it is the city of the great King. ³⁶And do not swear by your head, for you cannot make one hair white or black. ³⁷Let your word be 'Yes, Yes' or 'No, No'; anything more than this comes from the evil one.*

33. *Again, you have heard that it was said to those of ancient times, 'You shall not swear falsely, but carry out the vows you have made to the Lord.'* At first sight this appears to be citing either the Third Commandment on not taking the Lord's name in vain (Exod. 20:7; Deut. 5:11), or the Ninth Commandment on not bearing false witness (Exod. 20:16; Deut. 5:20). Philo took it to be the former; Krister Stendahl, the latter. The Old Testament otherwise permits swearing an oath, but it must be in the name of Yahweh (usually "As Yahweh lives"), not in the name of another god (Deut. 6:13; 10:20; Josh. 23:7; Amos 8:14; Jer.

5:7; 12:16). The Old Testament speaks about "swearing falsely" in Lev. 19:12 and Jer. 5:2.

It may be that Jesus is talking about neither commandment, nor about the swearing of oaths, but rather about making vows, since it says, but carry out the vows you have made to the Lord.' The law about making vows appears in Deut. 23:21-23. Vows are voluntary, and no one is required to make them, but if one does make a vow, presumably under oath, he or she must fulfill it with an appropriate offering, and do so quickly. But since "vow" and "oath" are used interchangeably in the tannaitic literature,[1] Jesus' teaching may be referring to any statement made under oath.

34-37. *But I say to you, Do not swear at all, either by heaven, for it is the throne of God, or by the earth, for it is his footstool, or by Jerusalem, for it is the city of the great King.' And do not swear by your head, for you cannot make one hair white or black. Let your word be 'Yes, Yes' or 'No, No'; anything more than this comes from the evil one.* The problem is an old one. People are careless in swearing oaths, rendering them empty. Jeremiah faced this problem, and said only if people swore oaths "in truth, in justice, and in uprightness," would nations realize the blessing of God's covenant with Abraham (Jer. 4:2). A Midrash cites this Jeremiah verse, going on to say that swearing by Yahweh's name even in truth may not be enough. One must also fear God and manifest other virtues of a godly life (Deut. 10:12), or else judgment will be the result. How much more, then, will judgment come upon those who swear in falsehood (*Num. Rab.* 22:1).

Here Jesus says not to swear at all, but to simply say "Yes, Yes" and "No, No." Anything more comes from evil (or the Evil One). The teaching is picked up in James 5:12. In the Talmud are these words: "Do not speak with your mouth what you do not mean in your

---

1. Lachs, *Rabbinic Commentary on the New Testament*, 100–101.

heart. . . . Let your nay and yea be both righteous" (*b. B. Bat.* 49a).[2] But there is no rabbinic ordinance or injunction never to swear an oath.[3] The Essenes disallowed oath taking except when entering the community, considering it worse than perjury (Josephus, *War* 2.8.6; cf. CD 15:1-4).[4] The truth, they said, does not need such support. Sirach has this word on oath taking:

> Do not accustom your mouth to oaths,
> nor habitually utter the name of the Holy One;
> For as a servant who is constantly under scrutiny
> will not lack bruises,
> So also the person who always swears and utters the Name
> will never be cleansed from sin.
> The one who swears many oaths is full of iniquity,
> and the scourge will not leave his house.
> If he swears in error, his sin remains on him,
> and if he disregards it, he sins doubly;
> If he swears a false oath he will not be justified,
> for his house will be filled with calamities.
> (Sir 23:9-11 NRSV)

Philo had this to say about swearing oaths:

> To swear not at all is the best course and most profitable in life, well-suited to a rational nature, which has been taught to speak the truth so well on each occasion that its words are regarded as oaths; to swear truly

---

2. See also *Slav. En.* 49:1; and *EncJud* 6:124.

3. B. Cohon, *Jacob's Well*, 56.

4. Joseph M. Baumgarten and Daniel R. Schwartz, "Damascus Document (CD)," in *The Dead Sea Scrolls: Hebrew, Aramaic, and Greek Texts with English Translations*, vol. 2, *Damascus Document, War Scroll, and Related Documents* (ed. James H. Charlesworth et al.; Princeton Theological Seminary Dead Sea Scrolls Project 2; Louisville: Westminster John Knox, 1995), 37–38; Chaim Rabin, *The Zadokite Documents* (2nd rev. ed.; Oxford: Clarendon, 1958), 70–73; Gaster, 95.

is only, as people say, a "second best voyage," for the mere fact of his swearing casts suspicion on the trustworthiness of the man. (*Decal.* 84; LCL)

Swearing by heaven, earth, Jerusalem, or the hairs on your head are all substitutes for the divine name in oaths and vows.[5] Heaven is God's throne and the earth is his footstool (Isa. 66:1). Jerusalem is the city of the "Great King," who is God (Pss. 47:2; 48:1-2; 95:3; Mal. 1:14). People today use "minced oaths" to avoid speaking the name of God, for example, "O my heavens" for "O my God," "For heaven's sake" in place of "For God's sake," and so on. Jesus says to avoid these as well.

---

5. Lachs, *Rabbinic Commentary on the New Testament*, 102.

13

How to Handle Insult (5:38-42)

38"You have heard that it was said, 'An eye for an eye and a tooth for a tooth.'
39 But I say to you, Do not resist an evildoer. But if anyone strikes you on the
right cheek, turn the other also; 40 and if anyone wants to sue you and take
your coat, give your cloak as well; 41 and if anyone forces you to go one mile,
go also the second mile. 42 Give to everyone who begs from you, and do not
refuse anyone who wants to borrow from you.

38. *You have heard that it was said, "An eye for an eye and a tooth
for a tooth."* This antithesis begins by citing the "law of retaliation"
(*lex talionis*) occurring in legal passages of the Old Testament (Exod.
21:23-25; Deut. 19:21; Lev. 24:18-20), where it is applied to cases
involving bodily injury or loss of life. In its full form it states: "life for
life, eye for eye, tooth for tooth, hand for hand, foot for foot, burn for
burn, wound for wound, stripe for stripe" (Exod. 21:23-25). Leviticus
24:18 adds that if a man kills another man's beast, he must supply a
replacement beast on the principle of "life for life."

This retribution formula is well attested in ancient Near Eastern law, where, as in the Bible, a limitation is placed on tribal vengeance that exacts a much greater price. The law of equivalent retaliation became standard in Babylon in the nineteenth and eighteenth centuries B.C.E. (Lipit-Ishtar Code; Code of Hammurabi), more than a thousand years before we encounter it in biblical law.[1] The Bible reflects the tribal standard in Gen. 4:23-24, where Lamech boasts to his wives:

> Adah and Zillah, hear my voice;
>> you wives of Lamech, listen to what I say:
> I have killed a man for wounding me,
>> a young man for striking me.
> If Cain is avenged sevenfold,
>> truly Lamech seventy-sevenfold.

In the ancient world, the law of equivalent retribution was seen to be humane; it was not considered "cruel and unusual" punishment, as it would be today. It simply mandated that punishment fit the crime. In Babylonian law, monetary compensation could be substituted for disfigurement, which became Jewish practice in the New Testament period when the principle was no longer taken literally.[2] Literal application of the *lex talionis* had been abolished by the rabbis, probably as early as the age of Jesus, although this cannot definitely be proved.[3] The rabbis substituted monetary compensation.[4] Jesus, then, in quoting this principle, would be thinking not only of people who

1. Tikva Frymer-Kensky, "Tit for Tat: The Principle of Equal Retribution in Near Eastern and Biblical Law," *BA* 43 (1980): 230–34.
2. Rashi on Deut. 19:21; David Daube, *Studies in Biblical Law* (Cambridge: Cambridge University Press, 1947), 106–10.
3. Montefiore, *Synoptic Gospels*, 2:70; Lachs, *Rabbinic Commentary on the New Testament*, 103–4.
4. David Daube, "Matthew v. 38f," *JThS* 45 (1944): 178–81; Daube, *New Testament and Rabbinic Judaism*, 255–57.

want to retaliate by inflicting bodily injury but of those wanting to sue in court and get a settlement in money.

39-41. But I say to you, Do not resist an evildoer. That is, do not resist through violent or legal means, even though the wrongdoer is evil. The examples following are all cases of insult where the law of retaliation should not be applied.[5] None of the evils inflicted is of great magnitude; as a matter of fact, all are relatively minor. None has to do with bodily injury, much less a loss of life. A person should therefore be meek under insult. The Old Testament says that vindication will come finally from God (Isa. 50:6-7; Prov. 20:22; 24:29). The rabbis, too, express admiration for one who makes no retort to the person who assails him (*b. Shab.* 88b), or who ignores a slight or a wrong (*b. Yom.* 23a).

But if anyone strikes you on the right cheek, turn the other also. The first indignity is a slap (with the back of the right hand) on one's right cheek, which in the ancient world would be reckoned as an "insult." Even today it is considered an insulting action in the Near East.[6] Note the "right cheek" (Luke 6:29 omits "right") as compared to the "right eye" in v. 29 and the "right hand" in v. 30. Here the right cheek is intentional, for a strike with the front of the hand would go to the left cheek if the assailant was right-handed. So it is the back of the right hand that is being used to strike a person on his right cheek.[7] The Mishnah takes a strike with the back of the hand as particularly insulting, the fine being double that of an ordinary strike (*m. B. Qam.* 8:6).

Jesus is saying that when someone insults you, you are not to respond in kind; that is, you are not to slap him or her on the cheek. Yet the action prescribed is one that will shame the other person,

5. Daube, "Matthew v. 38f," 180; Daube, *New Testament and Rabbinic Judaism*, 257.
6. Jeremias, *Sermon on the Mount*, 27.
7. Lachs, *Rabbinic Commentary on the New Testament*, 104.

which is what turning the other cheek does. It is as if to say, "Do it again! Here is my other cheek!"[8] Paul, in discussing this teaching and the one following about loving one's enemies, understands the shaming intent perfectly. Citing Prov. 25:21-22, he says that such an action "will heap burning coals upon their heads" (Rom. 12:20). The enemy will be nonplussed, but the conflict is unlikely to escalate. Paul says, "Do not be overcome by evil, but overcome evil with good" (Rom. 12:21).

This teaching on nonretaliation must not become a hard and fast principle made to apply to every conceivable indignity or violence done to a person. Jesus is talking about insult and indignities one can handle. He is not talking about violent attacks upon one's person, one's family, or one's country, which are infinitely more grave. He is also not issuing a sweeping call for pacifism in war or for nonresistance in every confrontational situation. One does have a right to self-defense (cf. Luke 22:36). Public justice is also outside Jesus' purview. He is not speaking about the order of civic communities, or the organization of states, only about how brothers and sisters of the kingdom should act toward each other and toward those outside their ranks.[9]

and if anyone wants to sue you and take your coat, give your cloak as well. The second indignity is also relatively minor, although it probably violates Old Testament law and ordinary common sense. A better translation: If someone should take your tunic (χιτών is a garment worn next to the skin, a shirt),[10] you should offer him also your coat (ἱμάτιον is an outer garment worn above the χιτών).[11] Why is the person taking the shirt off your back? Probably because

8. Betz (*Sermon on the Mount*, 290) calls turning the other cheek a "provocative invitation" and says it is a sign not of weakness but of moral strength.
9. Montefiore, *Synoptic Gospels*, 2:71-72.
10. Liddell and Scott, *Greek-English Lexicon*, 1993, s.v. χιτών.
11. Liddell and Scott, *Greek-English Lexicon*, 829, s.v. ἱμάτιον.

you have incurred a debt, and it is being seized as a pledge. Or maybe you have not paid a debt off. The text speaks about legal action. Very likely you are poor, or else the creditor would be seizing something more valuable.

Old Testament law aims at protecting the poor from overzealous creditors who want a coat when you have nothing else to give them (Exod. 22:26-27; Deut. 24:10-13). The coat is usually the last thing a person is forced to surrender, making the seizure of a tunic in Jesus' example extreme (Luke 6:29 reverses the garments, presumably assuming a robbery). According to Old Testament law, a widow's coat cannot be taken as a pledge under any circumstances (Deut. 24:17). If you happen to be poor, the creditor is obliged to return the coat before nightfall, since you have nothing else to sleep in (Deut. 24:12-13). Garments were commonly given as pledges (Prov. 20:16; 27:13), and in the Old Testament those who callously seize them from the poor come in for strong censure. Amos says that people in Israel "lay themselves down beside every altar, on garments taken in pledge" (Amos 2:8). Eliphaz accuses Job: "For you have exacted pledges from your family for no reason, and stripped the naked of their clothing" (Job 22:6). So, by offering to surrender your coat when the creditor asks for your shirt, you will be shaming him, and more than likely he will not take it.[12] This is another case of dealing with an evil person by giving him more than what he asks for. End of conflict.

and if anyone forces you to go one mile, go also the second mile. Being forced to walk a mile was another indignity, this one having come with the Roman occupation of Palestine. Roman soldiers could compel a non-Roman subject to carry his equipment one mile.[13] Simon the Cyrene, one will recall, a bystander along the road, was

---

12. Lapide, *Sermon on the Mount,* 110.
13. Stendahl, "Matthew," 777.

compelled to carry Jesus' cross (Matt. 27:32; Mark. 15:21). When such a thing happens, Jesus says you are to show your disdain for this loathsome practice by offering to do even more than what the person asks, and go a second mile. From this we get our current expression of "going the extra mile."

42. *Give to everyone who begs from you, and do not refuse anyone who wants to borrow from you.* Giving money to beggars and lending are outlays on a very small scale. Beggars typically receive crumbs or small change. Jesus is not talking about giving in to every request for money. He is simply telling his followers to be compassionate toward the poor, which is what Deuteronomic law requires. There one is admonished continually to share one's resources with the stranger, orphan, and widow, also with the resident Levite in town (Lev. 19:10; Deut. 15:7-11; 16:11, 14; 24:19-22). Jewish exhortations to practice charity are extensive, where charity includes not only giving money to the poor, but caring for all who are needy, particularly orphans and widows, visiting the sick, and comforting mourners.[14] The Mishnah says, Let your house be wide open; let the poor be members of your household (*m. Ab.* [= *P. Ab*] 1:5). And in the Talmud, "He who gives a small coin to a poor man obtains six blessings, and he who addresses to him words of comfort obtains eleven blessings" (*b. B. Bat.* 9b). But the rabbis also cautioned that in almsgiving there should be a limit, lest a man impoverish himself by living beyond his means and becoming a burden on society.[15]

Luther said that one must surely give to the poor, but one was not required to give what they ask for.[16] Calvin said much the same thing.[17]

---

14. B. Cohon, *Jacob's Well*, 62–64; C. G. Montefiore and H. Loewe, *A Rabbinic Anthology* (London: Macmillan, 1938), 412–39.

15. B. Cohon, *Jacob's Well*, 63.

16. McArthur, *Understanding the Sermon on the Mount*, 108.

17. McArthur, *Understanding the Sermon on the Mount*, 108–9; see chapter 3 above.

14

Love Your Enemies (5:43-48)

43"You have heard that it was said, 'You shall love your neighbor and hate your enemy.' 44But I say to you, Love your enemies and pray for those who persecute you, 45so that you may be children of your Father in heaven; for he makes his sun rise on the evil and on the good, and sends rain on the righteous and on the unrighteous. 46For if you love those who love you, what reward do you have? Do not even the tax collectors do the same? 47And if you greet only your brothers and sisters, what more are you doing than others? Do not even the Gentiles do the same? 48Be perfect, therefore, as your heavenly Father is perfect.

43. *You have heard that it was said, "You shall love your neighbor and hate your enemy."* This final antithesis deals with love toward others, asking at the beginning whether one should love one's neighbor and hate one's enemy. Some people are apparently living by this principle. Hans Dieter Betz thinks it is a popular assumption existing everywhere.[1] Jesus' listeners doubtless know Deuteronomy's teaching about love—God's love of Israel (Deut. 7:6-8; 10:15; 23:5), Israel's

---

1. Betz, *Sermon on the Mount*, 306.

obligation to love God (Deut. 6:5; 7:9; 10:12; 11:1, 13, 22), and the love and care Israel must show toward the poor, widows, orphans, strangers, and jobless Levites in town (Deut. 10:19; 14:27-29; 15:7-11; 16:11, 14; 24:19-21).[2] They also can be expected to know the teaching in Lev. 19:17-18:

> You shall not hate in your heart anyone of your kin; you shall reprove your neighbor, or you will incur guilt yourself. You shall not take vengeance or bear a grudge against any of your people, but you shall love your neighbor as yourself. I am the LORD.

This teaching does not have universal application, as Samuel Lachs points out.[3] In Lev. 19:34 one is also told to love the stranger (sojourner) as oneself, where the Israelite is reminded that he or she was a stranger (sojourner) in Egypt. This is fully in line with Deuteronomic teaching. But nowhere in the Old Testament or in the rabbinic literature is there an explicit command to love one's neighbor and hate one's enemy. The closest the Old Testament gets is in Ps. 139:21-22, where the Psalmist expresses hatred toward those who hate God, for which reason they are counted as his enemies. The Qumran literature, however, does command members of the community to love all that God has chosen and to hate all that he has rejected (1QS 1:3-4, 9-11; 9:16; CD 2:14-16), and to love the "sons of light" and hate the "sons of darkness." The *Manual of Discipline* says:

> [The Master of the Community] shall admit into the Covenant of Grace all those who have freely devoted themselves to the observance of God's precepts, that they may be joined to the counsel of God and may live perfectly before Him in accordance with all that has been revealed

---

2. William L. Moran, "The Ancient Near Eastern Background of the Love of God in Deuteronomy," *CBQ* 25 (1963): 77–87. On God's love for Israel and Israel's love for God in the rabbinic literature, see Montefiore and Loewe, *Rabbinic Anthology*, 58–85, 93–115. They say, "The Rabbis believed that God and Israel were united together by a passionate love on both sides" (p. 58).

3. Lachs, *Rabbinic Commentary on the New Testament*, 107.

concerning their appointed times, and that they may love all the sons of light, each according to his lot in God's design, and hate all the sons of darkness, each according to his guilt in God's vengeance. (1QS 1:7-11)[4]

These Jews thought of themselves as "children of light," who were required to hate all "children of darkness." But even here caution is required in assuming a reference by Jesus to the Essenes.[5]

44. *But I say to you, Love your enemies and pray for those who persecute you.* Enemies, of course, could well be non-Jews, but they could also be fellow Jews who are behaving as enemies—persecuting Jesus' followers or even plotting to take their lives. There is the well-known story of David repaying Saul with good when the latter was plotting to kill him (1 Sam. 24:19). The Psalmist knew well enemies close at hand (Psalms 23; 41; 55; 59; 143; etc.), so did Jeremiah (Jer. 11:18-23; 12:1-6; 20:7-12; 38:1-6; etc.), and Jews in all ages have had to reckon with enemies among their own people. The solution in the Old Testament was to leave vengeance to God (Deut. 32:35) and pray for one's deliverance, which is what one hears throughout the Psalms and from Jeremiah. *Slavonic Enoch* gives this advice:

> Every assault and every persecution and every evil word, endure for the sake of the Lord. If the injury and persecution happen to you on account of the Lord, then endure them all for the sake of the Lord. And if you are able to take vengeance with a hundred-fold revenge, do not take vengeance, neither on one who is close to you or on one who is distant from you. For the Lord is the one who takes vengeance, and he will be the avenger for you on the day of the great judgment, so that there may be no acts of retribution here from human beings, but only from the Lord. (*Slav. En.* 50:3-4)

---

4. G. Vermes, *The Complete Dead Sea Scrolls in English* (London: Penguin, 1997), 98–99. See also 1QS 9:21-22.

5. W. D. Davies, *The Setting of the Sermon on the Mount* (Cambridge: Cambridge University Press, 1964), 245–48; Betz, *Sermon on the Mount,* 304.

Love in the Old Testament and the New Testament is different from other love in that it can be commanded. In the New Testament, see especially John 15:12. The Old Testament has this law requiring charity toward an enemy:

> When you come upon your enemy's ox or donkey going astray, you shall bring it back. When you see the donkey of one who hates you lying under its burden and you would hold back from setting it free, you must help to set it free. (Exod 23:4-5; cf. Deut 22:4)

In Proverbs is this teaching:

> If your enemies are hungry, give them bread to eat;
> And if they are thirsty, give them water to drink;
> For you will heap coals of fire on their heads
> And the LORD will reward you. (Prov 25:21-22)

Paul cited this wisdom teaching in his letter to the Roman church (Rom. 12:20).

In the rabbinic literature, "neighbor" in Lev. 19:18 is interpreted more broadly, with the result that a universal interpretation of the teaching prevails (*Ab. R. Nat.* 2.26).[6] Lachs gives this example from the rabbinic literature as expounding the greatest principle in the Torah:

> R. Hanina, the deputy high priest, said of neighborly love that it is a thing on which the whole world depends. This command was given with an oath at Mount Sinai, "If thou hate thy neighbor who is as bad as thyself, I will exact payment from thee. If thou love thy neighbor, who is as good as thyself, I will have mercy on thee.[7]

There is also Jesus' parable of the Good Samaritan in Luke 10:29-37, which is told to answer the question, "Who is my neighbor?"

---

6. Lachs, *Rabbinic Commentary on the New Testament*, 107.
7. Lachs, *Rabbinic Commentary on the New Testament*, 107.

The story of a Confederate soldier carrying out the teaching of Prov. 25:21 during the Civil War is reported in *The Gettysburg Experience*,[8] a local magazine circulating in the town of Gettysburg, Pennsylvania. In December 11–13, 1862, General Robert E. Lee had held off the Union forces at Fredericksburg, Virginia, and on the day after the battle, as Union soldiers lay wounded and dying on Marye's Heights, crying for water, a young confederate soldier named Richard Kirkland asked General Kershaw for permission to leave the safety of his own position to carry water to the wounded Union soldiers. Kershaw thought it an extremely unwise and dangerous action, but nevertheless gave his consent.

> From his window at his headquarters, General Kershaw watched his young subordinate, just 19 years of age, climb over the wall, his body covered with canteens. He watched "with profound anxiety" as Kirkland began his errand of mercy. A few Union soldiers, believing that Kirkland meant to rob the dead, took shots at him, but fortunately, they missed their target. Richard hurried to the nearest sufferer, lifted his head, and poured the life-giving water onto parched lips. He placed the knapsack under his head, covered him hastily with his coat, and moved to the next wounded soldier. "By this time," General Kershaw remembered, "his purpose was well understood on both sides and the danger was over." From all parts of the field arose fresh cries of 'Water, water, for God's sake, water!' . . . The Union troops found their voice and cheered the angel of mercy. Richard Kirkland worked at his errand for an hour and a half. Many Federals on that field lived because of Kirkland's kind work.[9]

Kirkland died in a subsequent battle on Snodgrass Hill in northern Georgia. He is buried in Camden, South Carolina, and on his tombstone, flanked with canteens, is inscribed the words: "If thine enemy thirst, give him drink (Prov 25:21; Rom 12:20)."[10]

---

8. Diana Loski, "Two Carolina Gentlemen," *The Gettysburg Experience* (August 2006): 25–38.
9. Loski, "Two Carolina Gentlemen," 27–28.
10. Loski, "Two Carolina Gentlemen," 33.

Looking outside the Bible to wisdom teachings much older, we have among the excavated texts from ancient Mesopotamia this proverb:[11]

> Do not return evil to your adversary,
>> requite with kindness the one who does evil to you;
> Maintain justice for your enemy.
>> Be friendly to your enemy . . .;
> Give food to eat, beer to drink;
>> grant what is requested, provide for and treat with honor.
> At this one's god takes pleasure;
>> it is pleasing to Shamash, who will repay him with honor,
> Do good things, be kind all your days.

On praying for those who persecute you, there is an interesting story reported in the Talmud making precisely this point. Rabbi Meir, bothered by men who were causing him a great deal of trouble, prayed that they would die. But his wife asked him why he was praying that way, since the psalm he was reading ended by saying that the wicked will be no more (Ps. 104:35). Would it not be better if he prayed that his enemies should repent, then the wicked would be no more? He did that, and the troublemakers repented (*b. Ber.* 10a).

45. *so that you may be children of your Father in heaven.* The phrase "sons / children of your Father in heaven" is not found elsewhere in the New Testament, but in Deut. 14:1 Israelites are told that they are "sons / children of the LORD your God." Peacemakers are called "sons / children of God" in the Beatitudes (5:9), and, when praying, children of the kingdom are to begin, "Our Father in heaven" (6:9).

---

11. "Counsels of Wisdom," in *ANET*[3], 426, 595.

for he makes his sun rise on the evil and on the good, and sends rain on the righteous and on the unrighteous. The phrase has a nice chiasmus: evil/good/righteous/unrighteous.[12] On the idea that God showers goodness on all people, see Ps. 145:9: "The Lord is good to all, and his compassion is over all that he has made." The idea exists in the rabbinic literature, where it says, "God causes the sun to shine both upon Israel and upon the nations, for the Lord is good to all (*Pes. R.* 195).[13] But C. G. Montefiore qualifies this goodness: "God's goodness towards the bad is very temporary, according to the Gospel! Does He not send them, after their life on earth, to hell-fire and gnashing of teeth? . . . In the Talmud, too, the wicked are sent to hell or are annihilated.[14]

46. *For if you love those who love you, what reward do you have? Do not even the tax collectors do the same?* Luke has: "For even sinners love those who love them" (Luke 6:32). We are brought now to a love well below the love taught in the Bible. Jesus is citing a principle much along the lines of "You scratch my back and I'll scratch yours." It is common behavior, and there is nothing wrong with it— modern politicians and business people act according to this principle of reciprocity—nevertheless, it is inadequate for those aspiring to be children of the kingdom. What reward is there for this? Maybe a small one, or in God's economy none at all. The tax collectors, who were much despised in society because of their unethical behavior, and Jews, for the most part, employed by the Roman government, acted according to this principle. Matthew—who was himself originally a tax collector (9:9)—couples these individuals with sinners (9:10), Gentiles (18:17), and prostitutes (21:31-32). But the tax collector is lifted up in Jesus' parable of the Pharisee and the tax

---

12. Betz, *Sermon on the Mount,* 316.
13. This passage is quoted in Montefiore and Loewe, *Rabbinic Anthology,* 43.
14. Montefiore, *Synoptic Gospels,* 2:81–82.

collector (Luke 18:9-14) and becomes the prototype Christian convert.[15] Not only does Matthew leave his tax table to become Jesus' disciple, but there is Zacchaeus, whose life was turned around by Jesus and had salvation come to his house (Luke 19:1-10).

47. *And if you greet only your brothers and sisters, what more are you doing than others? Do not even the Gentiles do the same?* The term *Gentiles* occurs rather seldom in the New Testament.[16] It means "non-Jews," and in the Old Testament it refers usually to the "(heathen) nations." Jesus is calling here for a righteousness better than that of the Gentiles, just as he called earlier for a righteousness better than that of the scribes and Pharisees (5:20). Among Jews, great importance was attached to greeting one's fellow, and greeting him first. It was said of Rabbi Johanan ben Zakkai that no man ever gave him a greeting first, even a heathen in the street (*b. Ber.* 17a).

48. *Be perfect, therefore, as your heavenly Father is perfect.* Jesus concludes this portion of the Sermon by calling followers to be perfect as their heavenly Father is perfect, a verse summing up the entire set of antitheses.[17] The English word *perfect* is difficult and has led many—particularly in the Wesleyan tradition—into serious misunderstanding. The Greek term is τέλειος, a word expressing totality. Referring to sacrificial animals, it means "whole," "without blemish."[18] In the LXX, generally it means "undivided, complete, whole," translating Hebrew תמים (Deut 18:13), which has the same basic meaning.[19] With reference to both animals and people the terms can also mean "full-grown," "mature." The two terms, along

---

15. Betz, *Sermon on the Mount*, 319.

16. The term occurs only five times in the New Testament, three times in Matthew (5:47; 6:7; 18:17), once in Gal. 2:14, and once in 3 John 7.

17. Stendahl, "Matthew," 777; Betz, *Sermon on the Mount*, 320.

18. Liddell and Scott, *Greek-English Lexicon*, 1769, s.v. τέλειος; G. Delling, "τέλειος," in *TDNT* 8:67.

19. BDB, 1071, s.v. תָּמִים.

with a few others in the Old Testament, translate into English as "perfect," "whole," "righteous," "blameless," "upright," and so on. Krister Stendahl says that תמים does not imply "perfection" in a pedantic sense ("absolutely flawless"),[20] nor does it mean "sinless." "Perfect" in the Old Testament is always used of human beings (cf. Gen. 6:9; 17:1; Deut. 18:13), never of God.[21]

Genesis 6:9 says that "Noah was a righteous man, blameless (תמים; LXX: τέλειος) in his generation; Noah walked with God." In Gen 17:1, God says to Abraham: "I am God Almighty; walk before me, and be blameless (Heb. תמים)." The Midrash translates into English as: "Walk before me and be thou whole" (Gen. Rab. 46:4). The Talmud, quoting this verse, says that Abraham was called perfect in virtue of his carrying out the command to circumcise (b. Ned. 32a; see also Gen. Rab. 46:4). Jesus makes a similar demand on an otherwise good man in Matt. 19:21, saying, "If you wish to be perfect (Εἰ θέλεις τέλειος εἶναι), go, sell your possessions, and give the money to the poor, and you will have treasure in heaven; then come, follow me" Unfortunately, the man walked away disappointed. The present verse may build upon Deut. 18:13, where Israel is told, "You shall be blameless (Heb. תמים; LXX: τέλειος) before the LORD your God" (RSV).[22] Targum Neofiti paraphrases, "My people, children of Israel, you shall be perfect in good work with the Lord your God." James 1:4 (RSV) tells Christian believers, "And let steadfastness have its full effect, that you may be perfect and complete, lacking in nothing" (ἡ δὲ ὑπομονὴ ἔργον τέλειον ἐχέτω ἵνα ἦτε τέλειοι καὶ ὁλόκληροι ἐν μηδενὶ λειπόμενοι). The Didache says in turning the other cheek "you will be perfect" (1:4). Job was said to be a "blameless and upright" man (Job 1:1), and in the New Testament there is Nathaniel,

20. Stendahl, "Matthew," 777.
21. Lachs, Rabbinic Commentary on the New Testament, 110.
22. Massey, Interpreting the Sermon on the Mount, 45–48.

of whom Jesus said in astonishment when he saw him, "Here is truly an Israelite in whom there is no deceit" (John 1:47). None of these individuals was flawless; neither was Israel at its best, nor the Christian church at its best. So, paradoxically, we can agree with Paul when he says: "all have sinned and fall short of the glory of God" (Rom. 3:23).

The Old Testament and the rabbinic literature teach the *imitatio Dei*, which is the obligation of human beings to imitate God's actions by their actions.[23] In Christian tradition it is the *imitatio Christi* (Ignatius of Antioch; Polycarp; Francis of Assisi; Thomas à Kempis),[24] and in Pietistic hymns worshipers sing about "being like Jesus." The Jewish teaching is rooted in Gen. 1:27, which says that God created man and woman in his own image. In Deuteronomy, which has been called "Israel's book of *imitatio Dei*," [25] is the command to "walk in all (Yahweh's) ways" (Deut. 10:12; 11:22; 13:4; 26:17). In the Talmud, "walking after God" was taken to mean "walk(ing) after the attributes of the Holy One," where reference is made to God having *clothed the naked* Adam and Eve in the garden (Gen. 3:21), *visiting the sick* Abraham by the oaks of Mamre, where according to tradition he was suffering the pangs of circumcision (Gen. 18:1; cf. 17:23-27),[26] *comforting* Isaac with a blessing after the death of Abraham (Gen. 25:11), and *burying* Moses in the Moabite valley (Deut. 34:6) (*b. Sot.* 14a). We thus have passages in the Bible such as the present one, "Be perfect, therefore, as your heavenly Father is perfect"; "Be merciful, just as your Father is merciful" (Luke 6:36); and "You shall

---

23. Sidney Steiman, "Imitation of God (*Imitatio Dei*)" in *EncJud* 8:1292–93; Schechter, *Some Aspects of Rabbinic Theology*, 199–218; Abrahams, *Studies in Pharisaism and the Gospels*, 138–54; Moore, *Judaism*, 2:109–11; Montefiore, *Rabbinic Literature and Gospel Teachings*, 105. Martin Buber calls this imitation of the "invisible, incomprehensible, unformed, not to be formed" God "the central paradox of Judaism" (*Israel and the World*, 71).

24. Buber, *Israel and the World*, 68–71; cf. Abrahams, *Studies in Pharisaism and the Gospels*, 147.

25. Buber, *Israel and the World*, 75.

26. Buber, *Israel and the World*, 76; see *m. Tanḥ.* Genesis 4:3-4.

be holy, for I the LORD your God am holy" (Lev. 19:2; cf. Deut. 7:6; 14:2, 21). In Exodus, the Decalogue commands Israelites to take a Sabbath rest because God rested on the Sabbath after creating the world (Exod. 20:10-11). In Deuteronomy, Israel is told to act justly and charitably toward the orphan, the widow, and the sojourner because that is the way God acts (Deut. 10:18-19). Yahweh's charity to the poor and needy is also a recurring theme in the Psalms (Pss. 10:14, 17-18; 68:5; 146:9). Hans Dieter Betz says this concept of the "imitation of God" underlies not only the present verse but the whole of the Sermon on the Mount.[27]

In later Jewish literature, the greatness of God is juxtaposed with God's personal concern for the humble, the needy, and the distressed.[28] The rabbis therefore admonished Jews to imitate the qualities of divine mercy, forbearance, and kindness, but stopped short of counseling them to imitate God's attribute of stern justice.[29] In the *Mekhilta,* Rabbi Abba Shaul is quoted as saying, "O try to be like him (i.e., God)" (*Mekh. Shir.* 28:2, 3a).[30] In the writings of Philo, the doctrine of imitating God is associated with the Platonic idea of "becoming like God," as far as this is possible.[31] The doctrine of the *imitatio Dei* is discussed also by the great medieval Jewish philosopher Moses Maimonides,[32] for whom the key text is Jer. 9:23-24, where God is said to delight in "kindness, justice, and righteousness," and by the modern Jewish philosopher Martin Buber, who sees a connection between the Jewish doctrine and the Pythagorean school of the Greek philosophy.[33]

---

27. Betz, *Sermon on the Mount,* 325.
28. Moore, *Judaism,* 1:441.
29. *EncJud* 8:1292.
30. On Abba Shaul, see Buber, *Israel and the World,* 74–76.
31. Harry A. Wolfson, *Philo: Foundations of Religious Philosophy in Judaism, Christianity, and Islam* (2 vols.; Cambridge, MA: Harvard University Press, 1947), 2:194–95.
32. Moses Maimonides, *The Guide of the Perplexed* (trans. Shlomo Pines; Chicago: University of Chicago Press, 1963), 3:54 on pp. 632–38.

E. Stanley Jones takes this verse about becoming perfect as the center point of the Sermon on the Mount, saying that, except for the book of Revelation, where heaven is seen to be a release from present persecution, it is the main emphasis of the New Testament.[34] He finds thirty-three places in the New Testament where perfection is mentioned, for example, Matt. 19:21; 1 Cor. 13:10; Eph. 4:11-13; Phil. 3:12-14; Col. 1:28-29; Heb. 2:10; 1 John 4:18. Jones says the conception of "the complete life" may be better than "perfection," for the New Testament conception is "complete—plus."[35] He says that Wesley, who taught perfection, said that the perfection spoken of in the Sermon on the Mount is perfection only in love and not in character and conduct.[36] But Jones says that the perfection mentioned here is more far-reaching than that. The "therefore" beginning the verse does not merely point back to the preceding verse, but to the whole preceding forty-eight verses, which give us the content of this perfection.[37] John Wesley, who wrote a considerable amount on Christian perfection, said, "no living man is infallible or omniscient," and "sinless perfection is a phrase I never use."[38] Here Wesley is very much in line with Jewish thinking, for as Israel Abrahams says:

> In the Hebrew Bible God is far removed from man, though he is brought near by prayer. God's nature is, however, discriminated from human nature by Power, Wisdom, Eternity, Constancy, Uniqueness, Holiness. Judaism never has abandoned, never can abandon, this transcendental idea of God.[39]

---

33. Buber, *Israel and the World*, 66–77. This influence was noted earlier by I. Abrahams, *Studies in Pharisaism and the Gospels*, 138, where Pythagoras is credited with the precept "Follow God." Plato took the idea from the Pythagoreans, and Philo took it from Plato.

34. Jones, *Christ of the Mount*, 31–40.

35. Jones, *Christ of the Mount*, 36.

36. Jones, *Christ of the Mount*, 38–39.

37. Jones, *Christ of the Mount*, 41.

38. John Wesley, *Thoughts on Christian Perfection* (London: T. Cordeux, 1822), 6, 11.

39. Abrahams, *Studies in Pharisaism and the Gospels*, 149.

15

Beware of Public Piety (6:1-18)

6 [1]*"Beware of practicing your piety before others in order to be seen by them; for then you have no reward from your Father in heaven.* [2]*So whenever you give alms, do not sound a trumpet before you, as the hypocrites do in the synagogues and in the streets, so that they may be praised by others. Truly I tell you, they have received their reward.* [3]*But when you give alms, do not let your left hand know what your right hand is doing,* [4]*so that your alms may be done in secret; and your Father who sees in secret will reward you.*

[5]*"And whenever you pray, do not be like the hypocrites; for they love to stand and pray in the synagogues and at the street corners, so that they may be seen by others. Truly I tell you, they have received their reward.* [6]*But whenever you pray, go into your room and shut the door and pray to your Father who is in secret; and your Father who sees in secret will reward you.* [7]*When you are praying, do not heap up empty phrases as the Gentiles do; for they think that they will be heard because of their many words.* [8]*Do not be like them, for your Father knows what you need before you ask him.*

[9]*"Pray then in this way:*
Our Father in heaven,

> hallowed be your name.
> [10]Your kingdom come,
> your will be done, on earth as it is in heaven.
> [11]Give us this day our daily bread.
> [12]And forgive us our debts,
> as we also have forgiven our debtors.
> [13]And do not bring us to the time of trial,
> but rescue us from the evil one.
> (For the kingdom and the power
> and the glory are yours forever. Amen)[1]
> [14]For if you forgive others their trespasses, your heavenly Father will
> also forgive you; [15]but if you do not forgive others, neither will your
> Father forgive your trespasses. [16]And whenever you fast, do not look
> dismal, like the hypocrites, for they disfigure their faces so as to show
> others that they are fasting. Truly I tell you, they have received their
> reward. [17]But when you fast, put oil on your head and wash your face,
> [18]so that your fasting may be seen not by others but by your Father who
> is in secret; and your Father who seeks in secret will reward you.

These teachings on almsgiving (vv. 2-4), prayer (vv. 5-15), and
fasting (vv. 16-18) censure self-righteous public display of the three
cardinal virtues of Jewish piety (or righteousness), which gives no
honor to God. Other self-righteous acts of the scribes and Pharisees
are censured in chapter 23. Jewish piety lifted up the virtues of prayer,
charity, and repentance, with repentance associated with fasting (1
Kgs. 21:27; Joel 2:12; Jonah 3:5; Neh. 9:1) (*Ecc. Rab.* 5:6, 1).[2]
Penitence and fasting survived in the season of Lent in the Christian
church, becoming a forty-day preparation for the passion, death, and
resurrection of Jesus Christ.

1. NRSV has this in a footnote.
2. Lachs, *Rabbinic Commentary on the New Testament,* 112.

The present teachings expand upon Matt. 5:20, where Jesus says that the righteousness of his followers must exceed that of the scribes and Pharisees, or they will never enter the kingdom of heaven. Some manuscripts begin the verse with "but" (δέ), which creates a balance with the superior righteousness called for in 5:20.[3] Here a contrast in each case is set up between the spurious piety of display and a genuine piety that seeks to conceal itself.

6.1 *Beware of practicing your piety before others in order to be seen by them; for then you have no reward from your Father in heaven.* The Greek word for "piety" is δικαιοσύνη, which translates Hebrew צדקה, usually "righteousness." In later Hebrew, however, צדקה can also mean "liberality," where it becomes a technical term for almsgiving.[4] Jesus here is warning against carrying out the otherwise laudable act of almsgiving simply to be seen by others.[5] Almsgiving, along with other pious acts, is to honor God. No reward in heaven will there be for displays of self-righteous piety.

2. *So whenever you give alms, do not sound a trumpet before you, as the hypocrites do in the synagogues and in the streets, so that they may be praised by others.* The giving of alms is highly praised in Jewish tradition. Sirach says not to keep the poor man waiting for your alms (Sir. 29:8), and that almsgiving atones for sin (Sir. 3:30). The book of Tobit says:

> For almsgiving delivers from death, and keeps you from going into the Darkness. Indeed, almsgiving, for all who practice it, is an excellent offering in the presence of the Most High (Tob. 4:10-11).

And again:

---

3. Stendahl, "Matthew," 778.

4. Marcus Jastrow, *Dictionary of the Targumim, the Talmud Babli and Yerushalmi, and the Midrashic Literature* (2 vols.; London: W. C. Luzac; New York: G. Putnam's Sons, 1903; repr., New York: Pardes, 1950), 1263–64, s.v. צְדָקָה.

5. According to Jerome (*Commentary on Matthew*, 86), this is the definition of "hypocrite."

Prayer with fasting is good, but better than both is almsgiving with righteousness. A little with righteousness is better than wealth with wrongdoing. It is better to give alms than to lay up gold. For almsgiving saves from death and purges away every sin. Those who give alms will enjoy a full life, but those who commit sin and do wrong are their own worst enemies (Tob. 12:8-10).

But giving alms in order to be seen is not the piety Jesus wants. Chrysostom notes in this connection the parable of the Pharisee and the tax collector (Luke 18:9-14), where the Pharisee prays, 'God, I thank you that I am not like other people: thieves, rogues, adulterers, or even like this tax collector. I fast twice a week; I give a tenth of all my income.'[6] Jesus says it is better to give alms in secret, another very Jewish idea. The Talmud quotes Rabbi Eleazar as saying: "A man who gives charity in secret is greater than Moses our teacher" (*b. B. Bat.* 9b). Eleazar also reasoned that if it was right "to walk humbly" (Micah 6:8) in matters carried out publicly, for example, weddings and funerals, how much more in matters normally done privately, such as almsgiving? (*b. Suk.* 49b with note) The good rabbi went on to say that one who performs charity is greater than one who offers all his sacrifices (Prov. 21:3) and that the reward of charity (צדקה) depends entirely on the extent of the steadfast love (חסד) in it (Hos. 10:12; *b. Suk.* 49b). The rabbis thus taught that one is commanded to maintain needy persons; however, one is not commanded to make them rich (*b. Ket.* 67b).

"Sounding the trumpet" has been somewhat of a problem for interpretation. The "trumpet" is the *shofar* (שופר), a ram's horn used in worship (Ps. 98:6) and to warn of enemy attacks (Amos 3:6). But it has been unclear just how this horn was used in soliciting alms. Some, for example, Chrysostom,[7] and in modern times Hans Dieter Betz,[8]

---

6. John Chrysostom, *Homilies of S. John Chrysostom on the Gospel of Matthew*, 1:240 (Homily 19).
7. Chrysostom, *Homilies of S. John Chrysostom on the Gospel of Matthew*, 1:287 (Homily 19).

take the expression to be metaphorical. But Adolf Büchler argued a century ago that sounding the trumpet is not metaphorical at all, but referred to a specific act of fasting and public prayer for rain spoken in the streets.[9] On these occasions, the trumpet was sounded after each of the six benedictions, and alms were distributed to the poor. Today, Salvationists ring bells at Christmas calling for alms.

Samuel Lachs offers another explanation. He thinks that the trumpet referred to here is not the usual wind instrument but a horn-shaped receptacle for collecting money.[10] There were thirteen of these in the temple (*m. Sheq.* 6:1, 5; *b. 'Erub.* 32a), used for collecting money for various charitable purposes. Lachs thus interprets the verse to read: "Don't cause the collection box to be passed before you," which Jesus took to be an ostentatious show of charity. In the temple also were two chambers, one called the chamber of the secret [gifts], the other the chamber of the utensils (*m. Sheq.* 5:6).[11] Into the former, pious individuals put gifts secretly. The poor could then go in to the chamber and help themselves without having to confront the donor. After the destruction of the temple, these horn-shaped collection boxes were used outside the temple,[12] but it remains a question whether, in the time of Jesus, they were being ostentatiously paraded in the synagogues and in the streets?[13]

---

8. Betz (*Sermon on the Mount,* 356) calls it a "figure of speech," what Paul calls "boasting" (cf. 1 Cor. 5:6).
9. Adolf Büchler, "St Matthew VI 1-6 and Other Allied Passages," *JThS* 10 (1909): 266–70; Montefiore, *Synoptic Gospels,* 2:95–96; Stendahl, "Matthew," 778. See in this connection *b. Sanh.* 35a; *Gen. Rab.* 33:3; *Lev. Rab.* 34:4.
10. Lachs, *Rabbinic Commentary on the New Testament,* 112.
11. See also Geza Vermes, *Jesus the Jew: A Historian's Reading of the Gospels* (London: Collins, 1973), 78.
12. There was a horned-shaped box in the house of R. Judah to collect money for students of the Yeshiva (*b. Git.* 6b).
13. Betz (*Sermon on the Mount,* 360) notes too that the context here speaks of the synagogues, not the Jerusalem Temple.

hypocrites. Greek: οἱ ὑποκριταὶ. A hypocrite (ὑποκρῖτής) is "one who plays a part on the stage, an actor, a pretender,"[14] the term being used often by Matthew in describing the scribes and Pharisees (6:2, 5, 16; 23:13, 15, 23, 25, 27, 29). People judging others without first examining themselves are also called hypocrites in the Sermon (7:5). The term picks up on the verb "to be seen" (θεαθῆναι) in v. 1, which is related to the noun "theater" (θέατρον).[15] In the LXX ὑποκρῖτής means "impious" (Job 34:30; 36:13),[16] which comes close to the meaning here in Matthew. The term survives in the early church (*Did.* 8:1). Hypocrites are to be found among religious types in every age. Chrysostom gives this sobering reminder to Christians: "Here it were well to sigh aloud, and to wail bitterly: for not only do we imitate the hypocrites, but we have even surpassed them."[17] Jewish literature itself is highly critical of hypocritical behavior.[18]

Truly I tell you, they have received their reward. Hypocrites have a reward of recognition and repute on earth (Jerome; Stendahl); others have to wait for it until the coming age (Matt. 5:12; Mark 10:30; Luke 16:19-31). There may also be irony in Jesus' statement, that is, they are receiving a reward that does not amount to much (cf. Matt. 5:46).

3-4. *But when you give alms, do not let your left hand know what your right hand is doing, so that your alms may be done in secret; and your Father who sees in secret will reward you.* "Not letting your left hand know what the right hand is doing" is doubtless a proverb and does not mean that almsgiving should be done in such a way that the donor does not know what he is doing. Rather, the donor's knowledge of what he is doing should not be known to others but

---

14. Liddell and Scott, *Greek-English Lexicon*, 1886, s.v. ὑποκρῖτής.
15. Liddell and Scott, *Greek-English Lexicon*, 787, s.v. θέατρον.
16. Stendahl, "Matthew," 778.
17. Chrysostom, *Homilies of S. John Chrysostom on the Gospel of Matthew*, 1:306 (Homily 20).
18. See, for example, *Ps. Sol.* 4:7, 20. The latter verse says, "Let ravens peck out the eyes of the hypocrites."

should be kept secret.[19] One reason for giving alms in secret is in order not to shame the person receiving the alms. A Midrash on the closing verse of Ecclesiastes, "For God will bring every deed into judgment, including every secret thing, whether good or evil" (Eccles. 12:14), says that the school of R. Jannai took this verse to refer to a person who gives a poor man a coin publicly. It happened that R. Jannai saw a person give a poor man a coin publicly, and he said to him: "It had been better that you did not give it to him than to have given it to him and put him to shame" (b. Ḥag. 5a; Eccles. Rab. 12:14, 1).

and your Father who sees in secret will reward you. Here and in vv. 6, 18 some manuscripts add "openly" after "you" (KJV), which turns around the rabbinic teaching that people who sin in secret, thinking no one will see them (Job 24:15), find out to their sorrow that the Omnipresent One later proclaims it publicly (b. Sot. 3a, 9a). The Old Testament attests to the all-searching eyes of God, which penetrate places where people think he will not see (Amos 9:1-4; Jer. 7:11; 16:17; 23:24; Ezek. 8:12; Pss. 94:6-7; 139). Elsewhere Jesus speaks of good things done in secret eventually becoming public (Matt. 10:26-27; Luke 12:2-3).

your Father. On "Father," "Father in heaven" or "heavenly Father," which are pious substitutes for addressing God, see note for 6:9.

5. *And whenever you pray, do not be like the hypocrites; for they love to stand and pray in the synagogues and at the street corners, so that they may be seen by others. Truly I tell you, they have received their reward.* The sort of prayer Jesus has in mind is that uttered by the Pharisee in the parable of the Pharisee and the tax collector (Luke 18:11-12), although that took place in the Temple. Jews prayed standing up (b. Ber. 26b, 30a; T^{PsJ} Num 10:35) but were admonished not to

---

19. Betz, *Sermon on the Mount*, 359.

stand on a high place, for example, on a chair or on a footstool, but on some lowly place, as there is no elevation before God (cf. Ps. 130:1) (*b. Ber.* 10b). The usual place for communal prayer was the synagogue, although offerings at the Temple were accompanied by public prayers.[20] Peter and John were going up to the Temple at the hour of prayer, which was the ninth hour, when they met a lame man being carried there to ask for alms (Acts 3:1). On fast-days prayers were recited in the open (*b. Meg.* 26a). Individuals also prayed wherever they happened to be when the time of prayer was at hand, with certain exceptions, whether at work, while traveling, or under other conditions.[21] Since prayers took place at set times during the day (as in Islam), one stopped what one was doing and recited the prayer in a standing position (Muslims crouch down in prayer).

Jesus was not opposed to public prayers as such, but he realized the temptation to make it an occasion for self-display. The rabbis, too, were aware of this. A Midrash asks, "Is it permissible for a Jew standing at prayer to pray loudly? The Sages said, you might think that he may raise his voice, but Hannah long ago shows otherwise" (1 Sam 1:13) (*Deut. Rab.* 2:1).

6. *But whenever you pray, go into your room and shut the door and pray to your Father who is in secret; and your Father who sees in secret will reward you.* C. G. Montefiore says, "The Rabbis laid immense stress upon public or communal worship, upon praying *with* the community, upon not separating oneself *from* the community or congregation, but of always joining with them in prayer."[22] Nevertheless, pious Jews prayed in inner chambers with the door shut. Some had a chamber at the top of the house employed for

---

20. Stendahl, "Matthew," 778.

21. Montefiore, *Rabbinic Literature and Gospel Teachings*, 115–18; Lachs, *Rabbinic Commentary on the New Testament*, 115; cf. *m. Ber.* 4:5; *b. Ber.* 3a.

22. Montefiore, *Rabbinic Literature and Gospel Teachings*, 116; cf. *b. Ber.* 29b–30a.

private devotion.[23] One recalls Elisha's prayer behind closed doors that restored life to the son of the Shunammite woman (2 Kgs. 4:32-37). Daniel, too, is said to have gone to his room to pray privately (Dan. 6:10).[24] Beryl Cohon says that some of the finest prayers incorporated into the Jewish *Prayer Book* were, at the time of Jesus, said by pious Jews in an inner chamber with the doors shut.[25]

Jesus is not making private prayer an absolute rule;[26] his teaching here is aimed at persons posturing themselves in public prayer. Jesus would doubtless approve of public prayers if the spirit was right. He attended synagogue worship regularly (Luke 4:15-16; Matt. 13:54) and heard many pious prayers uttered there. And in his parable of the Pharisee and the tax collector, someone was on hand in the temple to hear the pious prayer of the tax collector, which enabled the fellow to return home justified (Luke 18:13-14). Chrysostom says, "What then, . . . ought we not to pray in church? Indeed we ought to pray by all means, but in such a spirit as this"; that is, as in the prayer Jesus gives. Chrysostom goes on to point out that one can also enter the closet for display, and then the closed doors will do him no good.[27] It is inconceivable that Jesus would have wanted the Lord's Prayer to be uttered only in private. The corporate nature of the prayer from beginning to end marks it as a prayer for public worship, and that is the way it has been used down through the ages.

and your Father who sees in secret will reward you. God answers prayer (Matt. 7:7-11; Luke 18:1-9), but not always giving the answer expected or hoped for. Jeremiah discovered this when interceding

23. Green, *Notes on the Sermon on the Mount*, 20.

24. Abrahams, *Studies in Pharisaism and the Gospels*, 102; Lachs, *Rabbinic Commentary on the New Testament*, 116.

25. B. Cohon, *Jacob's Well*, 78.

26. See K. Emmerich, "Prayer in the Inner Chamber," in *'And Other Pastors of Thy Flock': A German Tribute to the Bishop of Chichester* (ed. Franz Hildebrandt; Cambridge: Cambridge University Press, 1942), 6-18.

27. Chrysostom, *Homilies of S. John Chrysostom on the Gospel of Matthew*, 1:290 (Homily 19).

for the nation (Jer. 7:16-20; 11:14-17; 15:1-4), and faithful people throughout the ages have found the same to be true. Prayers of righteous persons have great power in their effect (James 5:16), but those uttered by the self-righteous, God will not hear (Luke 18:9-14).

Much discussion exists in the rabbinic literature about efficacious prayer. The rabbis believed in prayers being answered, but they also recognized that answered prayer is an act of divine grace, citing Exod. 33:19 (*Deut. Rab.* 2:1). They said a man must purify his heart and then pray. Is there such a thing as an impure prayer? No, however the one who prays to God with hands soiled from violence will not be answered. Why? Because his prayer is sinful. Since Job committed no violence, his prayer was pure (cf. Ps. 24:4) (*Exod. Rab.* 22). With God we also need not be impatient in prayer (Sir. 7:10). Unlike the unrighteous judge, God answers speedily (Luke 18:7-8).

7. *When you are praying, do not heap up empty phrases as the Gentiles do; for they think that they will be heard because of their many words.* The shift is now to a caricature of Gentile prayers, which are censured for being overly heavy with vain repetitions. The Greek is even more vivid: "Do not babble (βατταλογήσητε) empty phrases." Jewish prayers could be long,[28] but were not known for their excessive length. In some cases brevity was considered the better option (*m. Ber.* 1:4; *m. Yom.* 5:1; *b. Yom.* 53b). The Preacher said, "Never be rash with your mouth, nor let your heart be quick to utter a word before God, for God is in heaven, and you upon earth; therefore let your words be few" (Eccles. 5:2). Sirach said, "Babble not in the assembly of elders, and repeat not your words when you pray" (Sir 7:14 RSV). And in the Talmud, "A man's words should always be few in addressing the Holy One" (*b. Ber.* 61a). This applied all the more true to critical situations. Rabbi Joshua said, "He who is walking in

---

28. Long prayers are encouraged in *b. Ber.* 32b.

a dangerous place says a short prayer" (*m. Ber.* 4:4; *b. Ber.* 3a, 29b).
When the Israelites were descending into the Red Sea, and Moses was
said to be making a long prayer, God said to him, "My beloved ones
are drowning in the sea and you prolong your prayer before me!" (*b.
Sot.* 37a). Moses, actually, was remembered for both long and short
prayers, and his example was used to support long-winded prayers
and concise prayers of others (*b. Ber.* 34a).[29] Betz points out that pagan
(Gentile) prayers were not all like the ones described here, and that
non-Jewish sources also honored concise prayers.[30]

8. *Do not be like them, for your Father knows what you need before
you ask him.* That is, real needs, such as those petitioned for in the
Lord's Prayer, which God already knows.[31] God does not require
long prayers because he knows the need even before one lays it before
him (cf. Matt. 6:32). God knows all that may be known, the past and
the future (Sir. 42:18-20; Wis. 19:1). A Midrash says, Even before
a thought is formed in a man's heart, God knows it already (*Gen.
Rab.* 9:3; cf. Ps 139:4).[32] The rabbis believed in free will, but they
also accepted God's foreknowledge and just left it at that.[33] On the
efficacy of prayer, Israel Abrahams says, "If Rabbinism is firm in its
assertion that prayer *may* be answered, it is firmer still in its denial that
prayer *must* be answered. . . . Prayer was efficacious, but its whole
efficacy was lost if reliance was placed upon its efficacy."[34]

9. *Pray then in this way.* Jesus now gives a prayer his followers can
pray, which in Matthew appears at the center of the Sermon on the
Mount.[35] This may be intentional, and if so, it is climactic. The prayer

29. See Abrahams, *Studies in Pharisaism and the Gospels*, 102–3.
30. Betz, *Sermon on the Mount*, 365–67.
31. Betz, *Sermon on the Mount,* 368.
32. Cf. *Deut. Rab.* 2:17: "Sometimes God answers a prayer even before it is uttered" (cf. Isa. 65:24).
33. Montefiore and Loewe, *Rabbinic Anthology*, 36.
34. Abrahams, *Studies in Pharisaism and the Gospels*, 75.
35. Betz, *The Sermon on the Mount*, 373.

is recorded also in Luke 11:2b-4 and *Did.* 8:2. In Luke, the disciples say: "Lord, teach us to pray, as John taught his disciples" (Luke 11:1). It was common for rabbinic teachers to use or compose a favorite prayer form.[36] Sherman Johnson says regarding Jesus' prayer, "The prayer is thoroughly Jewish and nearly every phrase is paralleled in the *Kaddish* (Sanctification) and the *Eighteen Benedictions*; thus it is Jesus' inspired and original summary of his own people's piety at its best."[37] The *Kaddish* is a liturgy spoken in synagogue worship by mourners in memory or in honor of their departed.[38] The *Eighteen Benedictions (Shemoneh Esreh)* are also called the *Amidah.*

Prayer in Jewish tradition consists of three parts: praise, petition, and thanks,[39] which are preserved in the Eighteen (now Nineteen) Benedictions: (a) Three Blessings of *Praise* (1–3); (b) Twelve (now Thirteen) Blessings of *Petitions* (4–16); and (c) Three blessings of *Thanks* (17–19).[40] The three parts of the Lord's Prayer correspond not precisely but are still recognizably close:

1) Invocation: "Our Father in heaven"
2) Two sets of three petitions:
    a. Acknowledging attributes and promises of God:
        "Hallowed be your name"
        "Your kingdom come"
        "Your will be done on earth as it is in heaven"
    b. Petitions for human needs:

---

36. Abrahams, *Studies in Pharisaism and the Gospels*, 103-104.
37. Johnson, "Matthew," 309; cf. Betz, *Sermon on the Mount*, 372–73. On the *Kaddish* and *Eighteen Benedictions*, in *The Jewish Prayer Book*, see Israel Abrahams, *Annotated Edition of the Authorized Daily Prayer Book* (London: Eyre & Spottiswoode, 1914), lv–lxxi. Samuel Cohon says, too, that the Lord's Prayer bears a close resemblance to prayers current in Pharisaic circles ("Place of Jesus in the Religious Life of His Day," 94–95).
38. B. Cohon, *Jacob's Well*, 79–80.
39. Abrahams, *Studies in Pharisaism and the Gospels*, 107, who cites *Deut. Rab.* 2.
40. Abrahams, *Annotated Edition of the Authorized Daily Prayer Book*, lvii.

"Give us this day our daily bread"

"And forgive us our debts, as we forgive our debtors"

"And lead us not into temptation, but deliver us from evil"

3) Doxology: "For yours is the kingdom and the power and the glory forever. Amen."

Our Father in heaven. "Father in heaven" and "heavenly Father," which are substitute names for God used by pious Jews, appear more often in Matthew than in any other Gospel (cf. 5:16, 45; 7:21; 12:50; 26:39), or in any other book of the New Testament.[41] Luke begins simply with "Father." Beginning perhaps as early as the third century B.C.E., the divine name of Exod. 3:14-15, now vocalized "Yahweh," was not to be pronounced by pious Jews because it was considered too holy. Philo believes that the term "Father" is a substitute for ὁ ὤν in the LXX of Exod. 3:14.[42] Later, the term "Father" becomes important in the trinitarian doctrine of the Godhead, which makes an early appearance at the end of Matthew's Gospel (28:19-20).

God is addressed as "Father" in the Old Testament (Jer. 3:4; 31:9; Isa. 63:16; 64:8; Ps. 67:5; 89:26; 1 Chr. 29:10), and even more in the New Testament (Matt. 11:25; 12:50; 23:9; 25:34; 26:39; John 5:17-46; 14:9; 17:11; Acts 1:4; Rom. 1:7; etc.). The term occurs with unusual frequency in the Sermon on the Mount (sixteen times). As Betz points out, addressing God as Father is to address him as the God of creation (cf. Deut. 32:6; Isa. 64:8; Mal. 2:10).[43] The term "Father" appears in the apocryphal literature (Wis. 2:16; 14:3; Sir. 23:1, 4; 51:10; Tob. 13:4) and becomes rather frequent in the rabbinic literature. The Mishnah, Targums, and Midrashim all contain the

---

41. For discussion, see Massey, *Interpreting the Sermon on the Mount,* 1–32. In the LXX translation of Lev. 24:16, and later Targums on the verse, the capital offense of blaspheming the divine name was expanded to include even the pronunciation of it.

42. Massey, *Interpreting the Sermon on the Mount,* 19.

43. Betz, *Sermon on the Mount,* 368, 387.

expression "Father in heaven,"[44] which may indeed reflect the period of the New Testament.[45] "Our father who is in heaven" (אבינו שבשמים) occurs also in the Jewish *Prayer Book*.[46]

The Lord's Prayer uses the plural "Our Father," whereas rabbinic prayers sometime use the singular: "My Father who is in heaven."[47] Only by the fourth century C.E. did the rabbis seek to make it a rule that prayers must be in the plural.[48] Chrysostom places emphasis on the corporate nature of prayer, noting that Jesus does not say, "'My Father, who is in heaven,' but 'Our father,' offering up the supplication for the body in common, and nowhere looking to his own, but everywhere to his neighbor's good."[49] The Lord's Prayer is thus a corporate prayer, not a private one.

hallowed be your name. Jewish piety was accustomed not to name God without some expression of reverence.[50] The name of God is holy, as the invocation implies, and must be treated as such. God is holy in heaven (Isa. 6:1-3; Rev. 4:8-11), and it remains for people to make his name holy on earth. One way is to keep the Third Commandment (Exod. 20:7; Deut. 5:11).

10. *Your kingdom come.* May God's kingdom (= God's rule) come, as it did in ancient Israel (Deut. 33:5; Num. 23:21; Judg. 8:23; Ps. 24:7-10; etc.), but now and forever among all people. The language is eschatological: God's kingdom is established in heaven but not yet fully realized on earth (Matt. 11:12; Luke 16:16).[51] Mention of the

44. *M. Yom.* 8:9; T^{Nf} on Num. 20:21; T^{Nf} on Deut. 33:24; *Sifre Deut.* 306; *Exod. Rab.* 30:8.
45. Massey, *Interpreting the Sermon on the Mount*, 12–18.
46. Singer, *Daily Prayer Book*, 9, 70 (1992: 22, 120).
47. Abrahams, *Studies in Pharisaism and the Gospels*, 104.
48. Abrahams, *Studies in Pharisaism and the Gospels*, 104–5. See *b. Ber.* 29b-30a, where Abaye says one praying should always associate himself with the congregation, saying, for example, "May it be your will, O Lord *our* God, to lead *us* forth in peace etc."
49. Chrysostom, *Homilies of S. John Chrysostom on the Gospel of Matthew*, 1:293 (Homily 19); see also Betz, *Sermon on the Mount*, 388–89, who says "our Father" serves to join the worshiper together with other human beings.
50. Dibelius, *Sermon on the Mount*, 74.

"kingdom" is essential to any Jewish benediction prayer. The Talmud says, "Any benediction in which there is no mention of 'kingdom' is no benediction" (*b. Ber.* 40b). Targums to Isa. 31:4; 40:9; and Zech. 14:9 all await the defeat of Israel's enemies and the coming of God's kingdom upon the inhabitants of earth. A Midrash looks for the coming of the kingdom in the messianic age (*Cant. Rab.* 2:13). When God's kingdom comes in fullness, throughout the whole creation, evil will be overcome and Satan will be no more (*As. Mos.* 10:1).

your will be done, on earth as it is in heaven. May also God's will, carried out by holy ones in heaven, who stand at hand and foot ever ready to execute his words, become a reality on earth. For background, see the Prologue to the Blessing of Moses in Deut 33:2-5.[52]

11. Give *us this day our daily bread.* The last three petitions are concerned with human needs, and the most basic human need is that of "bread." Hebrew לחם can also mean "food." Proverbs 30:8 says, "feed me with the food (לחם) that I need. " Betz, however, thinks that the meaning here is even broader, referring to all the necessities for sustaining life.[53] The Greek word ἐπιούσιος is not attested in Greek literature before the Gospels, and its etymology is uncertain. "Daily" is the probable rendering. Jerome took it to mean "tomorrow's bread,"[54] but recognized that there are those who thought of it as the present day's food (cf. 6:34: "Do not worry about tomorrow"). Chrysostom says it is bread for one day, citing 6:34.[55] Betz renders the phrase, "Our daily bread give us today."[56] But Krister Stendahl says the bread is related to the future, and in the light of

51. Betz, *Sermon on the Mount*, 390.
52. See discussion of Deut. 33:1-5 in Lundbom, *Deuteronomy: A Commentary*, 919–25.
53. Betz, *Sermon on the Mount*, 377, 399.
54. Jerome, *Commentary on Matthew*, 88–89.
55. Chrysostom, *Homilies of S. John Chrysostom on the Gospel of Matthew*, 1:295–96 (Homily 19).
56. Betz, *Sermon on the Mount*, 379, 396.

the Qumran texts it may anticipate the messianic banquet (8:11). His translation: "Give us our bread today and tomorrow = day by day."[57] There could also be an allusion here to the manna in the wilderness, which was collected daily, but on the day before the Sabbath was collected for two days, since on the following day none could be gathered (Exod. 16:13-30).

12. And *forgive us our debts, as we also have forgiven our debtors.* Luke has "our sins" (Luke 11:4), but since "debts" (ὀφειλήματα) and "sins" (ἁμαρτίας) are often synonymous in Jewish liturgy,[58] the difference may not be that significant.[59] F. Charles Fensham thinks Jesus may have in mind the debt remission law in Deut. 15:2. In the ancient world it was common for a creditor to sell a debtor and/or his family into slavery. But this law in Deuteronomy remitted debts of a fellow Hebrew in the seventh year.[60] We are talking, then, about debts that cannot be repaid and must therefore be forgiven.[61] This petition asks God to forgive our (unrepayable) debts/sins,[62] which in light of Jesus' sacrificial death on the cross, becomes an accomplished fact for the world (John 3:16), fulfilling Jeremiah's new covenant promise (Jer. 31:31-34).[63]

There is no condition in this petition.[64] The two clauses are simply meant to hang together: we ask for God's forgiveness, and we are

57. Stendahl, "Matthew," 778; see earlier Stendahl, "Prayer and Forgiveness," SEÅ 22-23 (1957-58): 81-83.
58. B. Cohon, *Jacob's Well*, 82.
59. Abrahams, *Studies in Pharisaism and the Gospels*, 95; Augustine takes the two to be the same; see "Our Lord's Sermon on the Mount" in *Nicene and Post-Nicene Fathers*, 42; *Preaching of Augustine*, 119.
60. F. Charles Fensham, "The Legal Background of Mt. VI 12," *NovT* 4 (1960): 1-2. The debt remission law of Deuteronomy is taken to be the background also by Lachs, *Rabbinic Commentary on the New Testament*, 121-22.
61. Betz, *Sermon on the Mount*, 380.
62. *Exodus Rabbah* 31:1 says there is no creature that is not indebted to God; therefore, God must forgive former misdeeds.
63. See discussion of the new covenant passage in Lundbom, *Jeremiah 21-36*, 474-479.
64. Abrahams (*Studies in Pharisaism and the Gospels*, 95-96) thinks that Matthew does make a conditional connection between human forgiveness and God's, which he says is without Jewish

expected to forgive others. In rabbinic teaching, sins against God are forgiven on the Day of Atonement, where also the sins between one person and another are forgiven, but only if a one has become reconciled with his friend (*b. Yom.* 8:9). Abrahams notes that never does a synagogue prayer assign any limits to divine mercy, nor is human repentance a condition for God's pardon (except for what was just said about the Day of Atonement).[65] God's forgiveness is a unilateral act of mercy; he can and does forgive anyone at any time. Abrahams notes, however, what is said in Isa. 55:7, to which we might add Jer. 36:3 and Sir. 28:2-4. The latter says:

> Forgive your neighbor the wrong he has done,
>
> and then your sins will be pardoned when you pray.
>
> Does anyone harbor anger against another,
>
> and expect healing from the Lord?
>
> If someone has no mercy towards another like himself,
>
> can he then seek pardon for his own sins? (NRSV)

So, while it is true that God forgives a nation or an individual when they come to him in repentance, forgiveness can still be extended by God without prior repentance, which is the promise of the new covenant. It is the very nature of divine grace and mercy that it can be extended either with or without human merit.[66] One will recall Jesus' words on the cross: "Father, forgive them; for they do not know what they are doing" (Luke 23:34). Still, this is not the end of the matter. Jesus' parable of the unmerciful servant shows that, while God's forgiveness is prior and without condition, if the servant goes out and is unwilling to forgive his debtor, he is in for harsh judgment (Matt. 18:23-35).

---

parallel. But he depends here largely on vv. 14-15, Matt. 18:23-35; Mark 11:25-26; and Sir. 28:2.

65. Abrahams, *Studies in Pharisaism and the Gospels*, 97.

66. See David Noel Freedman and Jack R. Lundbom, "חנן *ḥnn*," in *TDOT* 5:22-36.

13. *And do not bring us to the time of trial.* Or: *And lead us not into temptation.* Perhaps the most difficult phrase in the Lord's Prayer, raising as it does the question of theodicy, that is, God's justification in light of evil in the world. The word translated "temptation" (πειρασμός) can also mean "trial" or "test,"[67] which are the more neutral terms used to translate Hebrew נסה in the LXX.[68] In the Old Testament God puts human individuals to the test, as we know from the story of Adam and Eve, from God's command that Abraham sacrifice his son, and from the trials that the good Job was made to endure. We see something similar happening when God tests Moses in the wilderness after the people have made a golden calf (Exod. 32:7-14; Deut. 9:13-14, 25-29). God proposes that the people be destroyed and he begin all over again with Moses. Moses wisely rejects the proposal, not only because of the deliverance of Israel from Egypt but, more importantly, because of God's unilateral covenant with Abraham to make his descendants as numerous as the stars of heaven and give them a land as an inheritance. It would be clearly wrong for God to undo this covenant, sworn in his own name. God then relents and Moses passes the test. Testings carried out by God occurred on other occasions, and continue to occur into the present day.

A Midrash says that God tests only according to the power of a person's endurance. Rabbi Jonathan used the example of a potter testing a clay vessel, a flax worker beating flax, or one yoking an ox. The potter will not test a defective vessel, lest with a single blow it break; the flax worker will not beat flax of inferior quality, lest it split; and one will not yoke a weak ox, only a strong one. Similarly, God does not test the wicked, only the righteous (but see Ps. 11:5) (*Gen. Rab.* 32:3). Paul makes a similar point when he tells the Corinthians,

---

67. Liddell and Scott, *Greek-English Lexicon*, 1355, s.v. πειρασμός.
68. BDB, 650, s.v. נסה.

"God is faithful, and he will not let you be tested / tempted beyond your strength, but with the testing / temptation will also provide the way out so that you may be able to endure it" (1 Cor. 10:13). In Luke, Jesus is quoted as saying, "Temptations to sin are sure to come, but woe to him by whom they come" (Luke 17:1 RSV), assuming a source of temptation other than God.

Still, it seems in the present petition that God may be the one who leads a person into testing / temptation, which comes dangerously close to the idea that evil originates with God. The Tempter par excellence is otherwise Satan (for example, Jesus is tempted by Satan in the wilderness; Matt. 4:1-11). The Greek word πειρασμός should probably be translated "temptation" here, since God can and does lead people into trials or testings, but he will not lead them into temptation, which is what the petition asks for. If one does translate the Greek as "trial" or "test," then Stendahl's paraphrase makes the best sense: "Do not put us to that ultimate test where no-one can stand" (cf. 24:22).[69] Stendahl says that the question whether God sends temptation is hardly involved; the accent is rather on the trial of the chosen one. But in Betz's view, the ultimate cause of temptation can only be God.[70]

James has a somewhat different view of God's testing, treating it as a "muscle-building" exercise preparing one for the crown of life (James 1:2-4, 12-15; 5:11). Compare Paul's view of suffering in Rom. 5:3-5. Perhaps building on Sir. 15:11-20, James rejects the idea that temptations come from God. He says:

> Let no one say when he is tempted, "I am tempted by God"; for God cannot be tempted with evil and he himself tempts no one; but each person is tempted when he is lured and enticed by his own desire. Then

---

69. Stendahl, "Matthew," 779.
70. See the excellent discussion in Betz, *Sermon on the Mount*, 410–13.

desire when it has conceived gives birth to sin; and sin when it is full
grown brings forth death. (James 1:13-15 RSV)

Nevertheless, good parallels to this petition exist in the Talmud and
Jewish *Prayer Book*. In a Talmudic prayer before going to bed the
supplant asks that God grant him to lie down in peace, and that God
not accustom him to transgression, not bring him into sin or iniquity
or contempt, and that the good inclination (יצר הטוב), not the evil
inclination (יצר הרע), have sway over him (*b. Ber.* 60b). In another
rabbinic prayer, the petitioner prays:

> May it be your will, O Lord, our God, to deliver us from the impudent
> and from impudence, from an evil man, from evil hap, from the evil
> impulse (יצר הרע), from an evil companion, from an evil neighbor,
> and from the destructive Accuser; from a hard lawsuit and from a hard
> opponent, whether he be a son of the covenant or not a son of the
> covenant. (*b. Ber.* 17a)

In the Jewish *Prayer Book* is this prayer: "Lead us not into sin or
transgression, iniquity, temptation or disgrace. Let not the evil
inclination dominate us."[71]

but rescue us from the evil one. Or: but rescue us from evil. Chrysostom
translates "from the Evil One" (cf. 5:37).[72] This brings in an allusion
to Satan, who always remains under God's rule (Betz: "God keeps
Satan on a leash") but nevertheless keeps busy tempting individuals
or finding fault with them (Job 1:6-12).[73] Betz thinks there is no
reference here to the devil, but rather to the subject matter of evil.[74]
Reference may also be to the rabbinic notion of the "evil inclination"
(יצר הרע), which is the propensity to sin in each individual.[75] In

71. Singer, *Daily Prayer Book*, 7 (1992: 18).

72. Chrysostom, *Homilies of S. John Chrysostom on the Gospel of Matthew,* 1:298 (Homily 19).

73. On Satan as the accuser of a person before God, see *Exod. Rab.* 31:2.

74. Betz, *Sermon on the Mount,* 380.

75. Abrahams, *Studies in Pharisaism and the Gospels,* 105; Lachs, *Rabbinic Commentary on the New Testament,* 122.

any case, interpretation here is no problem. We want or should want God's deliverance from evil or one causing evil. "Bring us not into temptation" and "deliver us from evil/the Evil One" are associated in Talmudic prayers (*b. Ber.* 60b).[76]

(For the kingdom and the power and the glory are yours forever. Amen.) The best and oldest ancient manuscripts of Matthew lack this doxology, and Luke 11:4 omits it. It is generally taken to be a later addition, quarried possibly from 1 Chron. 29:11.[77] However, it does appear in many Greek manuscripts and in the *Didache* (8:2), suggesting a date before 100 C.E. It was normal in Judaism to conclude prayers with a doxology. This one anticipates the messianic banquet, according to Stendahl, since "all the accounts of the institution of the Lord's Supper contain the eager look towards the coming of the kingdom" (cf. 26:29).[78]

14-15. *For if you forgive others their trespasses, your heavenly Father will also forgive you; but if you do not forgive others, neither will your Father forgive your trespasses.* Here a condition is put on God's forgiveness in v. 12, apparently building on the conclusion to the parable of the unmerciful servant (Matt. 18:28-35; cf. Mark 11:25-26).[79]

16. *And whenever you fast, do not look dismal, like the hypocrites, for they disfigure their faces so as to show others that they are fasting. Truly I tell you, they have received their reward.* In the Old Testament, fasting is a response to national emergencies, such as the death of a king (1 Sam. 31:13; 2 Sam. 1:12), a military defeat or military threat (Judg. 20:26; 2 Chron. 20:3; Jer. 36:6), a plague (Joel 1:14), or a drought

76. Abrahams, *Studies in Pharisaism and the Gospels,* 105.
77. Stendahl, "Matthew," 779; Lachs, *Rabbinic Commentary on the New Testament,* 122; Betz, *Sermon on the Mount,* 414, with reservations. In his view, the doxology derives from Jewish and Christian liturgy and was inserted into some manuscripts at a later time.
78. Stendahl, "Matthew," 779.
79. Jeremias, *Sermon on the Mount,* 25-26.

(Jer. 14:12). There is no clear evidence for fixed days of fasting in preexilic Israel or Judah, except possibly the Day of Atonement (Lev. 16:29, 31; 23:27, 32; Num. 29:7), where "afflict oneself" is thought to be a technical term for "carry out fasting."[80] Fixed days of fasting came in the postexilic period, when the destruction of Jerusalem was remembered (Zech. 7:3, 5; 8:19; Esther 9:31). At that time, the Day of Atonement also called for fasting and other privations (*m. Yom.* 8:1). A fast meant abstinence from food for the entire day, from sunrise to sunset (as Muslims do during the month of Ramadan). The Pharisees and John the Baptist also fasted on other days,[81] but Jesus did not lay this discipline on his disciples because the messianic age had dawned and they were friends of the bridegroom; it was therefore a time of joyous celebration (Matt. 9:14-17; Mark 2:18-22; Luke 5:33-38). Jesus, however, fasted during his forty days in the wilderness (Matt. 4:2), and told his disciples they would fast after he was gone. In the following verses he does permit fasting, but only with washed faces and anointed heads to keep the ritual secret. Fasting continues to be practiced in the church,[82] particularly during the forty days of Lent, but signs of mourning have returned.

Fasting comes dangerously close to the primitive (and pagan) idea, existing among people ancient and modern, of "excit[ing] the pity of a god by a spectacle of distress."[83] Such is a form of manipulation, forcing the god to act, the sort of thing practiced by the Baal prophets on Mount Carmel, who mutilated themselves in praying for rain

---

80. Lundbom, *Jeremiah 21–36*, 593.

81. S. Cohon ("Place of Jesus in the Religious Life of His Day," 96–97) calls these "extra fasts." Lachs (*Rabbinic Commentary on the New Testament*, 125) calls the fasts of the Pharisee in Luke 18:12 "private fasts," carried out twice a week, usually on Mondays and Thursdays (cf. *Did.* 8:1). On public fasts in Judaism, see Moore, *Judaism*, 2:55–69.

82. The *Didache* (8:1) says Christians should not fast with the "hypocrites" (Jews) on Mondays and Thursdays, but rather on Wednesday and Friday.

83. Moore, *Judaism*, 2:67. See also Alan Dundes, "Summoning Deity through Ritual Fasting," in Dundes, *Analytic Essays in Folklore* (The Hague and Paris: Mouton, 1975), 146–50.

(1 Kgs. 18:28). Desperate measures of this magnitude, as well as self-mutilations practiced in connection with rituals of mourning, were roundly condemned in the Old Testament as unbecoming of a people holy to the Lord God (Deut. 14:1-2). We have something similar in the modern day with prisoners going on hunger strikes to call attention to their plight and to force a change in their treatment, or effect a release.

they disfigure their faces. The ritual of grief and mourning included wearing sackcloth and putting ashes on the face to make one unsightly. Christians today have foreheads marked with ashes on Ash Wednesday. Jerome thought that the hypocrites disfigured their faces in order to feign sadness: though their heart was rejoicing, they wore a look of sorrow on the face.[84]

17-18. *But when you fast, put oil on your head and wash your face, so that your fasting may be seen not by others but by your Father who is in secret; and your Father who seeks in secret will reward you.* Jesus rejects the external display but permits fasting in secret with washed faces and heads anointed. Such will earn a reward from the Father. Jewish tradition forbade these symbols of joy as being inconsistent with fasting, especially on the Day of Atonement (*m. Yom.* 8:1).[85] Augustine, too, could not imagine fasting with washed face and an anointed head, so he took these precepts symbolically to refer to one's inner being.[86] David fasted over his sick child, but when the child died he ceased to fast, washed his face, and anointed himself (2 Sam. 12:15b-23). For a harsh critique of fasting in the Old Testament, see Isa. 58:1-14.

---

84. Jerome, *Commentary on Matthew*, 89.
85. S. Cohon, "Place of Jesus in the Religious Life of His Day," 96–97.
86. Augustine, "Our Lord's Sermon on the Mount," 47; *Preaching of Augustine*, 134.

Where Your Treasure Is (6:19-21)

¹⁹*"Do not store up for yourselves treasures on earth, where moth and rust consume and where thieves break in and steal;* ²⁰*but store up for yourselves treasures in heaven, where neither moth nor rust consumes and where thieves do not break in and steal.* ²¹*For where your treasure is, there your heart will be also.*

The remaining teachings of chapter 6 have a common theme, which is singleness of heart and vision in serving God and others. The first has to do with one's treasure, which Jesus says not to lay up on earth, but in heaven.

19. *Do not store up for yourselves treasures on earth, where moth and rust consume and where thieves break in and steal.* After rejecting excessive fasting for his disciples, Jesus now turns to a rejection of excessive indulgence in the accumulation of worldly possessions.[1] No lasting treasure can be stored on earth. Moths, then as today,

---

1. Betz, *Sermon on the Mount*, 429.

destroy unused woolen garments, and over time rust consumes metal objects. Krister Stendahl notes that the Greek word for "consume" (ἀφανίζει) is the same word that is translated "disfigure" in v. 16, and he thinks it could be a catchword bringing the two sayings together. Archaeologists have found hoards of coins hidden beneath floors and other secret places in ancient houses. Then, as now, thieves break in and steal. The Greek verb διορύσσουσιν (lit., "dig through") refers to entering houses made of mud-brick.

Jewish teachers are often uncomfortable with this portion of the Sermon. Gerald Friedlander calls it "The Un-Jewish Asceticism in the Gospels,"[2] believing that Jesus taught asceticism as the ideal rule of life, displayed an antipathy to wealth, and believed one should avoid all cares and ambitions. In his view, this was the dominant note struck in the Middle Ages as well as in the first four centuries of Christianity, with Origen and St. Francis being the most famous examples. Friedlander said the Jewish view was that "wealth *per se* is neither good nor evil."[3] Beryl Cohon agrees, saying that "depreciation of wealth and worldly goods as something intrinsically sinful is at variance with Rabbinic teaching. The Rabbis saw in wealth a means of doing good as well as evil."[4]

The caricature is overdrawn. Yes, Jesus warns here and elsewhere against an excessive reliance on riches, for example in the parable about the man who tears down barns to build larger ones (Luke 12:16-20), which in Luke's Gospel immediately precedes the teaching about "not being anxious for your life." This parable concludes: "So it is with those who store up treasures for themselves but are not rich toward God" (Luke 12:21). There is no evidence of asceticism in the Gospels.[5] Concluding one of the next teachings on

2. Friedlander, *Jewish Sources of the Sermon on the Mount*, 166–81.
3. Friedlander, *Jewish Sources of the Sermon on the Mount*, 169.
4. B. Cohon, *Jacob's Well*, 87.

"not worrying about your life," Jesus says, "and all these things will be given to you as well" (6:33). It is a question of priorities, not of living an ascetic life.

20. *but store up for yourselves treasures in heaven, where neither moth nor rust consumes and where thieves do not break in and steal.* No conflict here with Jewish teaching. Treasures laid up in heaven are exempt from perishability.[6] See Prov. 22:1-2:

> A good name is to be chosen rather than great riches,
>> and favor is better than silver or gold.
> The rich and the poor have this in common;
>> the LORD is the maker of them all.

And again, Prov. 30:7-8:

> Two things I ask of you;
>> Do not deny them to me before I die:
> Remove far from me falsehood and lying;
>> give me neither poverty nor riches;
>> feed me with the food that I need.

For the Psalmist, too, God's law is better than "thousands of gold and silver pieces" (Ps. 119:72). And from the prophet Jeremiah:

> Let not the wise man boast of his wisdom,
>> and let not the strong man boast of his strength,
>> and let not the rich man boast of his riches;
> But the one who boasts let him boast of this:
>> that he understands and knows me,

---

5. Adolf Harnack, *What Is Christianity?* (trans. Thomas Bailey Saunders; London: Williams & Norgate, 1901), 87–88.
6. Betz, *Sermon on the Mount*, 433.

for I Yahweh practice steadfast love,
justice and righteousness in the earth,
for in these I delight.
(Jer 9:23-24 AB)

In the Apocrypha and Pseudepigrapha is the oft-repeated idea that the person who works righteousness upon earth has a treasure in heaven/ with God. Sirach says:

Lay up your treasure according to the commandments
of the Most High,
and it will profit you more than gold.
Store up almsgiving in your treasury,
and it will rescue you from every disaster.
(Sir. 29:11-12 NRSV)

Laying up treasure here consists of almsgiving.[7] In Tobit, sharing one's possessions with others lays up a good treasure for some future day of necessity:

If you have many possessions, make your gift for them in proportion; if few, do not be afraid to give according to the little you have; so you will be laying up a good treasure for yourself against the day of necessity. (Tob. 4:8-9 NRSV)

See also *T. Levi.* 13:5: "Do righteousness, my son, upon earth, that you may have treasure in heaven," as well as other rabbinic writings.[8] Joachim Jeremias says regarding the present teaching, "It is not a question of contrasting earthly with heavenly treasure, but of the

---

7. See also *Vis. Ezra* 4-7, 8-10, 64 (*OTP* 1:587, 590); *T. Job* 9-13, 44 (*OTP* 1:842–44, 863).
8. *Exodus Rabbah* 31:3, 6; cf. *Slav. En.* 50:2-5; *2 Bar.* 14:12; *4 Ezra* 7:77; 8:33, 36.

place where the treasure is stored."[9] Samuel Lachs adds, "Wealth given away is wealth stored away."[10]

The theme of "heavenly treasure" was well known to Philo, who in light of Deut. 28:12 spoke about God's heavenly treasury of blessings and other good things.[11] Philo believed that the treasury of evil things were in ourselves; with God were only good things. Therefore, we cannot blame God for our sins (*Fug.* 79-80). Human beings can store up true wealth in heaven, whose adornment is wisdom and godliness, and have their store-houses filled because of the providence and good care of God (*Praem.* 104). What one must not do is hoard great stores of silver and gold in his house, "but bring it out for general use that he may soften the hard lot of the needy with the unction of his cheerfully given liberality" (*Spec. leg.* 4.74).

The rabbinic literature, too, contains the idea that a treasury exists in heaven where the pious have a store of good works.[12] The Talmud says that "all the works of Hillel were for the sake of heaven" (*b. Beṣ.* 16a). The wicked, by contrast, store up in this treasury an accumulation of evil deeds, which will be revealed on the great day of judgment.[13] A Midrash says that for one who treasures up religious acts and good deeds, behold, there is Paradise; while for the one who does not lay up righteous acts and good deeds, behold, there is Gehenna (*Gen. Rab.* 9:9).

The Gospel of Mark records an incident where a rich young man came to Jesus and asked what he must do to inherit eternal life. Jesus

---

9. Joachim Jeremias, *The Parables of Jesus* (rev. ed.; trans. S. H. Hooke; New York: Charles Scribner's Sons, 1963), 202 n. 50.

10. Lachs, *Rabbinic Commentary on the New Testament*, 126.

11. Massey, *Interpreting the Sermon on the Mount*, 167. See Philo, *Mig.* 121; *Deus.* 156; *Cher.* 48; *Her.* 76.

12. A. Marmorstein, *The Doctrine of Merits in Old Rabbinical Literature* (Jews' College, London: Publication 7; London: Jews College, 1920), 20-21. See *Deut. Rab.* 2:23; *Ecc. Rab.* 12:14, 1; *T. Levi* 13:5; *T. Naph.* 815.

13. See T^{Nf} and T^{PsJ} on Deut. 32:34.

cited the commandments. The man had observed them all from the time of his youth. Jesus then told him to go, sell his possessions and give the proceeds to the poor, and then he would have treasure in heaven. After that, he could become Jesus' disciple. The man departed crestfallen, for he had many possessions (Mark 10:17-22).

21. *For where your treasure is, there your heart be also.* Common wisdom. With the emphasis here being on singleness of heart and purpose, Søren Kierkegaard said that "purity of heart is to will one thing." [14]

14. Søren Kierkegaard, *Purity of Heart Is to Will One Thing* (trans. Douglas V. Steere; New York: Harper & Bros., 1948).

17

Single-Mindedness to God and Others
(6:22-24)

²²"The eye is the lamp of the body. So, if your eye is healthy, your whole body will be full of light; ²³but if your eye is unhealthy, your whole body will be full of darkness. If then the light in you is darkness, how great is the darkness! ²⁴No one can serve two masters; for a slave will either hate the one and love the other, or be devoted to the one and despise the other. You cannot serve God and wealth.

Here are two brief teachings, one on the healthy (or single) eye, the other on the impossibility of serving two masters—God and wealth (or Mammon). They lead into the final climactic teaching about seeking first the kingdom of heaven.

22-23. *The eye is the lamp of the body. So, if your eye is healthy, your whole body will be full of light; but if your eye is unhealthy, your whole body will be full of darkness.* We move now from the heart to the eye, both of which contribute disproportionately to bodily wholeness according to ancient psychology. The present teaching appears also in Luke 11:33–36, where it is combined with the "let your light shine" teaching of the Sermon (Matt. 5:15).

Ancient people understood the eye to be the aperture through which light was admitted into the body.[1] The body was something like a vessel that remained dark unless illuminated. A healthy eye illuminated the body; an unhealthy eye left the body in darkness.[2] The healthy eye is here called the "single (ἁπλοῦς) eye" in Greek, which was rendered into Latin as the "simple (simplex) eye." Greek ἁπλοῦς translates the Hebrew adjective תם, meaning "complete, sound, wholesome, having integrity, and so on (cf. Job 1:8; 2:3)."[3] The "single eye" is therefore a good, sound, healthy eye, which in the Bible denotes not so much a physical property of vision, but rather generous or liberal giving.[4] Someone with a "good eye" (טוב־עין) shares his bread with the poor (Prov. 22:9). The present teaching thus pairs nicely with the "treasures in heaven" teaching immediately preceding, which lifts up the generous giving of one's earthly possessions.

A "single eye" may also indicate single-mindedness, and, if so, a link is created with the next teaching on single-minded service to God. Still, the present teaching is difficult for the modern mind to grasp. We do not speak today of a "single/good/sound/healthy eye" in the way ancient people did, nor do we use "evil eye," which also figures into the interpretation, in ways the ancients did. The evil eye was diseased, or worse yet, possessed with magical power to cause disease.[5] In the Bible the "evil eye" denotes an envious, stingy, or

---

1. McKenzie, "Matthew," 74.
2. Betz, Sermon on the Mount, 451.
3. BDB, 1070, s.v. תם.
4. Benjamin W. Bacon, "The 'Single' Eye," The Expositor 8th Series 7 (1914): 279–84; Stendahl, "Matthew," 779.
5. On the ancient idea among primitive people that some individuals possess an "evil eye" that has the power to bewitch, and that these poisonous glances produce disease that eventually

grudging attitude on the part of one toward another (Prov. 23:6; 28:22; Tob. 4:7; Sir. 14:3-10).[6] Mention of the "evil eye" occurs only in Deuteronomy among the books of the Pentateuch (Deut. 15:9; 28:54, 56),[7] where reference is to a grudging attitude toward one in need. In our culture, generosity is expressed by the open palm, and its opposite by the closed fist.[8]

In the New Testament, Jesus tells a parable highlighting a grudging attitude toward a generous owner who overpaid hired laborers (Matt. 20:15). And in Mark 7:20-23, the "evil" or "sick" eye (ὀφθαλμὸς πονηρός) is listed together with evil thoughts, fornication, theft, murder, adultery, coveting, wickedness, deceit, licentiousness, slander, pride, and foolishness as evils coming from the heart that defile a person. The term is translated "envy" in the RSV, the more usual rendering, but it could also mean "closefistedness" or "greed."[9] In Rom. 12:8, Paul uses the adverb ἁπλῶς to mean "(giving with) generosity." James, too, speaks about God giving to all "generously (ἁπλῶς) and ungrudgingly" (James 1:5).

Jewish literature abounds in expressions of "the good eye" and "the evil eye," many of which refer, as in the Bible, to the opposite characteristics of generosity and envy/a grudging attitude.[10] The "good eye" is the "single eye," denoting single-mindedness or righteous living (T. Iss. 3:4).[11] The "evil eye" is the "evil inclination" (m. Ab. 2:11 [P. Ab. 2:15]). A generous spirit makes one a disciple of Abraham, which brings benefits both in this world and in the World

causes death, see Aaron Bray, "The Evil Eye among the Hebrews," in The Evil Eye: A Folklore Casebook (ed. Alan Dundes; New York and London: Garland, 1981), 45.

6. C. J. Cadoux, "The Evil Eye," ET 53 (1941–42): 354–55.

7. David Daube, "The Culture of Deuteronomy," Orita 3 (1969): 51.

8. Henry J. Cadbury, "The Single Eye," HTR 47 (1954): 73.

9. Cadoux, "Evil Eye," 355.

10. Friedlander, Jewish Sources of the Sermon on the Mount, 182; cf. m. Ab. 2:9 (P. Ab. 2:12-13); 2:11 (P. Ab. 2:15); and 5:13 (P. Ab. 5:16); b. B. Bat. 118a; b. Sot. 36b; Exod. Rab. 31:17.

11. Friedlander, Jewish Sources of the Sermon on the Mount, 184.

to Come. The grudging spirit makes one a disciple of Balaam, who will go on to inherit Gehenna (*m. Ab.* 5:19). But in some Talmudic texts the "evil eye" has become a malevolent power that harms people or causes their death, and amulets must be worn to ward off this power.[12] This is a widespread belief in ancient and certain modern cultures. The rabbinic literature contains both ideas side by side.[13]

If then the light in you is darkness, how great is the darkness! Another piece of common wisdom, which will be understood by everybody (cf. Job 18:5-6).

24. *No one can serve two masters; for a slave will either hate the one and love the other, or be devoted to the one and despise the other.* Single-mindedness is here transparent, where a seemingly proverbial statement lifts up the problem of divided loyalties. The sharp antithesis of "love" and "hate," what Søren Kierkegaard calls the "terrible battlefield" in a person's inner being,[14] is common in the Hebrew language (Gen. 29:30-31; Deut. 21:15-17; Mal. 1:2-3; Rom. 9:13), lacking as it does in particles expressing "more than" and "less than." There is also a chiasmus in the terms "hate/love/devoted/despise."[15] Luke 16:13 has "no slave can serve two masters," suggesting that Jesus has in mind a slave owned by two masters.[16] The idea has been questioned, but co-ownership of slaves at the time is possible.[17]

you cannot serve God and wealth. Or: "God and Mammon." The lesson to be drawn from this proverb is that the disciple cannot have divided loyalty. It is a trap leading to self-destruction. "Mammon"

12. See *b. B. Meş*, 107b; *b. Sanh.* 93a; *Gen. Rab.* 45:5; 53:13; *Lev. Rab.* 17:3; *Num. Rab.* 12:4.
13. Cadoux, "Evil Eye," 355.
14. Søren Kierkegaard, *Consider the Lilies* (trans. A. S. Aldworth and W. S. Ferrie; London: C. W. Daniel, 1940), 63.
15. Betz, *Sermon on the Mount*, 455.
16. Lachs, *Rabbinic Commentary on the New Testament*, 129.
17. Betz, *Sermon on the Mount*, 456.

(μαμωνᾶ) in the rabbinic literature refers to wealth, money, interest, and property,[18] and with property the connotation is not always bad.[19] Jerome notes that riches in Syriac are called "mammon."[20] Here the term is personified, becoming a pseudo-god.[21] "Jewish moralists point out that man's deepest love of God need not necessarily involve the hatred of wealth. One can serve God through one's wealth."[22] Nevertheless, Mammon can put one in opposition to God. What the Jewish sages warn against is becoming a slave to wealth, which includes money and other possessions (*T. Jud.* 18:6; 19:1; *T. Iss.* 4:1-6). This is the teaching in Sirach (31:5-11), who says that the person who loves gold (= mammon) will not be justified and will be led astray by it. But the rich person will be found blameless if he does not lust after gold. Sirach ends by saying that what counts will be acts of charity. The *Testament of Judah* says:

> Guard yourselves therefore, my children, against sexual promiscuity and love of money . . . for these things distance you from the law of God, blind the direction of the soul, and teach arrogance. They do not permit a man to show mercy to his neighbor. . . . For two passions contrary to God's command enslave him, so that he is unable to obey God: They blind his soul, and he goes about in the day as though it were night. (*T. Jud.* 18:2-6)[23]

Jerome says that one cannot serve Christ and riches at the same time, noting that Jesus does not say, "he who has riches," but "he who serves riches" (cf. 1 Tim. 6:10: "For the love of money is a root of all kinds of evil"). Kierkegaard notes that the birds and the lilies have not the anxiety of irresolution, fickleness, and disconsolateness, and

---

18. Lachs, *Rabbinic Commentary on the New Testament*, 130.
19. Stendahl, "Matthew," 779; cf. *m. Sanh.* 1:1; 3:1.
20. Jerome, *Commentary on Matthew*, 90.
21. Betz, *Sermon on the Mount*, 454-459.
22. Friedlander, *Jewish Sources of the Sermon on the Mount*, 186.
23. *OTP* 1:800.

can therefore be our teachers. The Christian, too, does not have these anxieties, for he has only one master.[24]

---

24. Søren Kierkegaard, "The Anxieties of the Heathen," in *Christian Discourses and the Lilies of the Field and the Birds of the Air and Three Discourses at the Communion on Fridays* (trans. Walter Lowrie; London: Oxford University Press, 1939), 83–93. See also the three discourses on "What it means to be a man" in Kierkegaard, *Consider the Lilies*.

18

Be Not Anxious about Your Life (6:25-34)

25"*Therefore I tell you, do not worry about your life, what you will eat or what you will drink, or about your body, what you will wear. Is not life more than food, and the body more than clothing?* 26*Look at the birds of the air; they neither sow nor reap nor gather into barns, and yet your heavenly Father feeds them. Are you not of more value than they?* 27*And can any of you by worrying add a single hour to your span of life?* 28*And why do you worry about clothing? Consider the lilies of the field, how they grow; they neither toil nor spin,* 29*yet I tell you, even Solomon in all his glory was not clothed like one of these.* 30*But if God so clothes the grass of the field, which is alive today and tomorrow is thrown into the oven, will he not much more clothe you—you of little faith?* 31*Therefore do not worry, saying, 'What will we eat?' or 'What will we drink?' or 'What will we wear?'* 32*For it is the Gentiles who strive for all these things; and indeed your heavenly Father knows that you need all these things.* 33*But strive first for the kingdom of God and his righteousness, and all these things will be given to you as well.* 34*So do not worry about tomorrow, for tomorrow will bring worries of its own. Today's trouble is enough for today.*

25. Therefore I tell you, do not worry about your life, what you will eat or what you will drink, or about your body, what you will wear. Is not life more than food, and the body more than clothing? This teaching appears also in Luke 12:22-33. It speaks about food, drink, and clothing, the most basic of human needs, and Jesus says not to be anxious about them. Søren Kierkegaard says the teaching is nevertheless addressed to the anxious: "Yea, in every line of this anxious gospel we can feel that it speaks not to the hale, not to the strong, not to the happy, but to the anxious."[1] Anxiety must not be passed over lightly, particularly among those living in poverty or near poverty. A Midrash says there is nothing in the world more grievous than poverty—the most terrible of all sufferings. One Jewish sage has said, "All sufferings are on one side, and poverty is on the other" (*Exod. Rab.* 31:12).

Jesus, in his parables and as a result of probing deeply into the lives of people, shows himself to be much concerned with worry, or the more serious ill, anxiety.[2] Yes, he perceived it among the poor, but he also saw worried looks on the faces of the rich, or those seeking to become rich.[3] Some were concerned with troubles that came with Roman occupation, or with talk about the end-times, or simply with ordinary and everyday concerns of life. In Luke the present teaching is preceded by the parable of the rich fool (Luke 12:16-21), which makes a silent tie-in between anxiety and the lust for riches. In God's economy, life consists of more than this.

Jesus and later New Testament writers would have people freed from worry and anxiety: Matt. 13:22/Mark 4:19/Luke 8:14 (parable of the sower); Matt. 10:19 (persecution); Luke 10:41 (Martha); Luke 21:34 (end-times); 1 Cor. 7:32-34 (marriage in crisis times); Phil.

---

1. Kierkegaard, *Consider the Lilies*, 14.
2. D. M. Baillie, "How Jesus Dealt with Worry (Mt. vi. 19-34)," *ET* 39 (1927–28): 443–47.
3. See Kierkegaard's essays on "the anxiety of poverty" and "the anxiety of abundance" in "The Anxieties of the Heathen" (*Christian Discourses*, 17–39).

4:6. Peter says, "Cast all your anxiety on him [God], because he cares for you" (1 Pet. 5:7). Paul is more positive—but only slightly so—in assessing anxiety about the affairs of the Lord (1 Cor. 7:32-34), his own concern for the churches (2 Cor. 11:28), and Timothy's anxiety for the welfare of the church at Philippi (Phil. 2:19-20). Kierkegaard thus concludes that Christians are to live without life's many anxieties.[4]

The Psalmist expresses anxiety over the wicked, but he rests assured that God will console his troubled soul, bring justice to bear, and destroy the wicked (Psalms 37; 55; 94). His advice:

> Cast your burden on the LORD,
>   and he will sustain you;
> he will never permit
>   the righteous to be moved. (Ps. 55:22)

Sirach, too, says that one should not be given over to anxiety; it brings premature old age (Sir. 30:24); if the anxiety is over wealth, it will keep one awake at night (Sir. 31:1-4). In the Talmud is another saying attributed to Sirach that does not exist in the book of Sirach that we possess. He says:

> Do not worry over tomorrow's evil, for you know not what today will bring forth. Tomorrow perhaps you will not be (alive), and you would have worried for a world which would not be yours. (b. Sanh. 100b)[5]

Tobit counsels his wife not to be anxious about their son while he is gone on a journey (Tob. 5:17-22; 10:1-7), and a Talmudic passage deals with a father's anxiety over perils that his daughter may face (b. Sanh. 100b). 2 Esdras 2:27 says one should not be anxious about

---

4. Kierkegaard, "Anxieties of the Heathen," 17–93.
5. See Montefiore, *Rabbinic Literature and Gospel Teachings*, 144.

the great day of tribulation and anguish, which is to come; some will weep and be sorrowful, but others will rejoice and have abundance.

26. *Look at the birds of the air; they neither sow nor reap nor gather into barns, and yet your heavenly Father feeds them.* Jesus bids one to look upward at the birds of the air. Kierkegaard says they can be our teacher—our silent teacher. The Psalmist notes that ravens are fed by God (Ps. 147:9), and Job notes, too, that birds, beasts, plants, and fish of the sea would tell you, if you asked them, that the life of every living thing rests secure in the hand of God (Job 12:7-10; 35:11; cf. Ps. 104:10-12). In the rabbinic literature, Rabbi Eleazar is reported to have said, "Have you ever seen a wild beast or a bird who has a trade? Yet they get along without difficulty" (*m. Qid.* 4:14).[6] It is true that birds, beasts, and other living creatures do not have to learn a trade; nevertheless, they still busy themselves getting food. T. H. Robinson says with regard to the birds, "Few men have to work as hard for their living as the average sparrow."[7] Birds also busy themselves with building nests, and feeding their young.

barns. Greek ἀποθήκας actually means "granaries" (Jer. 50:26; LXX 27:26).

Are you not of more value than they? An *a minori ad maius* ("How much more") argument, with Jesus building on the creation theology of Gen. 1:26-28 and, perhaps, on Psalm 8. Jesus elsewhere views humans as the apex of God's creation, ranking higher than many sparrows or a single sheep (Matt. 10:31; 12:12). For another *a minori ad maius* argument making the same point as here, see Jonah 4:10-11. Humans, too, are sustained by the care of a gracious God (Ps. 145:15-16), but, like the birds, are not to be indolent (2 Thess. 3:6-13).

---

6. See also *b. Qid.* 82b. The romantic Kierkegaard (*Consider the Lilies*, 54–57) wants to make the point, too, that "birds do not work."
7. Robinson, *Gospel of Matthew*, 59.

27. *And can any of you by worrying add a single hour to your span of life?* RSV: "add one cubit to his span of life." The cubit is a measurement of length, from the elbow to the tip of the middle finger (around eighteen inches). The word in the Greek (ἡλικία) refers to stature in Luke 2:52 and 19:3, but here it becomes a measurement of time. There is nothing unusual about applying a measurement of length to age in Ps. 39:5. Jesus asks rhetorically if anxiety will prolong life. The answer is obvious: No, it will not.

28. *And why do you worry about clothing? Consider the lilies of the field, how they grow; they neither toil nor spin.* Jesus now directs one's gaze downward, to the lilies growing at one's feet. Greek κρίνα τοῦ ἀγροῦ is "(white) lilies in the wild/field,"[8] an Old Testament Hebraism denoting "wild flowers" (Cant. 2:16; 4:5; 6:2-3; cf. Ps. 103:15 [LXX 102:15]: ἄνθος τοῦ ἀγροῦ). The Greek verb καταμανθάνω ("consider, examine closely")[9] occurs nowhere else in the New Testament but appears frequently in the LXX (e.g., Gen. 24:21). Kierkegaard lays particular emphasis on this word. He says:

> Consider the lily, look how it stands so graceful at thy foot, do not disdain it; is it not waiting for thee to rejoice in its loveliness? Look how it sways hither and thither, shaking itself free of everything, in order to retain its grace! Look how it freshens with the fresh breeze, and seems to move away, that it may resume its stillness and rejoice in its happy existence![10]

Our advice to hurried and over-busy people is, "Stop and smell the roses."

The lilies neither toil nor spin. Luke in some ancient manuscripts has "they neither spin nor weave" (Luke 12:27), which is the activity required in making clothes. Kierkegaard is impressed that both birds

---

8. Liddell and Scott, *Greek-English Lexicon*, 15, s.v. ἀγρός; 996, s.v. κρίνον.
9. Liddell and Scott, *Greek-English Lexicon,* 900.
10. Kierkegaard, *Consider the Lilies*, 42; cf. 16.

of the air and lilies of the field keep silent. "Silence shows deference to anxiety, and to the man who is anxious" (cf. Job 2:13).[11]

29. *yet I tell you, even Solomon in all his glory was not clothed like one of these.* Solomon became proverbial for his great wealth (1 Kgs. 10:14-29; 2 Chron. 9:13-28). Josephus recalls it (*Ant.* 8.190), and the rabbinic literature cites the lavish meals served at his table.[12] Much toil and spinning must have gone into making Solomon's elegant robes;[13] still, they are no match for the lilies of the field.

30. *But if God so clothes the grass of the field, which is alive today and tomorrow is thrown into the oven, will he not much more clothe you—you of little faith?* Lilies and wild flowers clothe the grass of the field, but all lasts only a short time, and is gone (Isa. 40:6-8). Kierkegaard says:

> Oh, truly there is beauty, and there is youth and loveliness, in Nature, truly there is endless variety, and thronging life, and there is gaity and joy; but there is also, as it were, a deep, unfathomable grief; yet none of the creatures out there even suspects it, and just this fact, that none of them suspects it, is what man finds pathetic. So to be lovely, so to bloom, so to flutter about, so to build with the beloved; so to live—and to die so![14]

Will not God then clothe his children? Another argument *a minori ad maius*. The idea of God clothing humans occurs early in the Bible (Gen. 3:21). But they, too, like the lilies of the field, are here today and gone tomorrow. It happens to the high and the lowly, often with great suddenness.[15] Sirach says, "The king of today will die tomorrow" (Sir. 10:19).[16]

11. Kierkegaard, *Consider the Lilies*, 14-15.
12. *M. B. Meṣ.* 7:1; *b. 'Erub.* 41a; *b. Ta'an* 29b; cf. 1 Kgs 10:5.
13. Betz, *Sermon on the Mount*, 478.
14. Kierkegaard, *Consider the Lilies*, 60.
15. See David Daube, *The Sudden in the Scriptures* (Leiden: Brill, 1964).
16. This aphorism is repeated in *b. Ber.* 32b.

you of little faith! A "mild reproach," says Kierkegaard, "far from wounding, far from vexing, far from casting down, [but] rather lifts up and gives encouragement."[17] "You of little faith" occurs a number of times in the rabbinic writings.[18] In the Talmud is this word attributed to R. Eliezer the Great:

> Whoever has a piece of bread in his basket and says, "What shall I eat tomorrow?" belongs only to them who are little in faith. (*b. Sot.* 48b)

Jesus is always astonished to see in people—often non-Jews—great faith (Matt. 8:10/Luke 7:9; 15:28; Mark 2:5), and he is just as astonished to find others with such little faith (Matt. 6:30/Luke 12:28; Matt 8:26/Luke 8:25; 14:31; 16:8; 17:20). Nevertheless, faith as little as a grain of mustard seed can uproot trees and move mountains (Matt. 21:21-22/Luke 17:5-6). Jesus wonders when the Son of man comes, will he find faith on earth? (Luke 18:8). The great man of faith in the Bible is Abraham (Romans 4; Gal. 3:6, 9; James 2:21-23; cf. Gen. 15:6; 22:1-14), and the great biblical passage on the march of the faithful is in Hebrews (Heb. 11:1—12:2).

31-32. *Therefore do not worry, saying, 'What will we eat?' or 'What will we drink?' or 'What will we wear?' For it is the Gentiles who strive for all these things; and indeed your heavenly Father knows that you need all these things.* Gentiles here are portrayed as anxious disbelievers in the providence of God. Paul has a somewhat different take on the Gentiles in Rom. 2:14-16. Kierkegaard says the birds and lilies do not have the anxieties of the "heathen" (= Gentiles), which are anxieties about poverty, abundance, lowliness, highness, presumption, self-torment, irresolution, fickleness, and disconsolateness.[19] In regard to

---

17. Kierkegaard, *Consider the Lilies*, 43–44.
18. Friedlander, *Jewish Sources of the Sermon on the Mount*, 194; cf. *b. Sot.* 48b; *b. Pes.* 118a; *b. 'Ar.* 15a; *b. Ber.* 24b.
19. Kierkegaard, "Anxieties of the Heathen," 17–93.

prayer, Jesus said earlier that God knows human needs even before they ask him (6:8). It is so with regard to food and drink.

33. *But strive first for the kingdom of God and his righteousness, and all these things will be given to you as well.* Better: "seek first" (RSV). Hans Dieter Betz points out that the disciples are to be "seekers," which precludes simply sitting and waiting for what God gives.[20] Kierkegaard says the flower does not seek anything.[21] He goes on to say that "seeking first" means making a beginning, for many a "hard beginning." Here in Matthew the word "righteousness," which occurs earlier in 5:6, 10, and 20, is added to "kingdom." Both are key terms in Matthew's Gospel and in the Sermon. They are brought together also in Paul, who says, "For the kingdom of God is not food and drink but righteousness and peace and joy in the Holy Spirit" (Rom. 14:17). Luke does not have "righteousness" (Luke 12:31). If the disciples seek first God's kingdom and righteousness, these other needs—and they are basic needs—will be taken care of. This is no invitation to live the ascetic life, not even as practiced by John the Baptist, for whom Jesus had the highest praise (11:7-11). Jesus is talking about priorities, and to get these straight is to live an abundant life.[22]

34. *So do not worry about tomorrow, for tomorrow will bring worries of its own. Today's trouble is enough for today.* Greek κακία is usually rendered "evil," but here is better translated "trouble." As Jerome points out, Jesus is talking not about the opposite of virtue but rather the toil and affliction and anguish of the world.[23]

---

20. Betz, *Sermon on the Mount*, 482–83.
21. Kierkegaard, *Consider the Lilies*, 67.
22. Dibelius (*Sermon on the Mount*, 49–50) does not think Jesus is promising worldly things for life in the here and now. The kingdom, in his view, has only eschatological meaning, and so Jesus is telling his followers "to seek the kingdom of God and nothing else." But if the kingdom comes before the end of the world, which it certainly does, one can seek it first and receive all one needs in the here and now.
23. Jerome, *Commentary on Matthew*, 92.

This verse is not found in Luke and appears to be a later addition. It has the sound of a proverb, particularly since sentiments of a similar nature occur in many wisdom texts. In the Old Testament is this proverb: "Do not boast about tomorrow, for you do not know what a day may bring " (Prov. 27:1). In the New Testament, James gives this cautionary word to those overly eager to increase their holdings:

> Come now, you who say, 'Today or tomorrow we will go to such and such a town and spend a year there, doing business and making money,' yet you do not even know what tomorrow will bring. What is your life? For you are a mist that appears for a while and then vanishes. (James 4:13-14)

This wisdom about tomorrow is old and widespread, found not only in classical sources but in texts from ancient Egypt.[24] From Egypt are these words of advice:

> Prepare not for the morrow before it arrives; one knows not what mischance may be in it. ("The Protests of the Eloquent Peasant," *ANET*[3], 409)

> One does not know what may happen, so that he may understand the morrow. ("The Instruction of Vizer Ptah-Hotep," *ANET*[3], 413)

> Do not spend the night fearful of the morrow. At daybreak what is the morrow like? Man knows not what the morrow is like. ("The Instruction of Amen-em-opet," *ANET*[3], 423)

The rabbis, too, taught that one should not be anxious over tomorrow:[25]

> Let not anxiety enter your heart, for it has slain many a person. (*b. Sanh.* 100b)

---

24. J. Gwyn Griffiths, "Wisdom about Tomorrow," *HTR* 53 (1960): 219–21.
25. Friedlander, *Jewish Sources of the Sermon on the Mount*, 209.

Moses said: Lord of the Universe, sufficient is the evil in the time thereof. (*b. Ber.* 9b)

19

———

Beware of Making Judgments (7:1-5)

7 ¹*"Do not judge, so that you may not be judged.* ²*For with the judgment you make you will be judged, and the measure you give will be the measure you get.* ³*Why do you see the speck in your neighbor's eye, but do not notice the log in your own eye?* ⁴*Or how can you say to your neighbor, 'Let me take the speck out of your eye,' while the log is in your own eye?* ⁵*You hypocrite, first take the log out of your own eye, and then you will see clearly to take the speck out of your neighbor's eye.*

1-2. *Do not judge, so that you may not be judged.* How one reads these words makes all the difference. One must not extrapolate the first two words, "Do not judge," and assume that this contains the essence of the teaching. Nor should one read the phrase in its entirety and conclude that people are to refrain from all judgments, lest they, too, be judged—by others, and more importantly by God. Both miss the point because they fail to grasp the idiom. What is more, they fail to interpret these initial words by what is said in the larger context of vv. 1-5.

Life requires that we make judgments, not only on evils of various description but on people behaving badly.[1] Paul is thinking along the same lines when he says to "speak the truth in love" (Eph. 4:15). In the present teaching, Jesus is simply issuing a warning—and a very important warning—that we not judge others in such a manner that the judgment ends up coming down upon our own head, applying rather to us than to the one we are judging. Paul tells the church in Rome, "Therefore you have no excuse, whoever you are, when you judge others; for in passing judgment on another you condemn yourself, because you, the judge, are doing the very same things" (Rom. 2:1). Jesus is teaching pretty much the same thing in the Golden Rule (7:12).

Jewish literature, on the whole, emphasized "judging favorably" rather than "not judging," where the goal was to assess another's conduct in a good way, that is, "on the side of merit."[2] Nevertheless, the Talmud contained these admonitions:

> Rabbi Nathan said: "Do not taunt your neighbor with the blemish you yourself have." (*b. B. Meṣ.*59b)

> Rabbi Hanan said: "He who invokes the judgment of Heaven against his fellow is himself punished first." (*b. B. Qam.* 93a)

For with the judgment you make you will be judged, and the measure you give will be the measure you get. "The "measure-for-measure" principle appears also in Mark 4:24 and Luke 6:37-38, where the latter has the same teaching as here. In the Old Testament it was the justice meted out to the Canaanite king Adonibezek, whose thumbs and big

---

1. This was recognized by Jerome (*Commentary on Matthew*, 92–93); see also George S. Hendry, "Judge Not: A Critical Test of Faith," *Theology Today* 40 (1983): 113, 119.
2. Montefiore, *Rabbinic Literature and Gospel Teachings*, 145.

toes were cut off as punishment for what he did to seventy other kings, making them pick up scraps of food under his table without aid of either (Judg. 1:6-7). The "measure-for-measure" principle was applied often by the rabbis, being found in the Targums (Gen. 38:25; Lev. 26:43; Isa. 27:8),[3] as well as in other Jewish literature.[4] Jesus employs it in his parable of the unmerciful servant (Matt. 18:23-35). This principle is basically the *lex talionis* ("law of retaliation") rule of the Old Testament (Exod. 21:23-25; Lev. 24:18-20; Deut. 19:21), also well attested in ancient Near Eastern law.[5]

3. *Why do you see the speck in your neighbor's eye, but do not notice the log in your own eye?* Hyperbole in a rhetorical question aimed at pointing up the hypocrisy in judgments people make. For more Oriental exaggeration in the teachings of Jesus, see Matt. 19:24: "It is easier for a camel to go through the eye of a needle than for someone who is rich to enter the kingdom of God"; and Matt. 23:24: "You strain out a gnat but swallow a camel." What does the "log" consist of? Obviously, the same thing represented by the "speck" (= wood splinter) in the neighbor's eye, or something similar. Betz says, "Human nature, being what it is, tends to exaggerate the flaws of others and to overlook one's own flaws. This is true especially among relatives and friends."[6]

neighbor. Or "brother" (RSV). In Matthew a "brother," except where a blood brother is meant, is a Christian brother (5:22-24, 47; 7:3-5; 18:15, 21).[7] Inclusive language of today would require that we add "sister." Betz thinks that in the Sermon it identifies fellow Jews outside the group of disciples.[8]

---

3. T^{Nf} Gen. 38:25; T^{Nf} Lev. 26:43; T Isa. 27:8.

4. Montefiore, *Rabbinic Literature and Gospel Teachings*, 144–45; Massey, *Interpreting the Sermon on the Mount*, 74–89; cf. Wis. 11:15-20; 12:23-27; 18:4-11; *m. Sot.* 1:7.

5. See Lundbom, *Deuteronomy: A Commentary*, 574–75, on Deut 19:21.

6. Betz, *Sermon on the Mount*, 492.

7. Davies, *Setting of the Sermon on the Mount*, 98.

4. *Or how can you say to your neighbor, 'Let me take the speck out of your eye,' while the log is in your own eye?* A follow-up rhetorical question, shifting now from seeing the speck to doing something about it. In the Talmud is preserved this exchange between a judge and a man: "If the judge said to a man, 'Take the splinter from between your eyes (or teeth),' he would retort, 'Take the beam from between your eyes'" (*b. B. Bat.* 15b).[9] The same exchange occurs elsewhere in the Talmud, where Rabbi Eleazar ben Azariah is said to have exclaimed, "I wonder if there is one in this generation who knows how to reprove" (*b. 'Ar.* 16b). Another Talmudic admonition is: "Trim yourselves, and then trim others" (*b. B. Bat.* 60b).

5. *You hypocrite, first take the log out of your own eye, and then you will see clearly to take the speck out of your neighbor's eye.* This is the necessary corrective to judgments that apply more to ourselves than to those we are judging. Judgments on others are permissible once a bit of self-examination has taken place. Our judgments will then be more reasonable and more gentle.

You hypocrite. The key word in Jesus' teaching. Hypocritical behavior is unacceptable to everyone. The subject of hypocrisy is given fuller treatment in chapter 23. On the term *hypocrite* in the Sermon and elsewhere in Matthew, see note for 6:2.

8. Betz, *Sermon on the Mount*, 492.
9. The Talmudic text has "your eyes," but some suggest that the original reading was "your teeth"; see George Brockwell King, "The Mote and the Beam," *HTR* 17 (1924): 393–404.

20

Give Not Away What is Holy (7:6)

[6]*"Do not give what is holy to dogs; and do not throw your pearls before swine, or they will trample them under foot and turn and maul you.*

6. *Do not give what is holy to dogs; and do not throw your pearls before swine, or they will trample them under foot and turn to maul you.* This saying has no apparent connection with what precedes. The two may be linked by catchwords: ἐκβάλω in 7:4–5, and βάλλω in 7:6.[1] The verse is chiastic in structure:[2]

Do not give what is holy to *dogs*;
and do not throw your pearls before *swine,*
or they [the *swine*] will trample them under foot
and [the *dogs*] will turn to maul you.

1. Betz, *Sermon on the Mount,* 495.
2. John Jebb, *Sacred Literature* (London: T. Cadell & W. Davies, 1820), 338–39; Lund, *Chiasmus in the New Testament,* 32; T. F. Glasson. "Chiasmus in St. Matthew vii. 6," *ET* 68 (1956–57): 302.

Swine are those who will trample pearls under foot, and (mad) dogs are those who will turn and maul you. Swine rend no one. On "dogs" as a metaphor for shameless and relentless persecutors, see Ps. 22:16-18, a passage that later came to be applied to the crucifixion of Christ. Dogs and swine were considered unclean animals in antiquity.[3] Both are spoken of disparagingly in 2 Pet. 2:22, where, as Jerome points out, the swine are unworthy of what is holy because after being washed they only return to wallowing in the mud.[4] Unthinkable, too, is a gold ring in a swine's snout (Prov. 11:22). Jerome interprets what 2 Pet. 2:22 says about dogs, that they return to their own vomit, to refer perhaps to people who have come to faith in Christ, but then return to (the vomit of) their former sins. Paul combines "dogs" with "evil workers" in Phil. 3:2, and in Rev. 22:15 "dogs" along with other evildoers are seen to be outside the heavenly Jerusalem.

The two animals were sometimes used in Jewish literature to refer metaphorically to the Gentiles (= nations, heathen), but, according to Israel Abrahams, only when referring to Gentile wickedness and idolatrous behavior.[5] Nations of the world are compared to dogs in Isa. 56:11, where they are said to be greedy but not wicked. Jesus used "dogs" in a disparaging sense when answering the Syrophoenician woman who wanted her demon-possessed daughter healed. He appeared unwilling at first, saying, "It is not fair to take the children's food and throw it to the dogs." But her response was quick and witty: "Yes, Lord, yet even the dogs eat the crumbs that fall from their masters' table." Jesus was astonished, commended her for having great

---

3. Augustine, "Our Lord's Sermon on the Mount" in *Nicene and Post-Nicene Fathers*, 57; *Preaching of Augustine*, 162; Stendahl, "Matthew," 780; Betz, *Sermon on the Mount*, 498. Dogs eat carrion (*Gen. Rab.* 45:9), making them unclean (cf. Deut. 14:12-18).

4. Jerome, *Commentary on Matthew*, 93.

5. Abrahams, *Studies in Pharisaism and the Gospels*, 195; cf. Montefiore, *Rabbinic Literature and Gospel Teachings*, 152.

faith, and then healed the daughter (Matt. 15:22-28; Mark 7:24-30). The "children" here are Jews, and the "dogs" Gentiles.[6] Samuel Lachs thinks that here in the Sermon "dogs" refers to the Samaritans, and "swine"—or wild boars, in his opinion—to the Romans.[7]

The question has often been asked why Jesus might not want his teachings given to everyone. An interesting passage in the rabbinic literature (*j. Ab. Zar.* ii. 8, 41d), which is based on a fanciful interpretation of Exod. 21:1, says the following:

> Even as a treasure must not be shown to everyone, so with the words of the Law: one must not go profoundly into them except in the presence of suitable people.[8]

On not showing treasures to everyone, one is reminded of Isaiah's rebuke to Hezekiah for showing all the royal treasures to visiting messengers of the Babylonian king (2 Kgs. 20:12-19).

In the Gospels, one's first impression is that Jesus wants the good news of the kingdom to get out to everyone. Does he not reach out to the Samaritan woman at Jacob's well, tell the parable of the Good Samaritan, heal finally the young girl in Tyre-Sidon, and in other ways view the messianic age as one where Gentiles are to be included in God's plan of salvation? Yes, but he does indicate, on certain occasions, that his ministry was only to "the lost sheep of the house of Israel" (Matt. 10:6; 15:24), and it seems he did not want certain of his teachings divulged to everyone.

When the disciples ask Jesus why he speaks in parables, he answers, "To you it has been given to know the secrets of the kingdom of heaven, but to them it has not been given" (Matt 13:10-11 ; cf. Luke 8:9-10). In the Lukan version, God's word to Isaiah at the time of his call is quoted: this word, though precious, will go to people who see

---

6. Betz, *Sermon on the Mount*, 498.
7. Lachs, *Rabbinic Commentary on the New Testament*, 139.
8. Montefiore, *Rabbinic Literature and Gospel Teachings*, 146.

but will not see, to people who will hear but not hear (Isa. 6:9-10). When the Seventy returned with glowing reports of the success of their mission, Jesus warned them about rejoicing in their own power over demons, but then prayed this prayer: "I thank you, Father, Lord of heaven and earth, because you have hidden these things from the wise and the intelligent and have revealed them to infants; yes, Father, for such was your gracious will" (Luke 10:21). On another occasion, Peter asked Jesus if he is telling a parable "for us or for everyone?" (Luke 12:41), again indicating that some teachings were only for the disciples, not for everyone.

Eusebius, the early church historian, made this statement: "Beware that nothing tempt you to divulge publicly what I disclose to you, nor cast it before the profane, either for the sake of renown, or gain, or any other unholy solicitation." He then quoted the pagan philosopher Porphyry (234–305 C.E.), who said about oracular secrets:

> Such communication must be imparted to those who regulate their lives, in order to promote the salvation of the soul. Let my communication be preserved as the "unutterable" of secrets, because the gods through oracles have not spoken with clearness concerning themselves, but through enigmas. (*Eus. Prep.* 89)

what is holy . . . pearls. What is it that is holy? We are not told. The "pearls" could be Jesus' teachings on the kingdom (13:45), or his teachings in the Sermon,[9] and, if so, we would have to assume that on some these teachings will be wasted. The *Didache* (9:5) interprets the present cautionary word to mean not admitting the unbaptized to the thanksgiving meal (= Eucharist). Betz thinks that for the early

---

9. Betz, *Sermon on the Mount*, 498.

church the imagery will be referring to heretics,[10] but that originally Jesus' cautionary word had to be more general.

10. Betz, *Sermon on the Mount*, 500.

21

Ask and It Will Be Given You (7:7-12)

7"Ask, and it will be given you; search, and you will find; knock, and the door will be opened for you. 8For everyone who asks receives, and everyone who searches finds, and for everyone who knocks, the door will be opened. 9Is there anyone among you who, if your child asks for bread, will give a stone? 10Or if the child asks for a fish, will give a snake? 11If you then, who are evil, know how to give good gifts to your children, how much more will your Father in heaven give good things to those who ask him! 12In everything do to others as you would have them do to you; for this is the law and the prophets.

7. *Ask, and it will be given you; search, and you will find; knock, and the door will be opened for you.* We are back now to prayer. Jesus is speaking here to people who do not pray, or who are reluctant to pray, the same audience to whom his parable of the persistent widow was told (Luke 18:1-8), and his parable of the importune friend at midnight, which in Luke immediately precedes the teaching given here (Luke 11:5-13). Not every request will be granted, or granted in

the way the petitioner asks, but God's goodness is ever available and should be actively sought. God answers prayer; the rabbis believed it, and so did Jesus.[1] On "ask, and it will be given you," see Ps. 2:8 and Deut. 32:7; on "search / seek, and you will find," see Prov. 8:17; Jer. 29:13; Isa. 55:6; 1 Chron. 28:9; 2 Chron. 15:2; Luke 15:8-9; and on "knock, and the door will be opened to you," see Cant. 5:2; Luke 12:36; 13:25; Acts 12:13; Rev. 3:20. The Talmud talks of "knocking at the gates of mercy," and they being opened to one (*b. Meg.* 12b).

8. *For everyone who asks receives, and he who searches finds, and for everyone who knocks the door will be opened.* A general truth, but not something to be made into an absolute rule. If it were made an absolute rule, Christianity would be reduced to pagan and primitive religion, where one seeks to manipulate the deity to get whatever one wants. Even then, manipulation will not get the desired result (cf. 1 Kgs. 18:25-29). Betz comments, "The saying calls attention to an astonishing fact: while doors are usually locked, they surprisingly open when one simply knocks at the door."[2]

9. *Is there anyone among you who, if your child asks for bread, will give a stone?* A rhetorical question, the answer to which is obvious: No one! But the Roman writer Seneca (d. 65 C.E.) had this to say about offering bad bread:

> Fabius Verrucosus used to say that a benefit rudely given by a hard-hearted man is like a loaf of gritty bread, which a starving man needs must accept, but which is bitter to eat. (*Benef.* 2.7.1)

10. *Or if the child asks for a fish, will give a snake?* Another rhetorical question. Two in succession have more impact than one. Jesus often gave two teachings in succession—sometimes three—to make a single point (Matt. 13:24-50; Luke 13:18-21; 14:27-33; 15:3-32).

---

1. Montefiore, *Rabbinic Literature and Gospel Teachings*, 147.
2. Betz, *Sermon on the Mount*, 504.

11. *If you then, who are evil, know how to give good gifts to your children, how much more will your Father in heaven give good things to those who ask him!* Another argument *a minori ad maius*, containing a gentle censure of human parents, even though he calls them "evil." In good Hebrew rhetorical style, Jesus himself supplies the answer his hearers are too embarrassed to give.[3] That humanity is evil is noted elsewhere in the Sermon (5:11, 39, 45; 6:13; 7:15, 18, 23), and yet good things come from people who are evil.[4]

12. *In everything do to others as you would have them do to you; for this is the law and the prophets.* The so-called Golden Rule, occurring also in Luke 6:31, which appears to develop from Lev. 19:18: "You shall love your neighbor as yourself."[5] The Rule may also be rooted in the "law of retaliation" (*lex talionis*), although the two are not the same. If the Golden Rule were recast in terms of the law of retaliation, it would go: "Do to others as they do to you,"[6] and the Rule calls for considerably more than this.

In this commandment the whole of the Sermon is summed up.[7] And more. Hans Dieter Betz says that here the Sermon is pointing beyond itself, referring not only to the ethical discussions of 5:17–7:11 but to an endless number of other issues. The Rule is a general principle for all ethical decision making. Betz goes on to point out that humanity being what it is, there will be some "risk

---

3. On the figure of *hypophora* in Jeremiah, where the prophet answers his own rhetorical questions, often double questions, see Lundbom, *Hebrew Prophets*, 193–94; cf. Lundbom, *Jeremiah 37–52: A New Translation with Introduction and Commentary* (AB 21C; New York: Doubleday, 2004), 591.

4. Betz, *Sermon on the Mount*, 506.

5. T^{PsJ} Lev. 19:18: "You shall love your neighbor, so that what is hateful to you, you shall not do to him"; cf. Augustine, "Our Lord's Sermon on the Mount" in *Nicene and Post-Nicene Fathers*, 59; *Preaching of Augustine*, 170; George Brockwell King, "The 'Negative' Golden Rule," *JR* 8 (1928): 274, who thinks Hillel may have had Lev. 19:18 in mind when he came up with his negative form of the dictum.

6. Betz, *Sermon on the Mount*, 512–13.

7. Davies, "Matthew 5, 17–18," 430.

taking" in following the Rule, but one must nevertheless take the risk.[8] The Rule in negative form occurs in Tobit: "And what you hate, do not do to anyone" (Tob. 4:15), also in the dictum of Hillel: "What is hateful to you, do not to your neighbor; that is the whole Torah, while the rest is commentary: go and learn it" (b. Shab. 31a). Hillel gave this as an answer to a heathen proselyte who wanted to learn the whole Torah while standing on one foot. Philo repeated the same principle,[9] and so did Rabbi Akiba.[10] Sirach's equivalent, like the Golden Rule, was positive: "Judge your neighbor's feelings by your own" (Sir. 31:15). Admonitions of a similar nature occur in the Pseudepigrapha (Slav. En. 61:1; Let. Arist. 207), Targums,[11] Mishnah, Talmud (b. B. Meṣ. 59b; b. B. Qam. 93a), and also in non-Jewish literature.[12] In the Mishnah:

> Eliezer says: "Let the respect owing to your fellow be as precious to you as the respect owing to yourself." (m. Ab. 2:10 [P. Ab. 2:14])

In classical literature the following have been preserved:

> Aristotle: "For a man is supposed not to reproach others with what he does himself." (Art Rhet. ii 6:19)

> Herodotus: "I will not myself do that which I account blameworthy in my neighbor." (Hist. 3.142)

> And: "I will not do that which I blame in you." (Hist. 7.136)

> Isocrates: "Do not do to others that which angers you when they do it to you." (Nic. 61)

---

8. Betz, *Sermon on the Mount*, 516–19.

9. Abrahams, *Studies in Pharisaism and the Gospels*, 21, although he does not think Philo's source is Jewish.

10. Montefiore and Loewe, *Rabbinic Anthology*, 172–73.

11. T^{PsJ} on Lev 19:34, regarding the sojourner: "so that what you hate for yourself you will not do to him."

12. Abrahams, *Studies in Pharisaism and the Gospels*, 18–29; King, " 'Negative' Golden Rule," 268–79.

There has been much discussion over the relative merits of the positive and negative forms of the dictum, and which, if any, is better. It is generally concluded that, while there may well be psychological support for extolling the good, there is really little difference between the two, and one should not be considered superior to the other. Both say essentially the same thing.[13]

for this is the law and the prophets. That is, the Golden Rule summarizes everything known thus far about God's will for humankind, similar to Hillel's "this is the whole Torah . . . the rest is commentary." Paul, quoting Lev. 19:18, says, "love is the fulfilling of the law" (Rom. 13:9-10).

13. King, " 'Negative' Golden Rule," 275–77.

22

Enter Through the Narrow Gate (7:13-14)

[13]*"Enter through the narrow gate; for the gate is wide and the road is easy that leads to destruction, and there are many who take it.* [14]*For the gate is narrow and the road is hard that leads to life, and there are few who find it.*

13. *Enter through the narrow gate; for the gate is wide and the road is easy that leads to destruction, and there are many who take it.* The road is "broad" (not "easy") that leads to destruction. This segment of Sermon on the Mount teaching appears also in Luke 13:24. The "two ways" teaching is a wisdom theme, well known from the Old Testament and elsewhere. It occurs in Psalm 1 and dominates the early chapters of Proverbs, where men are warned against following the way of fools and taking the path to houses of seductive women, being told instead to walk in integrity and fall in love with Lady Wisdom (Proverbs 1–9). We have the teaching also in Joshua's speech to Israel just before his death. He says to the people:

Choose this day whom you will serve, whether the gods your ancestors served in the region beyond the River, or the gods of the Amorites in whose land you are living; but as for me and my household, we will serve the LORD. (Josh. 24:15)

And then there is the mighty Elijah, who says to the people:

How long will you go limping with two different opinions? If the LORD is God, follow him, but if Baal, then follow him. (1 Kgs. 18:21)

"Walking in the way" has strong ethical implications in the Old Testament,[1] especially in Deuteronomy, where "walking in the Lord's way" applies broadly to the whole of life, whether of individuals or the Israelite nation. It translates into loving, serving, and fearing the Lord, but above all it means keeping the commandments (Deut. 5:33; 6:7; 8:6; 10:12; 11:19, 22; etc.). Walking in the Lord's way leads to life, increase, and blessing (Deut. 30:16); turning aside, seen most blatantly in going after other gods, leads to death (Deut. 11:28). In Psalm 119, too, blessing comes to the one who walks in the law of the Lord (v. 1).

The best example of a "two ways" teaching in the Old Testament occurs in Deut. 30:15-20, where Moses tells the Israelite people assembled in the plains of Moab:

See, I have set before you today life and prosperity, death and adversity. If you obey the commandments of the LORD your God[2] that I am commanding you today, by loving the LORD your God, walking in his ways, and observing his commandments, decrees, and ordinances, then you shall live and become numerous, and the LORD your God will bless you in the land that you are entering to possess. But if your heart turns away and you do not hear, but are led astray to bow down to other gods and serve them, I declare to you today that you shall perish; you shall not live long in the land that you are crossing the Jordan to enter and

---

1. James Muilenburg, *The Way of Israel: Biblical Faith and Ethics* (New York: Harper & Row, 1961).
2. Supplied with the LXX.

possess. I call heaven and earth to witness against you today that I have set before you life and death, blessings and curses. Choose life so that you and your descendants may live, loving the LORD your God, obeying him, and holding fast to him; for that means life to you and length of days, so that you may live in the land that the LORD swore to give to your ancestors, to Abraham, to Isaac, and to Jacob.

Jeremiah recasts the Deuteronomic teaching in an oracle to King Zedekiah, where the way to life becomes surrendering to the Babylonians, and the way to death becomes holding out in Jerusalem (Jer. 21:8-10). Other "two ways" teachings are found in Jer. 6:16 and 42:7-22.

The "two ways" teaching occurs a number of times in the pseudepigraphical literature.[3] In the *Testament of Abraham* is a near parallel to the teaching here. The archangel Michael takes Abraham in a chariot to the first gate of heaven:

> And Abraham saw two ways. The first way was strait and narrow and the other broad and spacious. [And he saw there two gates. One gate was broad], corresponding to the broad way, and one gate was strait, corresponding to the strait way. And outside the two gates of that place, they saw a man seated on a golden throne. And the appearance of that man was terrifying, like the Master's. And they saw many souls being driven by angels and being led through the broad gate, and they saw a few other souls and they were being brought by angels through the narrow gate. . . . And when [the wondrous one] sees many souls entering through the strait gate, then he arises and sits on his throne rejoicing and exulting cheerfully, because the strait gate is (the gate) of the righteous, which leads to life, and those who enter through it come into Paradise. . . . And when he sees many souls entering through the broad gate, then he pulls the hair of his head and casts himself on the ground crying and wailing bitterly; for the broad gate is (the gate) of the sinners, which leads to destruction and to eternal punishment. (*T. Abr.* 11)[4]

---

3. See *Slav. En.* 30:15 (*OTP* 1:152); *Sib. Or.* 8: 399-401 (*OTP* 1: 427); *4 Ezra* 7:3-15 (*OTP* 1:536–37); *T. Abr.* 11 (*OTP* 1:888); *T. Ash.* 1:3-9 (*OTP* 1:816–17).
4. *OTP* 1:888.

The "two ways" teaching occurs in other Jewish literature, at Qumran, in the Targums, and in writings of the early church.[5] Many examples are known also from Greek literature and philosophy.[6] The Qumran *Manual of Discipline* (1QS 1:1-15) admonishes members of the sect to "no more walk in the stubbornness of a guilty heart, [but] walk blamelessly before God"; and to "love the children of light and hate the children of darkness."[7] Another Qumran text has turned up (4Q473) containing the "two ways" teaching. The relevant lines:

> He sets [before you life and death(?) . . . before you are] t[wo] ways, one goo[d and one evil. If you walk in the good way He will guard you(?)] and bless you. But, if you walk in the [evil] way, [He will curse you and revile you(?), and evil] He will br[ing] upon you and destroy you [. . .], and blight, snow, ice, and hai[l . . .] with all the angel[s of destruction(?) . . .][8]

Philo has thoughts on the "two ways," where for him the "way to virtue" is the road of choice and, in the end, he found the road to be easily traveled. He says:

> But there are some men of diligence and effort, who at first think the way leading to virtue rough and steep and difficult, but for whom later on the all-bountiful God renders it a highway, transforming the bitterness of their toil into sweetness. (*Post.* 154 [LCL])

In another work:

> But the roads of sound-sense and self mastery and of all the other virtues, if not untrodden, are at all event unworn; for scanty is the number of those that tread them, that have genuinely devoted themselves to the

---

5. Sebastian Brock, "The Two Ways and the Palestinian Targum," in *A Tribute to Geza Vermes: Jewish and Christian Literature and History* (ed. Philip R. Davies and Richard T. White; JSOTSup 100; Sheffield: JSOT Press, 1990), 139–52.

6. Betz, *Sermon on the Mount*, 521–22.

7. Gaster, *Dead Sea Scriptures*, 47–48. Gaster notes that the Zadokite Document talks, too, about "walking in proper paths" (pp. 71–74).

8. T. Elgvin, "4Q473," in George J. Brooke et al., in consultation with James C. VanderKam, *Qumran Cave 4.XVII: Parabiblical Texts, Part 3* (DJD 22; Oxford: Clarendon, 1996), 292–94.

pursuit of wisdom, and entered into no other association than that with the beautiful and noble, and have renounced everything else whatever. (*Agr.* 104 [LCL])

Again, in discussing the incident in which Eli, the priest at Shiloh, thought the godly Hannah to be drunk (1 Sam. 1:15):

> For to the varlet, who thought to make a mock of her, for to him and to every fool the way to virtue seems rough and painful and ill to tread, and to this one of the old writers [i.e., Hesiod] has testified in these words:
> "Vice you may take by squadrons, but there lies
> 'Twixt you and virtue (so hath God ordained)
> Sore travail. Long and steep the road to her
> And rough at first; but—reach the top—and she,
> So hard to win! is now an easy prize." (*Ebr.* 150 [LCL])

Early Christians were said to belong to "the Way," which doubtless developed out of the teaching on the "two ways (Acts 9:2; 19:9; 24:14, 22). In the *Didache* (1:1-2) the "two ways" develops from the Golden Rule (v. 12):

> There are two paths, one of life and one of death, and the difference between the two paths is great. Path of life: love the God who made you, and second, love your neighbor as yourself. And whatsoever you do not want to happen to you, do not do to another.

For John Wesley the narrow road leading to heaven is the way of lowliness, mourning, meekness, holy desire, love of God and one's neighbor, doing good, and suffering evil for Christ's sake, the very things Jesus lifts up in the Beatitudes and in the Sermon. Those not teaching these are false prophets. False prophets teach the way of pride, of levity, of passion, of worldly desire, of loving pleasure more than God, of unkindness to one's neighbor, of unconcern for good works, and suffering no evil or persecution for righteousness' sake.[9]

---

9. John Wesley, *A Caution against False Prophets: A Sermon (Matt. vii. 15-20).* (London: New Chapel and at Mr. Wesley's Preaching Houses in Town and Country, 1789), 4–5. Betz (*Sermon*

In the nineteenth century the individual Christian life was depicted by many as a journey to the promised land, which was heaven. It developed classical form in John Bunyan's *The Pilgrim's Progress*, one of the most widely read books in the eighteenth and nineteenth centuries, and still read today with profit.[10] In this work, Pilgrim journeys from this world to the World to Come: setting out, encountering various dangers along the way, but finally arriving safely in the desired country.

Hymnody of the period, in the Pietistic and Evangelical tradition, reflects the same theme of "life as a pilgrimage." One verse of Isaac Watts's "Come We That Love the Lord":

> The hill of Zion yields a thousand sacred sweets
> Before we reach the heavenly fields,
> Before we reach the heavenly fields,
> Or walk the golden streets,
> Or walk the golden streets.
> We're marching to Zion, beautiful, beautiful Zion.
> We're marching upward to Zion, the beautiful city of God.
> (*CovH* 1950 #368)

Swedish Pietists sang O. A. Ottander's hymn, "As Pilgrims in This World" (Vi bo ej här):

> As pilgrims in this world where life is fleeting,
> We journey on to meet our dearest Friend.
> Keep thou, O Lord, our hearts from false affections,
> And lead us onward to the journey's end.

---

on the Mount, 521) says that the sayings of the Sermon on the Mount are not the way itself, but "trailmarkers pointing out the way"; the way itself is "the life to be lived by the disciples in obedience to the instructions of the Sermon on the Mount."

10. John Bunyan, *The Pilgrim's Progress: From This World, to That Which Is to Come* (London: J. Clarke, 1741).

Well may you ask if I can now be truly
A child of God, the Lord's devoted bride,
But here you see in me my human frailties [Swedish: "in my traveling clothes"].
Some day you'll see my spirit glorified [Swedish: "in my white robes"].
(trans. Obed Johnson; *CovH* 1950 #502)

Lina Sandell's "Strait Is the Gate to All That Come" is based on the passage here:

Strait is the gate to all that come,
And narrow is the way
Which leads unto the heav'nly home,
Where yet is room for thee,
Where yet is room for thee

In heav'n, where God his own shall take,
There's also room for thee.
In Jesus' name, for Jesus' sake,
The gates shall opened be,
The gates shall opened be.

Now God be praised, that even I
May in that city dwell,
Where peace shall reign eternally
And all with me be well,
And all with me be well.
(trans. Augustus Nelson; *CovH* 1950 #516)

With the present teaching combining a "two roads" and a "two gates" theme, Betz asks whether the gates are at the beginning of the journey or at the end.[11] The answer is not indicated in the biblical text, but Betz decides that they stand at the end of the roads, which is doubtless correct. It is certainly so in the *Testament of Abraham*, in Bunyan's *Pilgrim's Progress*, and in much eighteenth- and nineteenth-century Christian theology. The gate at the end of road on which the righteous travel is the heavenly Jerusalem, and the gate at the end of the road on which the wicked travel opens into the hell of eternal punishment.

14. *For the gate is narrow and the road is hard that leads to life, and there are few who find it.* The road leading to life is "confined," (not "hard"). On the many and the few, see Matt. 22:14. Krister Stendahl points out that, while the narrow door and confined road are hard to find, no stress is put here on the road being hard to walk (*pace* RSV).[12]

---

11. Betz, *Sermon on the Mount*, 521-523.
12. Stendahl, "Matthew," 780.

23

Beware of False Prophets (7:15-20)

¹⁵*"Beware of false prophets, who come to you in sheep's clothing but inwardly are ravenous wolves.* ¹⁶*You will know them by their fruits. Are grapes gathered from thorns, or figs from thistles?* ¹⁷*In the same way, every good tree bears good fruit, but the bad tree bears bad fruit.* ¹⁸*A good tree cannot bear bad fruit, nor can a bad tree bear good fruit.* ¹⁹*Every tree that does not bear good fruit is cut down and thrown into the fire.* ²⁰*Thus you will know them by their fruits.*

15. *Beware of false prophets, who come to you in sheep's clothing but inwardly are ravenous wolves.* Interpreters often connect this teaching with the previous one, assuming that when walking along the way one will meet travelers among whom will be prophets, some genuine, and some false. Sermons preached in England during the seventeenth

and eighteenth centuries made the connection,[1] and it survives in more recent interpretations.[2]

The problem of false prophecy is an old one. Deuteronomy has two tests for false prophecy: (1) in 13:1-5, where the false prophet is one who, despite success in performing signs and wonders, leads people in the way of other gods; and (2) in 18:18-22, where the false (Yahweh) prophet is the one whose word does not come true. The problem of false prophecy emerged in the early monarchy but became acute in the time of Jeremiah, at which time prophets were still prophesying by Baal (Jer. 2:8). But even more troublesome were Yahweh prophets who had not been sent and, as a result, were not getting the message right (Jer. 23:16-17, 18, 21-22, 31-32; 28:1-17; 29:8-9, 23; etc.), or who were behaving immorally (23:10-11, 14; 29:21-23).[3] The term *false prophet* never appears in the Hebrew Old Testament; the term ψευδοπροφήτης ("false prophet") occurs in the LXX.[4] The true prophet, by implication, is one who leads people "in the way of Yahweh," gets Yahweh's message right, and behaves with integrity.

In postexilic Judaism, the last prophets were said to be Haggai, Zechariah, and Malachi, after which the Holy Spirit departed from Israel.[5] But by the New Testament period things had changed. John the Baptist was widely taken to be a prophet (Matt. 11:9-14; 14:5; 21:26; Mark 11:32; Luke 7:24-26; 20:6), and Jesus, too, was confessed by many as a prophet (Matt. 21:11, 46; Mark 6:15; 8:28; Luke 7:16; 9:8, 19; 24:19; John 4:19; 6:14; 7:40, 52; 9:17). He even took himself

---

1. See the sermon preached by Stephen Denison at Paul's Croffe on February 11, 1627, "But Beware of False Prophets (Matt. 7:15)," in *The White Wolfe* (London: George Miller, 1627), 3; also John Wesley's sermon *A Caution against False Prophets*, 2–4.

2. For example, Betz, *Sermon on the Mount*, 527.

3. Lundbom, *Hebrew Prophets*, 138–56.

4. See LXX Jer. 33:7, 8, 11, 16; 34:9; 35:1; 36:1, 8 (= MT Jer. 26:7, 8, 11, 16; 27:9; 28:1; 29:1, 8); also LXX Zech. 13:2.

5. See b. *Sanh.* 11a; b. *Sot.* 48b; b. *Yom.* 9b; *Cant. Rab.* 8:9, 3.

to be a prophet (Matt. 13:57; Mark 6:4; Luke 4:24; 13:33; John 4:44). The New Testament knows of other prophets, some of whom were genuine (Matt. 10:41; Acts 11:27; 13:1; 15:32; 21:10-14; 1 Cor. 14:29-32), some of whom were false (Acts 13:6; Titus 1:10-16). Paul takes prophecy as one of the bona fide gifts of the Spirit (1 Cor. 12:10; 14:39-40), and prophets have an appointed office in the body of Christ—a very important office, second only to that of apostles (1 Cor. 12:28; Eph. 4:11). There is also talk in the New Testament about true prophets who will arise in the future (Matt. 23:34; Luke 11:49) and false prophets sure to deceive people in the end-times. They will perform signs and wonders (cf. Deut. 13:1-3) but in the end will suffer eternal punishment (Matt. 24:11, 24; Mark 13:22; Rev. 16:13; 19:20; 20:10).

Other Christian documents attest to prophets being active in the early church, some genuine, and some not (*Did.* 11–15; *Eus. Hist.* 3.37.1). Justin Martyr tells Trypho the Jew:

> You should realize the fact that among us Christians the charisms of prophecy exist down to the present day, that the gifts that previously resided among your people have now been transmitted to us. (*Dial. Trypho* 82)

The *Shepherd of Hermas* says that false prophets are destroying the understanding of the double-minded, but not the faithful (*Shep. Herm.* Commandment 11). The *Didache* says that false prophets performing signs and wonders (cf. Deut. 13:1), who are sheep turned into wolves, will arise in the end-times (*Did.* 16:3-4). It also sets forth tests for discerning prophets currently itinerating; for example, they may not stay as houseguests more than two days, and they may not ask for money (*Did.* 11:5; cf. Micah 3:5-6). Eusebius reports false prophets who are speaking in ecstasy (*Eus. Hist.* 5.17.2-4).

The prophets warned against here in the Sermon are within the Christian community. Krister Stendahl thinks they are false teachers and that vv. 13–22 all refer to the eschatological crisis facing the New Testament church.[6] Hans Dieter Betz, too, thinks the false prophets are teachers of heresy,[7] which would compare to the false prophets in Jeremiah's time who did not get the message right. Augustine's collection of (false) heretics numbered eighty-eight.[8]

Sheep are a common metaphor throughout the Bible, but wolves appear also, only less frequently, portraying vicious individuals who prey on others (Zeph. 3:3; Ezek. 22:27; Matt. 10:16; Luke 10:3). Here in the Sermon it is individuals coming dressed in sheep's clothing who inwardly are ravenous wolves. As such they are even more dangerous, for they are hard to detect. We all know the tale of Little Red Riding Hood. Clothing, of course, became a distinguishing mark of John the Baptist and, before him, the prophet Elijah. Both dressed in simple garments that wore rough against the skin, making a statement against the nice attire of kings and a generation caught up in the ways of wickedness (2 Kgs. 1:8; Matt. 3:4; 11:7–9; Mark 1:6). Prophets coming in "sheep's clothing" will be well attired and will appear harmless. But they will not be harmless.

The clothing here may simply be used figuratively, however, and dress may not be an issue at all. But the false prophets, at minimum, will appear gentle and harmless but in reality will be exceedingly harmful. On hypocrisy between the outer and inner person, where the Pharisees and scribes come in for censure, see Matt. 23:27–28. The

---

6. Stendahl, "Matthew," 780; Betz (*Sermon on the Mount*, 527), however, while he does recognize that vv. 21–23 look ahead to the end-times, thinks the present teaching on the false prophets seems uninterested in them.

7. Betz, *Sermon on the Mount*, 536; Jerome (*Commentary on Matthew*, 94), too, thinks the false prophets are heretics.

8. Cited in Denison, "But Beware of False Prophets (Matt. 7:15)," 9–10.

Talmud says regarding a scholar: Any scholar whose inside is not like his outside is no scholar. . . . He is called abominable (*b. Yom.* 72b).

16. *You will know them by their fruits.* This is repeated at the end of the saying (v. 20), serving as an *inclusio.* Compare a similar teaching in Luke 6:44a. This is how we know the false prophets. Good and bad trees, good and bad vines—and the fruit of both were used often in the Bible to symbolize good and bad individuals (Matt. 3:10; 13:31-32; Jude 12). In the Old Testament, and also among the rabbis, the "fruit" test was not in teaching but in deeds.[9] Jeremiah was concerned about bad deeds in his expression "fruits of his/your doings" (Jer. 17:10; 21:14; 32:19). In Matt. 12:33-37 and Luke 6:45, the "fruit" of the tree refers to a person's conduct. Sirach 27:6 says too, "Its fruit discloses the cultivation of a tree; so a person's speech discloses the cultivation of his mind" (NRSV). A Midrash asks: "What is the fruit of the righteous?" and gives a slightly expanded answer: "Life, religious actions, and good deeds" (*Gen. Rab.* 30:6). The same holds true with workers of iniquity: "by their works those who speak lying blasphemies are recognized" (*Slav. En.* 42:14). Teaching may have become the "fruit" of prophets later in the church, but not here. Jesus is calling for good deeds. Wesley says the good fruit is holiness, the bad fruit sin and wickedness.[10]

Jeremiah makes his analogy between trees and the whole of a person's life:

Cursed is the man who trusts in mortals,
    and makes flesh his strength,
    and from Yahweh his heart turns away.
For he shall become like a juniper in the Arabah.

9. Montefiore, *Rabbinic Literature and Gospel Teachings*, 153: "the test is the deed."
10. Wesley, *Caution against False Prophets*, 7.

It will not see when the good comes,

. . . .[11]

It inhabits scorched places in the wilderness,
    a salt land not inhabited.

Blessed is the man who trusts in Yahweh,
    and Yahweh becomes his trust.
For he shall become like a tree transplanted by water;
    by a stream, it shall shoot out its roots.

It will not fear when the heat comes,
    for its leaves become luxuriant.
In the year of drought it will not worry,
    for it will not stop bearing fruit. (Jer. 17:5-8 AB)

Are grapes gathered from thorns, or figs from thistles? More rhetorical questions, the answers to which are "No!" Compare a different version in Luke 6:44b. James asks: "Can a fig tree, my brothers and sisters, yield olives, or a grapevine figs? No more can salt water yield fresh" (James 3:12)

17. *In the same way, every good tree bears good fruit, but the bad tree bears bad fruit.* On trees and their roots, see Matt. 3:10; 15:13; John 15:1-11; and Rom. 11:16-24. The bad (or evil) fruit is not rotten (*pace* Betz), just so bitter it cannot be eaten.[12]

18. *A good tree cannot bear bad fruit, nor can a bad tree bear good fruit.* Compare Matt. 12:33 and Luke 6:43. Hebrew רע can mean "bad" or "evil." Greek σαπρός, when used metaphorically, can also mean "bad," the opposite of καλός, "good."[13] Betz translates the Greek as

---

11. A colon of poetry appears here to have fallen out.
12. Lachs, *Rabbinic Commentary on the New Testament*, 148.
13. Liddell and Scott, *Greek-English Lexicon*, 1583, s.v. σαπρός.

"rotten,"[14] which does not seem right. Although fruit can rot on an unhealthy tree, more often it rots after having been picked and allowed to sit too long (Jer. 24:2-3). The fruit here is still on the tree, and it is bad, bitter, and potentially poisonous fruit.

In Isaiah's "Song of the Vineyard" (5:1-7), Yahweh says he carefully planted Israel as a choice vine, but when he came looking for grapes, he found it had yielded wild grapes. Fruit here was bad conduct: bloodshed and a cry, instead of justice and righteousness. Similarly, in a prophecy from Jeremiah, Yahweh expresses wonderment that he could have planted Israel as a choice vine, wholly pure seed it was, and then found to his great sorrow that it turned degenerate, becoming a wild vine (Jer. 2:21). In nature such things do not happen. The "vine" imagery in the Song of Moses in Deuteronomy is more in accord with the natural order. There the enemies of Yahweh are said to be a vine from Sodom, grown on the fields of Gomorrah, having fruit bitter that is poisonous (Deut. 32:32-33).

19. *Every tree that does not bear good fruit is cut down and thrown into the fire.* In the New Testament, nonbearing trees or trees not yielding good fruit are cursed or cut down (Matt 3:10; 21:19; Mark 11:12-14; Luke 3:9; 13:6-9). A cutting occurred earlier with the two branches of a once luxuriant Israel, thus fulfilling the prophecies of Isaiah and Jeremiah. And Jesus says another cutting is taking place now. John the Baptist preached the same bad news earlier (Matt. 3:10; Luke 3:9).

20. *Thus you will know them by their fruits.* A repetition of v. 16 (*inclusio*). In a Midrash, fruit-bearing trees were asked, "Why is your sound not audible?" They replied, "We do not need it, our fruits testify for us" (*Gen. Rab.* 16:3). Wesley says, however, that we should

14. Betz, *Sermon on the Mount*, 531, 538.

hear the false prophets out, even if we do not follow them, for not all of their teaching will be bad (cf. Matt. 23:2-3).[15]

15. Wesley, *Caution against False Prophets*, 8–9.

———

Hearing and Doing Is Everything (7:21-27)

²¹*"Not everyone who says to me, 'Lord, Lord,' will enter the kingdom of heaven, but only the one who does the will of my Father in heaven.* ²²*On that day many will say to me, 'Lord, Lord, did we not prophesy in your name, and cast out demons in your name, and do many deeds of power in your name?'* ²³*Then I will declare to them, 'I never knew you; go away from me, you evildoers.'* ²⁴*Everyone then who hears these words of mine and acts on them will be like a wise man who built his house on rock.* ²⁵*The rain fell, the floods came, and the winds blew and beat on that house, but it did not fall, because it had been founded on rock.* ²⁶*And everyone who hears these words of mine and does not act on them will be like a foolish man who built his house on sand.* ²⁷*The rain fell, and the floods came, and the winds blew and beat against that house, and it fell—and great was its fall!"*

21. *Not everyone who says to me, "Lord, Lord," will enter the kingdom of heaven, but only the one who does the will of my Father in heaven.* Verses 21-23 and 24-27 may be two short sayings combined, but they fit together, as they do also in Luke (Luke 6:46-49). Jesus is

acknowledged as "Lord" by certain people, but this is not the defining mark of discipleship, either now or at the last judgment. Jesus will be Judge at the last judgment;[1] now he is Teacher (or Rabbi) for all who would enter the kingdom. Doing the will of God the Father, which is a common expression in the rabbinic literature,[2] means *doing* the teaching that is given here in the Sermon on the Mount, and doing it with a passion. The Mishnah says, "Be strong as a leopard, swift as an eagle, fleet as a gazelle, and brave as a lion, to carry out the will of your Father who is in heaven" (*m. Ab.* 5:20). "Doing" is always the bottom line in Jewish thinking. It is so in Deuteronomy (Deut. 4:5, 14; 5:1, 27, 31-32; 6:1; etc.), and we see it elsewhere in the Old Testament (Exod. 19:7-8; Lev. 18:5). Ezekiel applied the "doing principle" to himself as watchman over Israel (Ezek. 33:3-16). In Luke, the parable of the two houses is preceded by these words: "Why do you call me 'Lord, Lord,' and do not do what I tell you? I will show you what someone is like who comes to me, hears my words, and acts on them" (Luke 6:46-47).

22. *On that day many will say to me, "Lord, Lord, did we not prophesy in your name, and cast out demons in your name, and do many deeds of power in your name?"* "That day" is the final day of the Lord's appearing, which will be a day of judgment. Jesus is speaking as the Messiah and Judge.[3] Some appearing before him will be in for a surprise, as they have prophesied, cast out demons, and done many mighty works in Jesus' name.

23. *Then I will declare to them, 'I never knew you; go away from me, you evildoers.'* But these individuals have not done the will of the Father and practiced Jesus' teaching in their own lives, for which reason Jesus will reject them in the strongest of terms. An echo

1. Friedlander, *Jewish Sources of the Sermon on the Mount*, 257.
2. Lachs, *Rabbinic Commentary on the New Testament*, 150.
3. Montefiore, *Synoptic Gospels*, 2:124.

of Luke 13:27, where Ps. 6:8 is quoted: "Depart from me, all you workers of evil." "I never knew you" is a rabbinic expression of rejection, an exaggerated one, meaning, "It will be as if I never knew you," or "I don't want to know you, stay away!" (*b. 'Erub.* 53a; *b. M. Qat.* 16a). Jesus, of course, had prior knowledge of these individuals, but now he wants nothing more to do with them. Sirach says that only at the end of life is one truly defined: "Call no one happy before his death; by how he ends a person becomes known" (Sir 11:28 NRSV). The expression "I do not know you" occurs also at the conclusion of the parable of the wise and foolish maidens, where the foolish maidens are denied entrance to the messianic banquet (Matt. 25:12).

24-25. *Everyone then who hears these words of mine and acts on them will be like a wise man who built his house on rock. The rain fell, the floods came, and the winds blew and beat on that house, but it did not fall, because it had been founded on rock.* On the parable of two houses, compare Luke 6:48-49. On "hearing and doing," see Deut. 5:1 ("Hear . . . and be careful to do them" RSV); 5:27 (and we will hear and do it" RSV); and elsewhere in Deuteronomy.[4] "He who hears and does" is a thoroughly Jewish and rabbinic idea.[5] Matthew carries forth this important biblical teaching in 21:28-32; 23:1-3; 25:31-36, and elsewhere. Wise and foolish builders are a common motif in biblical and rabbinic thought (Prov. 12:7; 14:11; Ezek. 13:8-16; 1 Cor. 3:10-15). This parallel to the present teaching occurs in the rabbinic literature:

> Elisha ben Abuyah says: "One in whom there are good works, who has studied much Torah, to what may he be likened? To a person who builds first with stones and afterward with brick: even when much water comes and collects by their side, it does not dislodge them. But

---

4. Massey, *Interpreting the Sermon on the Mount*, 117.
5. Montefiore, *Synoptic Gospels*, 2:125.

one in whom there are no good works, though he studied Torah, to what may he be likened? To a person who builds first with bricks and afterward with stones: even when a little water gathers, it overthrows them immediately" (*Ab. R. Nat.* 24)[6]

Archaeologists excavating ancient city walls have discovered three or more courses of stone at the base, and then mud-brick from that point upward.

In Matthew, Jesus tells Peter, "You are Peter [Πέτρος = "rock"], and on this rock I will build my church, and the gates of Hades will not prevail against it" (Matt. 16:18). For Paul, Christ is the rock (Rom. 9:32-33; 1 Cor. 10:4; cf. 1 Pet. 2:7-8). In the Old Testament Israel's "Rock" is God (Deut. 32:4, 15, 18, 30-31; Ps. 18:2, 31, 46; etc.).

26-27. *And everyone who hears these words of mine and does not act on them will be like a foolish man who built his house on sand. The rain fell, and the floods came, and the winds blew and beat against that house, and it fell—and great was its fall!* The Zadokite Document from Qumran speaks disparagingly about "builders of a rickety wall."[7]

the foolish man. Greek: ἀνδρὶ μωρῷ. The word for "foolish" is from the same root as "lost its taste" (μωρανθῇ) in 5:13. In biblical thought, foolishness stands next to godlessness in keeping people from the kingdom (Matt. 25:1-12).

---

6. Cited in Lachs, *Rabbinic Commentary on the New Testament*, 151.
7. Gaster, *Dead Sea Scriptures*, 81.

25

And the Crowds Were Astonished (7:28-29)

28"Now when Jesus had finished saying these things, the crowds were astounded at his teaching, 29for he taught them as one having authority, and not as their scribes.

28-29. *Now when Jesus had finished saying these things, the crowds were astounded at his teaching, for he taught them as one having authority, and not as their scribes.* Although Jesus is giving this teaching primarily to his disciples (5:1), the crowds have been listening in, and they are astonished at the authority with which Jesus teaches. Scribes argued from tradition; Jesus is here speaking in his own name ("But I say to you" in 5:22, 28, 32, 34, 39, 44; cf. 28:18-20).[1]

---

1. Jerome, *Commentary on Matthew*, 98; Daube *New Testament and Rabbinic Judaism*, 55–62; 205–23; Stendahl, "Matthew," 780.

Appendix: Jewish, Christian, and Classical Authors Cited

1. Jewish

Hillel. Hillel (the Elder) was the greatest of the sages and scholars in the Second Temple period. His dates are from the first century B.C.E. to the beginning of the first century C.E. While tradition has him active for forty years, from 30 B.C.E. to 10 C.E., his dates seem certainly to be between 10 B.C.E. and 10 C.E., when he died. Hillel therefore lived during the reigns of King Herod and the Roman emperor Augustus. Born in Babylonia, Hillel came in the prime of manhood to Jerusalem to study biblical exposition and Jewish tradition, and he soon rose to prominence there. Among the Pharisees and scribes, he became the greatest authority in ethics and religion, also in civic law and economic matters. He is said to have had eighty students in his House of Hillel, a school more liberal than the rival House of Shammai. Hillel was a man of humility, not given to anger, and a pursuer of peace.

Josephus. Flavius Josephus was a Jewish historian whose dates are from c. 37 to 101 C.E. Born and raised in a wealthy aristocratic family in Jerusalem, he studied the Torah as a young man, but at the outbreak of the Jewish War against the Romans (66) was appointed commander of the Jewish forces in Galilee. When Jotapata fell in the decisive battle of 67, he fled with forty men to a cave but survived to surrender to Vespasian, who spared his life. Granted freedom once Vespasian became emperor in 69, Josephus became interpreter for Vespasian's son, Titus, and witnessed the sack of Jerusalem (70). He then went to Rome and was granted Roman citizenship. In Rome he wrote his two most important works, *The Jewish War* (c. 75), and *Jewish Antiquities* (c. 94).

Philo. Philo Judaeus (of Alexandria), whose dates are from c. 20 B.C.E. to 50 C.E., was a preeminent Jewish philosopher whose vast literary output—in Greek, not Hebrew—was preserved by the Christian church, where he exercised great influence among the Church Fathers. Apart from Josephus, no ancient Jewish source mentions Philo. He belonged to a noble family of Alexandrian Jewry that had connections with the Herodian dynasty and the Roman court. Philo had great erudition in classical literature and classical and contemporary philosophy; he had a thorough training in rhetoric and a broad knowledge of general science.

Maimonides. Moses Maimonides (1135–1204), known also as Rambam (Rabbi Moses ben Maimon), was the leading Jewish figure in the post-Talmudic era and one of the greatest thinkers of all time. He was a rabbinic authority, philosopher, codifier of Jewish law, and, later in life, a royal physician, in which capacity he also achieved fame. Born in Cordoba, Spain, Maimonides left there with his family because of persecution of the Jews in 1160, to settle in Fez, the medieval capital of Morocco. But in 1165 he left Fez and went to

Acra in Palestine. While sojourning there, he toured Jerusalem and the holy land. In 1166, he went to Egypt and, after a short stay in Alexandria, settled in Fustat, a section of Cairo. After the tragedy of his brother David's death in 1169, he made the medical profession his livelihood and became the royal physician to Grand Vizer Al Qadi al Fadil, later to Sultan Saladin. Maimonides died in Cairo on December 12, 1204, and was buried finally in Tiberius. His two most important works are *Mishneh Torah* (1180) and *Guide of the Perplexed* (1190).

2. Christian

Justin Martyr. Saint Justin Martyr, an early Christian philosopher and apologist, was born of pagan Greek parents in Palestine, in the city of Neapolis (modern Nablus), sometime around 100 c.e. He studied with various teachers at Ephesus and, after being converted to Christianity, taught Christian philosophy there. Sometime after 135, he left Ephesus for Rome. About 165, in the reign of Marcus Aurelius, he was denounced after disputing with a cynic philosopher and martyred for his Christian faith. Between the apostles and Irenaeus, he ranks as the greatest figure in the early church.

Eusebius. Eusebius of Caesarea (in Palestine), who became bishop of that city in c. 314 after the persecutions had ended, was known as an apologist, biblical exegete, and preeminent early church historian. Born c. 260, presumably in Caesarea, he was baptized as an adult, after which he entered the ranks of the clergy. Caesarea is where Origen had been for many years, and because of his influence the city had become a center of Christian learning. Eusebius drew upon the large library of Pamphilus in Caesarea, which contained works of Origen and an original of the Hexapla. He also used the library of

Bishop Alexander in Jerusalem. Eusebius was present at the Council of Nicaea in 325, holding a prominent position at the right hand of Constantine. His important writings include an *Onomasticon* in biblical topography, numerous commentaries, and an *Ecclesiastical History*, which was a vindication of Christianity against heathen and heretics. He died c. 339 or 340.

Gregory of Nyssa. Saint Gregory of Nyssa was one of the three Cappadocian Fathers. Born in Caesarea (modern Kayseri, Turkey) between 335 and 340, he went on to become a philosopher, rhetorician, and mystic. He spent time in a monastery but was then consecrated bishop of Nyssa, a suffragan of Caesarea in Cappadocia, in 372. Gregory played a major role in the Council of Constantinople in 381 and died sometime after 394 in Constantinople.

Chrysostom. John of Antioch (c. 347–407), surnamed Chrysostom (*chrysostomos* = "golden-mouthed"), was bishop of Constantinople and the greatest preacher of the patristic era. Born of educated upper-class Christian parents and raised at Antioch in Syria, John received the finest rhetorical education available. After his baptism as an adult (c. 367 or later), he became a lector devoting himself to Scripture in a monastery near Antioch. For two years he lived an ascetic life in the hills near Antioch, but when his health failed, he returned to the city in 378, where he began his extraordinary career as writer, liturgist, and preacher. John preached for years in Antioch. In 398, he was forced to accept consecration as bishop of Constantinople, which was not successful. Twice he was deposed and exiled. Chrysostom died in exile in 407 at Comana, an obscure village of Pontus in Asia Minor. He was made a saint in the Eastern Church, where he ranks as one of its greatest figures. His most valuable writings are the *Homilies* on various books of the Bible, but his outspoken criticism of Jews and Judaizing Christians taking part in Jewish festivals and other Jewish observances has led to the charge of that he was anti-Semitic, but this may be to employ anachronistic terminology to the historical context in which he lived.

Jerome. Saint Jerome (345–419), the greatest Scripture scholar of the Church Fathers, was born at Stridon in northeast Italy c. 345. At the age of twelve he was sent to Rome to study grammar, rhetoric, and the liberal arts under Donatus. He went to Antioch, spent two years in the desert near Aleppo, but fell sick and returned to Antioch. In 382, he traveled to Rome and became secretary to Pope Damasus I. Jerome did some writing there. Then, in 386 he settled in Bethlehem, where he remained the rest of his life. His monastery was burned by vandals in 416, and he died three years later. Jerome was the most learned man of his age. He translated the Hebrew Bible into Latin (the Vulgate) and wrote numerous commentaries (the Twelve Prophets, Daniel, Isaiah, Ezekiel, Jeremiah 1–32, and Matthew) and other important works.

Augustine. Saint Augustine (354–430), bishop and doctor of the church, was the most dominant figure in Western Christianity, retaining influence in subsequent years, during the Protestant Reformation, and even up to the present time. He was born in North Africa in 354, and was given a classical Roman education at Thagaste, after which he studied rhetoric at Carthage. In 383, he went to Rome and was appointed professor of rhetoric in Milan. In Milan he met Bishop Ambrose, became a Christian in 386 after reading Romans, and was baptized the following year by Ambrose. Augustine went to

Hippo (present-day Annaba, Algeria) in 391 to establish a monastery. He became bishop of Hippo and wrote much there; he also kept busy, however, with other activities of his office. Of his many important works, the best known are his *Confessions* and *City of God*. He also wrote a commentary on *The Lord's Sermon on the Mount*. Augustine died in Hippo in 430 at the age of seventy-six.

3. Greek

Isocrates. Isocrates (436–338 B.C.E.) was an Athenian orator of central importance in the golden age of Greece. He received a first-rate education, and his speeches provide important political commentary on events of the fourth century B.C.E. He was the son of a wealthy Athenian family, and, like Plato, a follower of Socrates, with whom he was acquainted. Early on he was also influenced by the sophist teachers Prodicus and Gorgias. In 392, he set up his own school of rhetoric, taking on no more than nine students at a time, and his main aim was to teach them how to argue. For a substantial fee he also wrote speeches for others to argue their cases in court.

Plato. Plato (429–347 B.C.E.) came from a wealthy Athenian family and rose to be one of the great thinkers of ancient Greece. The major influence on him was Socrates, whose trial he reports in the *Apology* and whose death is recounted in the *Phaedo*. Plato was a student of Socrates, which accounts for his writings being in dialogue form. He never presents ideas as his own, always forcing the reader to make up his own mind. He was a philosopher primarily, but also a mathematician. Plato founded an academy in Athens, where his most famous student was Aristotle.

Herodotus. This Greek historian is called the "Father of History"; he recorded the Greco-Persian Wars and looked ahead to the great war between Athens and Sparta (Peloponnesian War), fought in 431–404 B.C.E. Herodotus came from Halicarnassus (present-day Bodrum on the Aegean coast of Turkey), which was under Persian rule. Little is known of his birth and early life. He may have been born c. 484 B.C.E., just before the Persian Wars, and is said to have died in the 420s at less than sixty years of age. He received a Greek liberal arts education in grammar, gymnastic training, and music, after which he traveled extensively, spending an extended time in Egypt. He is said to have gone to Athens in 447. The *History* was his only work, and it includes also a wealth of geographical and ethnographical material. We do not know when the work was completed, perhaps by 425.

Aristotle. Aristotle (384–322 B.C.E.) was born at Stagira in Chalcidice (thirty-four miles east of present-day Thessaloniki) into a prominent Greek family, his father being personal physician to King Amyntas of Macedon. At seventeen he went to Athens to enter Plato's Academy (367), remaining there twenty years until Plato's death in 347. Aristotle went on to become one of the great philosophers and teachers of rhetoric in ancient Greece, making, among other things, practical application of Plato's philosophical theories. He was also the teacher of Alexander the Great. Aristotle wrote on many subjects, but one of his great achievements was to develop syllogistic reasoning into a system in his *Prior Analytics I.* Another was to bring deductive logic into the study of rhetoric, stressing the importance of the enthymeme (a truncated syllogism, with one premise omitted) in argumentation. He called the enthymeme "the strongest of rhetorical proofs."

4. Roman

Seneca (The Younger). Lucius Annaeus Seneca (4 B.C.E. to 65 C.E.), the second son of Seneca the rhetorician, became the most important public and literary figure in Rome in the age of Nero. Born at Corduba (modern Cordoba, Spain) c. 4 B.C.E., he was taken as an infant to Rome, where he was educated in rhetoric and philosophy. He entered upon a senatorial career, becoming an eloquent speaker, and gained the quaestorship under Tiberius. But he suffered ill health. For eight years he was banished to Corsica, although while there he wrote and studied. Then Agrippina, wife of Claudius, secured his recall in 49 and appointed him tutor to her young son, the future emperor Nero. From this point on Seneca's fortunes were linked with those of Nero. After gaining honor, wealth, and power, his influence weakened, and in 62 he sought obscurity. Then in 65 he was charged with complicity in the conspiracy of Piso and was forced to commit suicide. During his life, Seneca achieved great renown in Latin literature, writing both prose and poetry; and he attained remarkable rhetorical skill. He was probably the most brilliant and independent thinker of his day. In philosophy his interest was purely ethical. Discourses of his were said to be Stoic sermons.

Pliny (The Elder). Pliny the Elder (23/24–79 C.E.) was born in Novum Comum, Galilia Cisalpina (modern-day Como, Italy), into an upper-class family and received a classical education in literature, oratory, and law. He went on to become a prolific Roman scholar and writer. Pliny also received military training and, at twenty-three, was appointed a cavalry commander. His last assignment was commander of a fleet in the Bay of Naples. Pliny wrote some seventy-five books, being best known for his thirty-seven volume *Natural History*, published in 77, which was an encyclopedic work of all that the Romans knew about the natural world.

Bibliography

Reference Works

Abrahams, Israel. *Annotated Edition of the Authorized Daily Prayer Book.* London: Eyre & Spottiswoode, 1914.

Apostolic Fathers. *The Apostolic Fathers,* vol. 1. Translated by Kirsopp Lake. Loeb Classical Library. Cambridge, MA: Harvard University Press, 1952. Contains *The Didache* and *Clement of Rome.*

——. *The Apostolic Fathers,* vol. 2. Translated by Bart D. Ehrman. Loeb Classical Library. Cambridge, MA: Harvard University Press, 2003. Contains *The Shepherd of Hermas.*

Aristotle. *Aristotle XIX: The Nicomachean Ethics.* Translated by H. Rackham. Loeb Classical Library. Cambridge, MA: Harvard University Press, 1968.

——. *The 'Art' of Rhetoric.* Translated by John Henry Freese. Loeb Classical Library. Cambridge, MA: Harvard University Press, 1967.

Braude, William G. *The Midrash on Psalms.* 2 vols. Yale Judaica Series 13. New Haven: Yale University Press, 1959.

Brooke, George, et al., in consultation with James C. VanderKam. *Qumran Cave 4.XVII: Parabiblical Texts, Part 3.* Discoveries in the Judaean Desert 22. Oxford: Clarendon, 1996.

Brown, Francis, S. R. Driver, and Charles A. Briggs. *A Hebrew and English Lexicon of the Old Testament.* Based on the Lexicon of William Gesenius. Oxford: Clarendon, 1907. Reprint, 1957.

Brownlee, William Hugh. *The Dead Sea Manual of Discipline.* Bulletin of the American Schools of Oriental Research Supplementary Studies 10-12. New Haven: American Schools of Oriental Research, 1951.

Cathcart, Kevin J., and Robert P. Gordon, eds. *The Targum of the Minor Prophets.* Aramaic Bible 14. Wilmington, DE: Michael Glazier, 1989.

Charles, R. H. *The Apocrypha and Pseudepigrapha of the Old Testament* 2 vols. Oxford: Clarendon, 1913.

Charlesworth, James H., ed. *The Old Testament Pseudepigrapha* 2 vols. Garden City, NY: Doubleday, 1983–85.

Charlesworth, James H., et al., eds. *The Dead Sea Scrolls: Hebrew, Aramaic, and Greek Texts with English Translations.* Vol. 1, *Rule of the Community and Related Documents.* Princeton Theological Seminary Dead Sea Scrolls Project 1. Louisville: Westminster John Knox, 1994. Contains *The Rule of the Community,* by Elisha Qimron and James H. Charlesworth.

———, eds. *The Dead Sea Scrolls: Hebrew, Aramaic, and Greek Texts with English Translations.* Vol. 2, *Damascus Document, War Scroll, and Related Documents.* Princeton Theological Seminary Dead Sea Scrolls Project 2. Louisville: Westminster John Knox, 1995. Contains *Damascus Document,* by Joseph M. Baumgarten and Daniel R. Schwartz; and *War Scroll,* by Jean Duhaime.

Chilton, Bruce D. *The Isaiah Targum.* Aramaic Bible 11. Wilmington, DE: Michael Glazier, 1987.

Clarke, Ernest G. *Targum Pseudo-Jonathan: Numbers.* Aramaic Bible 4. Collegeville, MN: Liturgical Press, 1995.

———. *Targum Pseudo-Jonathan: Deuteronomy.* Aramaic Bible 5B. Collegeville, MN: Liturgical Press, 1998.

Daniell, David, ed. *Tyndale's New Testament.* New Haven: Yale University Press, 1989.

Dupont-Sommer, André. *The Essene Writings from Qumran.* Translated by Geza Vermes. Oxford: Basil Blackwell, 1961.

Epstein, I., *The Babylonian Talmud.* 34 vols. London: Soncino, 1935-48.

Eusebius. *Eusebius: The Ecclesiastical History I: Books 1–5.* Translated by Kirsopp Lake. Loeb Classical Library. Cambridge, MA: Harvard University Press, 1965.

Freedman, H., and Maurice Simon, eds. *Midrash Rabbah.* 10 vols. London: Soncino, 1939.

Gaster, T. H. *The Dead Sea Scriptures.* Rev. and enlarged ed. Garden City, NY: Doubleday, 1964.

Gregory of Nyssa. *The Lord's Prayer. The Beatitudes.* Translated by Hilda C. Graef. Ancient Christian Writers 18. Westminster, MD: Newman, 1954.

Guggenheimer, Heinrich W. *The Jerusalem Talmud.* Studia Judaica 18-21. Volumes I-IV. Berlin and New York: de Gruyter, 2000–2002.

Herodotus. *Herodotus II: Books 3–4.* Translated by A. D. Godley. Loeb Classical Library. Cambridge, MA: Harvard University Press, 1963.

———. *Herodotus III: Books V–VII.* Translated by A. D. Godley. Loeb Classical Library. Cambridge, MA: Harvard University Press, 1963.

Isocrates. *Isocrates I.* Translated by George Norlin. Loeb Classical Library. Cambridge, MA: Harvard University Press, 1966. Contains the oration "To Nicoles."

Jastrow, Marcus. *A Dictionary of the Targumim, the Talmud Babli and Yerushalmi, and the Midrashic Literature.* 2 vols. London: W. C. Luzac; New York: G. Putnam's Sons, 1903. Reprint, New York: Pardes, 1950.

Jerome, St. *Commentary on Matthew.* Translated by Thomas P. Scheck. Fathers of the Church 117. Washington, DC: Catholic University of America Press, 2008.

John Chrysostom. *The Homilies of S. John Chrysostom, Archbishop of Constantinople, on the Gospel of Matthew.* 3 vols. Library of the Fathers of the Holy Catholic Church 11, 15, 34 Oxford: John Henry Parker, 1843–51.

Josephus. *Josephus I: The Life; Against Apion.* Translated by H. St. J. Thackeray. Loeb Classical Library. Cambridge, MA: Harvard University Press, 1966.

———. *Josephus II: The Jewish War: Books 1–3.* Translated by H. St. J. Thackeray. Loeb Classical Library. Cambridge, MA: Harvard University Press, 1967.

Justin Martyr. *St. Justin Martyr: Dialogue with Trypho.* Edited by Michael Slusser. Translated by Thomas B. Falls. Selections from the Fathers of the Church 3. Washington, DC: Catholic University of America Press, 2003.

Kittel, Gerhard, and Gerhard Friedrich, eds. *Theological Dictionary of the New Testament.* Translated by Geoffrey W. Bromiley. 10 vols. Grand Rapids: Eerdmans, 1964–76.

Liddell, Henry George, and Robert Scott. *A Greek-English Lexicon.* 9th ed. with revised supplement. Oxford: Clarendon, 1996.

Maher, Michael. *Targum Pseudo-Jonathan: Leviticus.* Aramaic Bible 3. Collegeville, MN: Liturgical Press, 1994.

Mansoor, Menahem. *The Thanksgiving Hymns.* Studies on the Texts of the Desert of Judah 3. Leiden: Brill, 1961.

McNamara, Martin. *Targum Neofiti 1:* Genesis. Aramaic Bible 1A. Collegeville, MN: Liturgical Press, 1992.

———. *Targum Neofiti 1: Leviticus.* Aramaic Bible 3. Collegeville, MN: Liturgical Press, 1994.

———. *Targum Neofiti 1: Numbers.* Aramaic Bible 4. Collegeville, MN: Liturgical Press, 1995.

———. *Targum Neofiti 1: Deuteronomy.* Aramaic Bible 5A. Collegeville, MN: Liturgical Press, 1997.

Neusner, Jacob. *The Mishnah: A New Translation*. New Haven: Yale University Press, 1988.

———, trans. *Mekhilta according to Rabbi Ishmael: An Analytical Translation*. 2 vols. Brown Judaic Studies 148, 154. Atlanta: Scholars Press, 1988.

Newsom, Carol, Hartmut Stegemann, and Eileen Schuller. *Qumran Cave 1.III: 1QHodayot a, with Incorporation of 4QHodayot a–f and 1QHodayot b*. Discoveries in the Judaean Desert 40. Oxford: Clarendon, 2009.

Philo. *Philo II*. Translated by F. H. Colson and G. H. Whitaker. Loeb Classical Library. Cambridge, MA: Harvard University Press, 1968. Contains *De Cherubim* ("On the Cherubim"); and *De Posteritate Caini* ("On the Posterity and Exile of Cain").

———. *Philo III*. Translated by F. H. Colson and G. H. Whitaker. Loeb Classical Library. Cambridge, MA: Harvard University Press, 1960. Contains *Quod Deus Immutabilis Sit* ("On the Unchangeableness of God"); *De Agricultura* ("On Husbandry"); and *De Ebrietate* ("On Drunkenness").

———. *Philo IV*. Translated by F. H. Colson and G. H. Whitaker. Loeb Classical Library. Cambridge, MA: Harvard University Press, 1968. Contains *De Migratione Abrahami* ("On the Migration of Abraham"); and *Quis Rerum Divinarum Heres* ("Who Is the Heir of Divine Things").

———. *Philo V*. Translated by F. H. Colson and G. H. Whitaker. Loeb Classical Library. Cambridge, MA: Harvard University Press, 1968. Contains *De Fuga et Inventione* ("On Flight and Finding").

———. *Philo VI*. Translated by F. H. Colson. Loeb Classical Library. Cambridge, MA: Harvard University Press, 1966. Contains *De Vita Mosis* ("On the Life of Moses").

———. *Philo VII*. Translated by F. H. Colson. Loeb Classical Library. Cambridge, MA: Harvard University Press, 1958. Contains *De Decalogo* ("On the Decalogue") and *De Specialibus Legibus* ("On the Special Laws").

———. *Philo VIII.* Translated by F. H. Colson. Loeb Classical Library. Cambridge, MA: Harvard University Press, 1960. Contains *De Praemiis et Poenis* ("On Rewards and Punishments").

Plato. *Plato I.* Translated by Harold Northfowler. Loeb Classical Library. Cambridge, MA: Harvard University Press, 1966. Contains *Phaedo.*

Pliny. *Natural History VIII: Books 28–32.* Translated by W. H. S. Jones. Loeb Classical Library. Cambridge, MA: Harvard University Press, 1963.

Pritchard, James B., ed. *Ancient Near Eastern Texts Relating to the Old Testament.* 3rd ed. Princeton: Princeton University Press, 1969.

Rabin, Chaim. *The Zadokite Documents.* 2nd rev. ed. Oxford: Clarendon, 1958.

Seneca. *Seneca: Moral Essays III.* Translated by John W. Basore. Loeb Classical Library. Cambridge, MA: Harvard University Press, 1964. Contains *De Beneficiis* ("On Benefits").

Schaff, Philip, ed. *The Nicene and Post-Nicene Fathers,* Vol. 6, *Saint Augustine.* Grand Rapids: Eerdmans, 1974. Contains "The Sermon on the Mount."

Singer, Simeon, ed. *The Authorized Daily Prayer Book of the United Hebrew Congregations of the British Empire.* 9th ed. London: Eyre & Spottiswoode, 1912. American reprint, New York: Bloch, 1944. Enlarged Centenary Edition, ed. Rabbi Lord Jakobovitz. Cambridge: Press Syndicate of the University of Cambridge, 1992. Originally 1890.

Stec, David M. *The Targum of Psalms.* Aramaic Bible 16. Collegeville, MN: Liturgical Press, 2004.

Street, Henry. *Leaves from Eusebius.* London: Edward Bull, 1842. Contains "The Evangelical Preparation."

Tacitus. *Tacitus II: The Annals: Books 1–3.* Translated by John Jackson. Loeb Classical Library. Cambridge, MA: Harvard University Press, 1962.

Townsend, John T. *Midrash Tanḥuma I.* Hoboken, NJ: Ktav, 1989. Contains Genesis.

Vermes, Geza. *The Complete Dead Sea Scrolls in English.* London: Penguin, 1997.

Wolfson, Harry A. *Philo: Foundations of Religious Philosohy in Judaism, Christianity, and Islam.* 2 vols. Cambridge, MA: Harvard University Press, 1947.

Books and Articles

Abrahams, Israel. *Studies in Pharisaism and the Gospels.* Second Series. Cambridge: Cambridge University Press, 1924.

Arndt, Johann. *True Christianity.* Translated byPeter Erb. New York: Paulist, 1979.

Augustine, Saint. "Our Lord's Sermon on the Mount," translated by William Findlay, revised by D. S. Schaff. Iin *Nicene and Post-Nicene Fathers of the Christian Church,* vol. 6, *Augustin: Sermon on the Mount, Harmony of the Gospels, Homilies on the Gospels,* edited by Philip Schaff, 1–63. 1887. Reprint, Grand Rapids: Eerdmans, 1980.

———. *The Preaching of Augustine: Our Lord's Sermon on the Mount.* Translated byFrancine Cardman. Edited by Jaroslav Pelikan. Preacher's Paperback Library. Philadelphia: Fortress Press, 1973.

Bacon, Benjamin W. "The 'Single' Eye." *The Expositor* 8th Series 7 (1914): 275–88.

———. *Studies in Matthew.* New York: Henry Holt, 1930. Matthew 5–7 is discussed in "The First Book," 165–86.

Baillie, D. M. "How Jesus Dealt with Worry (Mt. vi. 19-34)." *Expository Times* 39 (1927–28): 443–47.

Barclay, William. *The Beatitudes and the Lord's Prayer for Everyman.* New York and Evanston: Harper & Row, 1968.

Barton, John. "Imitation of God in the Old Testament." In *The God of Israel,* edited by Robert P. Gordon, 35–46. University of Cambridge Oriental Publications 64. Cambridge: Cambridge University Press, 2007.

Best, Ernest. "Matthew V. 3." *New Testament Studies* 7 (1960–61): 255–58.

Betz, Hans Dieter. *Essays on the Sermon on the Mount.* Translated by L. L. Welborn. Philadelphia: Fortress Press, 1985.

———. *The Sermon on the Mount: A Commentary on the Sermon on the Mount, Including the Sermon on the Plain (Matthew 5:3—7:27 and Luke 6:20-49).* Hermeneia; Minneapolis: Fortress Press, 1995.

Black, Matthew. "The Beatitudes." *Expository Times* 64 (1952–53): 125–26.

Bonhoeffer, Dietrich. *The Cost of Discipleship.* New York: Macmillan, 1963.

Boring, M. Eugene. "The Gospel of Matthew." In *The New Interpreter's Bible,* edited by Leander E. Keck, 8:89–505. 13 vols. Nashville: Abingdon, 1995.

Branscomb, Bennett H. *Jesus and the Law of Moses.* New York: Richard R. Smith, 1930. Chapter 6 on "The Antithesis."

Bray, Aaron. "The Evil Eye among the Hebrews." In *The Evil Eye: A Folklore Casebook,* edited by Alan Dundes, 44–54. New York and London: Garland, 1981.

Brock, Sebastian. "The Two Ways and the Palestinian Targum." In *A Tribute to Geza Vermes: Essays on Jewish and Christian Literature and History,* edited by Philip R. Davies and Richard T. White, 139–52. Journal for the Study of the Old Testament: Supplement Series 100. Sheffield: JSOT Press, 1990.

Buber, Martin. *Israel and the World.* 1948. Reprint, Syracuse, NY: Syracuse University Press, 1997.

Büchler, Adolf. "St Matthew VI 1-6 and Other Allied Passages." *Journal of Theological Studies* 10 (1909): 266–70.

Bunyan, John. *The Pilgrim's Progress: From This World, to That Which Is to Come.* London: J. Clarke, 1741.

Cadbury, Henry J. "The Single Eye." *Harvard Theological Review* 47 (1954): 69–74.

Cadoux, C. J. "The Evil Eye." *Expository Times* 53 (1941–42): 354–55.

Calvin, John. *Calvin's* Institutes: *Abridged Edition.* Edited by Donald K. McKim. Louisville: Westminster John Knox, 2001.

———. *Commentary on a Harmony of the Evangelists, Matthew, Mark, and Luke I.* Translated by William Pringle. Grand Rapids: Baker Books, 2003.

Carleton, James G. "The Idiom of Exaggerated Contrast." *The Expositor* 4th Series 6 (1892): 365–72.

Charles, R. H. "The Beatitudes." *Expository Times* 28 (1916–17): 536–41.

Cohon, Beryl D. *Jacob's Well: Some Jewish Sources and Parallels to the Sermon on the Mount.* New York: Bookman Associates, 1956.

Cohon, Samuel S. "The Place of Jesus in the Religious Life of His Day." *Journal of Biblical Literature* 48 (1929): 82–108.

Cotter, W. E. P. "The Meek." *Expository Times* 33 (1921–22): 280.

Crisler, B. Cobbey. "The Acoustics and Crowd Capacity of Natural Theaters in Palestine." *Biblical Archaeologist* 39 (1976): 128–41.

Cross, Frank Moore, Jr. *The Ancient Library of Qumran and Modern Biblical Studies.* Rev. 3rd ed. Sheffield: Sheffield Academic Press, 1995. Originally 1958.

Daube, David. "The Culture of Deuteronomy." *Orita* 3 (1969): 27–52.

———. *The Exodus Pattern in the Bible.* London: Faber & Faber, 1963.

———. "Matthew v. 38f." *Journal of Theological Studies* 45 (1944): 177–87.

———. *The New Testament and Rabbinic Judaism.* London: University of London and Athlone Press, 1956. "Ye Have Heard—But I Say unto You," 55–62.

———. "The New Testament Terms for Divorce." *Theology* 47 (1944): 65–67.

———. "Three Questions of Form in Matthew V." *Journal of Theological Studies* 45 (1944): 21–31.

———. *Studies in Biblical Law*. Cambridge: Cambridge University Press, 1947.

———. *The Sudden in the Scriptures*. Leiden: Brill, 1964.

Davies, W. D. *Invitation to the New Testament*. Garden City, NY: Doubleday, 1966.

———. "Matthew 5, 17-18." In *Mélanges bibliques rédigés en l'honneur de André Robert*, 428–56. Travaux de l'Institut Catholique de Paris 4. Paris: Bloud & Gay, 1957.

———. *The Sermon on the Mount*. Cambridge: Cambridge University Press, 1969.

———. *The Setting of the Sermon on the Mount*. Cambridge: Cambridge University Press, 1964.

Deatrick, Eugene P. "Salt, Soil, Savior." *Biblical Archaeologist* 25 (1962): 41–48.

Denison, Stephen. "But Beware of False Prophets (Matt. 7:15)." In Stephen Denison, *The White Wolfe*. London: George Miller, 1627.

Derrett, J. Duncan M. *The Sermon on the Mount: A Manual for Living*. Northampton: Pilkington, 1994.

Dibelius, Martin. *The Sermon on the Mount*. John C. Shaffer Lectures at the Divinity School of Yale University 1937. New York: Charles Scribner's Sons, 1940.

Dodd, C. H. "The Beatitudes." In *Mélanges bibliques rédigés en l'honneur de André Robert*, 404–10. Travaux de l'Institut Catholique de Paris 4. Paris: Bloud & Gay, 1957.

———. *The Epistle of Paul to the Romans*. London: Hodder & Stoughton, 1932.

———. *The Interpretation of the Fourth Gospel*. Cambridge: Cambridge University Press, 1953.

Dumbrell, W. J. "The Logic of the Role of the Law in Matthew V 1-20." *Novum Testamentum* 23 (1981): 1–21.

Dundes, Alan. "Summoning Deity through Ritual Fasting." In Alan Dundes, *Analytic Essays in Folklore*, 146–50. The Hague and Paris: Mouton, 1975.

Eichrodt, Walther. *Theology of the Old Testament*. Translated by J. A. Baker. 2 vols. London: SCM, 1961–67.

Embree, Edwin Rogers. "A Conversation in Peking." *Atlantic Monthly* 146 (1930): 561–68.

Emmerich, K. "Prayer in the Inner Chamber." In *'And Other Pastors of Thy Flock': A German Tribute to the Bishop of Chichester*, edited by Franz Hildebrandt, 6–18. Cambridge: Cambridge University Press, 1942.

Fensham, F. Charles. "The Legal Background of Mt. VI 12." *Novum Testamentum* 4 (1960): 1–2.

Fenton, J. C. *The Gospel of St. Matthew*. Pelican New Testament Commentaries. Baltimore: Penguin, 1963.

———. "Inclusio and Chiasmus in Matthew." In *Studia evangelica: Papers Presented to the International Congress on "The Four Gospels in 1957" Held at Christ Church, Oxford*, edited by Kurt Aland, 174–79. Texte und Untersuchungen zur Geschichte der altchristlichen Literatur 73. Berlin: Akademie-Verlag, 1959.

Filson, Floyd V. *A Commentary on the Gospel according to St. Matthew*. Harper's New Testament Commentaries. New York: Harper & Brothers, 1960.

Fitzmyer, Joseph A. "Divorce among First-Century Palestinian Jews." In *H. L. Ginsberg Volume*, edited by Menahem Haran, 103–10. Eretz-Israel 14. Jerusalem: Israel Exploration Society, 1978.

Flusser, D. "Blessed Are the Poor in Spirit . . . ." *Israel Exploration Journal* 10 (1960): 1–13.

Freedman, David Noel. "Deliberate Deviation from an Established Pattern of Repetition in Hebrew Poetry as a Rhetorical Device." In *Proceedings of the Ninth World Congress of Jewish Studies (Jerusalem, August 4–12, 1985). Division A: The Period of the Bible*, 45–52 Jerusalem: World Union of Jewish Studies, 1986. Reprinted in David Noel Freedman, *Divine Commitment and Human Obligation,* 2:205–12.

———. "Divine Commitment and Human Obligation." *Interpretation* 18 (1964): 419–31. Reprinted in David Noel Freedman, *Divine Commitment and Human Obligation,* 1: 168–78.

———. *Divine Commitment and Human Obligation: Selected Writings of David Noel Freedman,* edited by John R. Huddlestun. 2 vols. Grand Rapids: Eerdmans, 1997.

———. "Prolegomenon." In George Buchanan Gray, *The Forms of Hebrew Poetry,* vii–lvi. New York: Ktav, 1972. Reprinted in *David Noel Freedman, Pottery, Poetry, and Prophecy: Studies in Early Hebrew Poetry,* 23–50. Winona Lake, IN: Eisenbrauns, 1980.

Freedman, David Noel, and Jack R. Lundbom. "חנן." In *Theological Dictionary of the Old Testament,* edited by G. J. Botterweck, Helmer Ringgren, and H.-J. Fabry, 5:22–36. 15 vols. Grand Rapids: Eerdmans, 1974–.

Friedlander, Gerald. *The Jewish Sources of the Sermon on the Mount.* 1911. Reprint, New York: Ktav, 1969.

Frost, Robert. *Selected Poems.* Middlesex: Penguin, 1973.

Frymer-Kensky, Tikva. "Tit for Tat: The Principle of Equal Retribution in Near Eastern and Biblical Law." *Biblical Archaeologist* 43 (1980): 230–34.

Fullerton, Kemper. "Raka," *Expository Times* 15 (1903–4): 429–31.

Gandhi, Mohandas K. *Gandhi's Autobiography.* Translated by Mahadev Desai. Washington, DC: Public Affairs Press, 1960.

———. *What Jesus Means to Me.* Edited by R. K. Prabhu. Ahmedabad: Navajivan, 1959.

Glasson, T. F. "Chiasmus in St. Matthew vii. 6." *Expository Times* 68 (1956–57): 302.

———. *Moses in the Fourth Gospel.* Studies in Biblical Theology 10. Naperville, IL: Allenson, 1963.

Green, H. B. "The Structure of St. Matthew's Gospel." In *Studia evangelica IV: Papers Presented to the Third International Congress on New Testament Studies.* Part 1, *The New Testament Scriptures,* edited by F. L. Cross, 47–59. Berlin: Akademie Verlag, 1968.

Green, S. G. *Notes on the Sermon on the Mount.* London: Sunday School Union, 1879.

Griffiths, J. Gwyn. "Wisdom about Tomorrow." *Harvard Theological Review* 53 (1960): 219–21.

Gruber, Mayer. "The Tragedy of Cain and Abel: A Case of Depression." *Jewish Quarterly Review* 69 (1978): 89–97.

Guelich, Robert A. "Interpreting the Sermon on the Mount." *Interpretation* 41 (1987): 117–30.

———. "Mt 5:22: Its Meaning and Integrity." *Zeitschrift für die neutestamentliche Wissenschaft* 64 (1973): 39–52.

Hammer, Reuven. Sifre: *A Tannaitic Commentary on the Book of Deuteronomy.* Yale Judaica Series 24. New Haven: Yale University Press, 1986.

Harnack, Adolf. *What Is Christianity?* Translated by Thomas Bailey Saunders. London: Williams & Norgate, 1901.

Harrington, Daniel J. "The Sermon on the Mount: What Is It?" *The Bible Today* 36 (1998): 280–86.

Hendrickx, Herman. *The Sermon on the Mount.* Rev. ed. London: Geoffrey Chapman, 1984.

Hendry, George S. "Judge Not: A Critical Test of Faith." *Theology Today* 40 (1983): 113–29.

Herzog, Frederick. *European Pietism Reviewed.* Princeton Theological Monograph Series 50. San Jose, CA: Pickwick, 2003.

Jackson, Bernard S. "Liability for Mere Intention in Early Jewish Law." *Hebrew Union College Annual* 42 (1971): 197–225.

Jebb, John. *Sacred Literature.* London: T. Cadell & W. Davies, 1820.

Jeremias, Joachim. *New Testament Theology,* vol. 1. Translated by John Bowden. New Testament Library. London: SCM, 1971.

———. *The Parables of Jesus.* Rev. ed. Translated by S. H. Hooke. New York: Charles Scribner's Sons, 1963.

———. *The Sermon on the Mount.* Translated by Norman Perrin. London: University of London, Athlone Press, 1961.

Johnson, Sherman E. "Matthew." In *The Interpreter's Bible,* edited by George A. Buttrick, 7:231–625. 12 vols. New York: Abingdon-Cokesbury, 1956.

Jones, E. Stanley. *The Christ of the Mount.* London: Hodder & Stoughton, 1931.

Keck, Leander E. "The Sermon on the Mount." In *Jesus and Man's Hope,* edited by Donald G. Miller and Dikran Y. Hadidian, 2:311–22. 2 vols. Pittsburgh: Pittsburgh Theological Seminary, 1970–71.

Kierkegaard, Søren. *Christian Discourses and the Lilies of the Field and the Birds of the Air and Three Discourses at the Communion on Fridays.* Translated by Walter Lowrie. London: Oxford University Press, 1939. Originally 1848. Contains "The Anxieties of the Heathen" (pp. 7–93).

———. *Consider the Lilies.* Translated by A. S. Aldworth and W. S. Ferrie. London: C. W. Daniel, 1940. The second part of "Edifying Discourses in a Different Vein" (1847).

———. *Purity of Heart Is to Will One Thing.* Translated by Douglas V. Steere. New York: Harper & Bros., 1948. Originally 1846.

King, George Brockwell. "The Mote and the Beam." *Harvard Theological Review* 17 (1924): 393–404.

———. "The 'Negative' Golden Rule." *Journal of Religion* 8 (1928): 268–79.

Kingsbury, Jack Dean. *The Parables of Jesus in Matthew 13.* Richmond: John Knox, 1969.

Kissinger, Warren S. *The Sermon on the Mount: A History of Interpretation and Bibliography.* Metuchen, NJ: Scarecrow, 1975.

Knox, John. "Ethical Obligation in the Realm of Grace." *Shane Quarterly* 15 (1954): 55–93.

Lachs, Samuel Tobias. *A Rabbinic Commentary on the New Testament.* Hoboken, NJ: Ktav, 1987.

Lapide, Pinchas. *The Sermon on the Mount: Utopia or Program for Action?* Translated by Arlene Swidler. Maryknoll, NY: Orbis Books, 1986.

Lieber, David L. "Divorce (In the Bible)" in *EncJud* 6: 122-125.

Liebreich, Leon. "The Compilation of the Book of Isaiah." *Jewish Quarterly Review* 46 (1956): 259–77.

Lindberg, Carter, ed. *The Pietist Theologians: An Introduction to Theology in the Seventeenth and Eighteenth Centuries.* Oxford: Blackwell, 2005.

Lohr, Charles H. "Oral Techniques in the Gospel of Matthew." *Catholic Biblical Quarterly* 23 (1961): 403–35.

Loski, Diana. "Two Carolina Gentlemen." *The Gettysburg Experience* (August 2006): 25–38.

Lund, Nils W. *Chiasmus in the New Testament.* Chapel Hill: University of North Carolina Press, 1942. Reprint, Peabody, MA: Hendrickson, 1992.

———. "The Influence of Chiasmus upon the Structure of the Gospels." *Anglican Theological Review* 13 (1931): 27–48.

———. "The Influence of Chiasmus upon the Structure of the Gospel according to Matthew." *Anglican Theological Review* 13 (1931): 405–33.

———. *Outline Studies in the Book of Revelation.* Chicago: Covenant Book Concern, 1935.

———. *Studies in the Book of Revelation.* Chicago: Covenant Press, 1955.

Lundbom, Jack R. "At What Elevation Is Jesus' Sermon on the Mount?" *Currents in Theology and Mission* 36 (2009): 440–54.

———. *Biblical Rhetoric and Rhetorical Criticism.* Hebrew Bible Monographs 45. Sheffield: Sheffield Phoenix Press, 2013.

———. "Closure in Mark's Gospel." *Seminary Ridge Review* 9, no. 1 (2006): 33–41. Reprinted in Lundbom, *Biblical Rhetoric and Rhetorical Criticism*, 323–31.

———. "Contentious Priests and Contentious People in Hosea IV 1-10." *Vetus Testamentum* 36 (1986): 52–70. Reprinted in Lundbom, *Biblical Rhetoric and Rhetorical Criticism*, 216–31.

———. *Deuteronomy: A Commentary*. Grand Rapids: Eerdmans, 2013.

———. *The Hebrew Prophets*. Minneapolis: Fortress Press, 2010.

———. *Jeremiah 1–20: A New Translation with Introduction and Commentary*. Anchor Bible 21A. New York: Doubleday, 1999. Reprint, New Haven: Yale University Press, 2009.

———. *Jeremiah 21–36. A New Translation with Introduction and Commentary*. Anchor Bible 21B. New York: Doubleday, 2004.

———. *Jeremiah 37–52. A New Translation with Introduction and Commentary*. Anchor Bible 21C. New York: Doubleday, 2004.

———. *Jeremiah: A Study in Ancient Hebrew Rhetoric*. Society of Biblical Literature Dissertation Series 18. Missoula, MT: Society of Biblical Literature and Scholars Press, 1975; 2nd ed., Winona Lake, IN: Eisenbrauns, 1997.

———. "Poetic Structure and Prophetic Rhetoric in Hosea." *Vetus Testamentum* 29 (1979): 300–308. Reprinted in *Prophecy in the Hebrew Bible: Selected Studies from Vetus Testamentum*, edited by David E. Orton, 139–47. Brill's Readers in Biblical Studies 5. Leiden: Brill, 2000. Reprinted also in Lundbom, *Biblical Rhetoric and Rhetorical Criticism*, 232–39.

———. "Structure in the Song of Moses (Deuteronomy 32.1-43)." In Lundbom, *Biblical Rhetoric and Rhetorical Criticism*, 131–49.

———. "What about Divorce?" *The Covenant Quarterly* 36, no. 4 (November 1978): 21–27.

———. *Writing Up Jeremiah: The Prophet and the Book*. Eugene, OR: Cascade Books, 2013.

Luther, Martin. *Luther's Works.* Vol. 21, *The Sermon on the Mount (Sermons) and The Magnificat.* Edited by Jaroslav Pelikan. St. Louis: Concordia, 1956.

Luz, Ulrich. *Matthew 1–7: A Commentary.* Translated by James E. Crouch. Hermeneia. Minneapolis: Fortress Press, 2007.

Maimonides, Moses. *The Guide of the Perplexed.* Translted by Shlomo Pines. Chicago: University of Chicago Press, 1963.

Marmorstein, A. *The Doctrine of Merits in Old Rabbinical Literature* (Jews' College, London: Publication 7. London: Jews College, 1920.

Massey, Isabel Ann. *Interpreting the Sermon on the Mount in the Light of Jewish Tradition as Evidenced in the Palestinian Targums of the Pentateuch: Selected Themes.* Studies in the Bible and Early Christianity 25. Lewiston, NY: Edwin Mellen, 1991.

Matthias, Markus. "August Hermann Francke (1663–1727)." In *The Pietist Theologians: An Introduction to Theology in the Seventeenth and Eighteenth Centuries,* edited by Carter Lindberg, 100–114. Oxford: Blackwell, 2005.

McArthur, Harvey K. *Understanding the Sermon on the Mount.* New York: Harper & Bros., 1960.

McEleney, Neil J. "The Beatitudes of the Sermon on the Mount/Plain." *Catholic Biblical Quarterly* 43 (1981): 1–13.

———. "The Principles of the Sermon on the Mount." *Catholic Biblical Quarterly* 41 (1979): 552–70.

McKenzie, John L. "The Gospel according to Matthew." In *The Jerome Biblical Commentary II,* edited by Raymond E. Brown et al., 62–114. Englewood Cliffs, NJ: Prentice-Hall, 1968.

M'Neile, Alan Hugh. *The Gospel according to St. Matthew.* London: Macmillan, 1952.

Meistad, Tore. *Martin Luther and John Wesley on the Sermon on the Mount.* Pietist and Wesleyan Studies 10. Lanham, Md. and London: Scarecrow, 1999.

Montefiore, C. G. *Rabbinic Literature and Gospel Teachings.* London: Macmillan, 1930.

———. *The Synoptic Gospels.* 2 vols. 2nd rev. ed. London: Macmillan, 1927. Originally 1909. Vol 2 on Matthew.

Montefiore, C. G., and H. Loewe. *A Rabbinic Anthology.* London: Macmillan, 1938.

Moore, George Foot. *Judaism in the First Centuries of the Christian Era: The Age of the Tannaim.* 2nd ed. 2 vols. Cambridge, MA: Harvard University Press, 1927. Reprint, New York: Schocken, 1971.

Moran, William. "The Ancient Near Eastern Background of the Love of God in Deuteronomy." *Catholic Biblical Quarterly* 25 (1963): 77–87.

Muilenburg, James. "Form Criticism and Beyond." *Journal of Biblical Literature* 88 (1969): 1–18. Reprinted in *Hearing and Speaking the Word: Selections from the Works of James Muilenburg,* edited by Thomas F. Best, 27–44. Scholars Press Homage Series. Chico, CA: Scholars Press, 1984. Reprinted also in *Beyond Form Criticism: Essays in Old Testament Literary Criticism,* edited by Paul R. House, 49–69. Sources for Biblical and Theological Study 2. Winona Lake, IN: Eisenbrauns, 1992.

———. "Isaiah." In *The Interpreter's Bible,* edited by George A. Buttrick, 5:381–773. 12 vols. New York: Abingdon-Cokesbury, 1951–57.

———. *The Way of Israel: Biblical Faith and Ethics.* New York: Harper & Row, 1961.

Nauck, Wolfgang. "Salt as a Metaphor in Instruction for Discipleship." *Studia Theologica* 6 (1952): 165–78.

Niebuhr, Reinhold. *An Interpretation of Christian Ethics.* New York: Meridian Books, 1956.

Olson, Mark K. *John Wesley's Theology of Christian Perfection: Developments in Doctrine and Theological System.* Fenwick, MI: Truth in Heart, 2007.

Olsson, Karl A. *By One Spirit.* Chicago: Covenant Press, 1962.

Peabody, Francis Greenwood. "The Peace-Makers." *Harvard Theological Review* 12 (1919): 51–66.

Pelikan, Jaroslav. *Jesus through the Centuries: His Place in the History of Culture.* New Haven: Yale University Press, 1985.

———. "Pietism." In *Dictionary of the History of Ideas: Studies of Selected Pivotal Ideas,* edited by Philip P. Wiener, 3:493–95. 5 vols. New York: Charles Scribner's Sons, 1973–74.

Pope, Marvin H. *Song of Songs: A New Translation with Introduction and Commentary.* Anchor Bible 7C. Garden City, NY: Doubleday, 1977.

Rabello, Alfredo Mordechai. "Divorce of Jews in the Roman Empire." *The Jewish Law Annual IV,* edited by Bernard S. Jackson, 79–102. Leiden: Brill, 1981.

Rad, Gerhard von. *Deuteronomy: A Commentary.* Old Testament Library. London: SCM, 1966.

Robinson, Theodore H. *The Gospel of Matthew.* Garden City, NY: Doubleday, Doran, 1928.

Sattler, Gary R. *God's Glory, Neighbor's Good: A Brief Introduction to the Life and Writings of August Hermann Francke.* Chicago: Covenant Press, 1982.

Schechter, Solomon. *Some Aspects of Rabbinic Theology.* London: Adam & Charles Black, 1909.

———. "Some Rabbinic Parallels to the New Testament." *Jewish Quarterly Review* O.S. 12 (1899–1900): 415–33.

Schereschewsky, Ben Zion (Beno). "Divorce (In Later Jewish Law)" in *EncJud* 6: 125-135.

Schuele, Frederick E. "Living Up to Matthew's Sermon on the Mount: An Approach." In *Christian Biblical Ethics: From Biblical Revelation to Contemporary Christian Praxis,* edited by Robert J. Daly, 200–210. New York: Paulist, 1984.

Schweitzer, Albert. *The Mystery of the Kingdom of God: The Secret of Jesus' Messiahship and Passion.* Translated by Walter Lowrie. New York: Macmillan, 1950. Originally 1901.

Skibbe, Eugene M. "Pentateuchal Themes in the Sermon on the Mount." *Lutheran Quarterly* 20 (1968): 44–51.

Smith, David. "Raka!" *Expository Times* 15 (1903–4): 235–37.

Smith, George Adam. *The Early Poetry of Israel in Its Physical and Social Origins.* Schweich Lectures, 1910. London: Henry Frowde, Oxford University Press, 1912.

Spener, Philip Jacob. *Pia Desideria.* Translated by Theodore G. Tappert. Philadelphia: Fortress Press, 1964.

Steiman, Sidney. "Imitation of God (*Imitatio Dei*)." In *EncJud* 8:1292–93.

Stein, K. James. "Philipp Jakob Spener (1635–1705)." In *The Pietist Theologians: An Introduction to Theology in the Seventeenth and Eighteenth Centuries,* edited by Carter Lindberg, 84–99. Oxford: Blackwell, 2005.

Stendahl, Krister. "Matthew." In *Peake's Commentary on the Bible,* edited by Matthew Black and H. H. Rowley, 769–98. New York: Thomas Nelson and Sons, 1962.

———. "Prayer and Forgiveness." *Svensk Exegetisk Årsbok* 22–23 (1957–58): 75–86.

Strecker, Georg. *The Sermon on the Mount.* Translated by O. C. Dean Jr. Nashville: Abingdon, 1988.

Sutcliffe, E. F. "One Jot or Tittle, Mt. 5.18." *Biblica* 9 (1928): 458–60.

Tappert, Theodore G., ed. *The Book of Concord.* Philadelphia: Muhlenberg, 1959.

Thielicke, Helmut. *Life Can Begin Again: Sermons on the Sermon on the Mount.* Translated by John W. Doberstein; London: James Clarke, 1963.

Thomas à Kempis. *The Imitation of Christ.* Translated by Joseph N. Tylenda. Wilmington, DE: Michael Glazier, 1984.

——. *The Imitation of Christ.* Edited and abridged by Paul Simpson McElroy. Mount Vernon, NY: Peter Pauper, 1965.

Tolstoy, Leo. *My Religion.* Translated by Huntington Smith. London: Walter Scott, 1889.

——. *Resurrection.* Translated by Rosemary Edmonds. London: Penguin, 1966.

Troyat, Henri. *Tolstoy.* Translated by Nancy Amphoux. New York: Penguin, 1970.

Trueblood, Elton. *The Humor of Christ.* New York: Harper & Row, 1964.

VanderWeele, Tyler J. "Some Observations Concerning the Chiastic Structure of the Gospel of Matthew." *Journal of Theological Studies* 59 (2008): 669–73.

Vermes, Geza. *Jesus the Jew: A Historian's Reading of the Gospels.* London: Collins, 1973.

Viviano, Benedict T. "The Sermon on the Mount in Recent Study." *Biblica* 78 (1997): 255–65.

Vogt, Peter. "Nicholas Ludwig von Zinzendorf (1700–1760)." In *The Pietist Theologians: An Introduction to Theology in the Seventeenth and Eighteenth Centuries,* edited by Carter Lindberg, 207–23. Oxford: Blackwell, 2005.

Wallmann, Johannes. "Johann Arndt (1555–1621)." In *The Pietist Theologians: An Introduction to Theology in the Seventeenth and Eighteenth Centuries,* edited by Carter Lindberg, 21–37. Oxford: Blackwell, 2005.

Weeden, Theodore J. *Mark—Traditions in Conflict.* Philadelphia: Fortress Press, 1971.

Weinfeld, Moshe. "The Charge of Hypocrisy in Matthew 23 and in Jewish Sources." *Immanuel* 24–25 (1990): 52–58.

Wernberg-Møller, P. "A Semitic Idiom in Matt. V. 22." *New Testament Studies* 3 (1956–57): 71–73.

Wesley, John. *A Caution against False Prophets: A Sermon (Matt. vii. 15-20).* London: New Chapel and at Mr. Wesley's Preaching Houses in Town and Country, 1789.

———. "Christian Perfection." In *The Works of John Wesley,* edited by Albert C. Outler, 2:97–121. Nashville: Abingdon, 1985.

———. "On Perfection." In *The Works of John Wesley,* edited by Albert C. Outler, 3:71–87. Nashville: Abingdon, 1985.

———. *A Plain Account of Christian Perfection.* Peabody, MA: Hendrickson, 2007.

———. "The Scripture Way of Salvation." In *The Works of John Wesley,* edited by Albert C. Outler, 2:153–69. Nashville: Abingdon, 1985.

———. *Thoughts on Christian Perfection.* London: T. Cordeux, 1822. A pamphlet published originally at Bristol, October 16, 1759.

———. *The Works of John Wesley,* edited by Albert C. Outler. Nashville: Abingdon, 1984–.

———. *The Works of John Wesley V.* London: Wesleyan Conference Office, 1872. Reprint, Grand Rapids: Zondervan, n.d. Sermons 21–33 on "Sermon on the Mount."

Wilder, Amos N. *Eschatology and Ethics in the Teaching of Jesus.* New York: Harper & Bros., 1939.

———. "The Teaching of Jesus, II. The Sermon on the Mount." In *The Interpreter's Bible,* edited by George A. Buttrick, 7:155–64. 12 vols. New York: Abingdon-Cokesbury, 1951–57.

Windisch, Hans. *The Meaning of the Sermon on the Mount.* Translated by S. MacLean Gilmour. Philadelphia: Westminster, 1951. Originally 1937.

Wood, W. S. "The Salt of the Earth." *Journal of Theological Studies* 25 (1923–24): 167–72.

Yaron, Reuven. "The Restoration of Marriage." *Journal of Jewish Studies* 17 (1966): 1–11.

Index of Authors

Index of Scripture References

Proverbs